Divine Revelation and Human Practice

Divine Revelation and Human Practice

RESPONSIVE and IMAGINATIVE PARTICIPATION

TONY CLARK

 CASCADE *Books* • Eugene, Oregon

DIVINE REVELATION AND HUMAN PRACTICE
Responsive and Imaginative Participation

Copyright © 2008 Tony Clark. All rights reserved. Except for brief quotations in critical publications or reviews, no part of this book may be reproduced in any manner without prior written permission from the publisher. Write: Permissions, Wipf and Stock Publishers, 199 W. 8th Ave., Suite 3, Eugene, OR 97401.

Cascade Books
A Division of Wipf and Stock Publishers
199 W. 8th Ave., Suite 3
Eugene, OR 97401

Scripture quotations are from the New Revised Standard Version Bible, copyright © 1989 by the Division of Christian Education of the National Council of the Churches of Christ in the USA and used by permission.

ISBN 10: 1-55635-516-5
ISBN 13: 978-1-55635-516-5

Cataloging-in-Publication data:

Clark, Tony.
    Divine revelation and human practice : responsive and imaginative participation / Tony Clark.

    xvi + 228 p.; 23 cm.

    ISBN 10: 1-55635-516-5
    ISBN 13: 978-1-55635-516-5 (alk. paper)

    1. Revelation. 2. Knowledge, Theory of. 3. Barth, Karl, 1886–1968. 4. Polanyi, Michael, 1886–1964. 5. Kaufman, Gordon D. 6. Torrance, Alan. I. Title.

BT127.2 C55 2008

Manufactured in the U.S.A.

For the first mate
and the three crew members

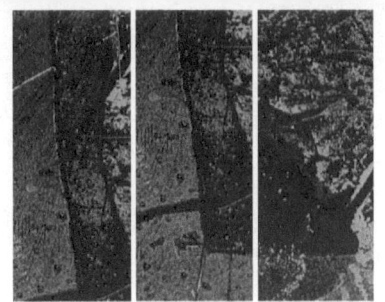

Contents

Acknowledgements ix
Bibliographic Note x
Foreword by Trevor Hart xi
Introduction xiii

1 An Exposition of Karl Barth's Doctrine of Revelation 1

2 Critical Engagement with Barth 37

3 Michael Polanyi's Theory of Knowledge 77
     Excursus: Polanyi and Religion 125

4 Barth and Polanyi in Conversation 145

5 Revelation and Participation 171

6 Revelation and Imagination 197

7 Closing Remarks 223

Bibliography 225

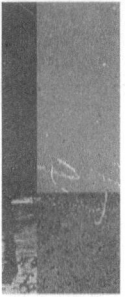

Acknowledgements

I WISH TO EXPRESS my heartfelt thanks to colleagues, friends, and family who have, in various ways, contributed to the writing of this book. I owe an immense debt of gratitude to Trevor Hart, Michael Partridge, and Jeremy Begbie of the University of St. Andrews. I have benefited greatly from their comments on various drafts of the text and their consistent encouragement. Alan Torrance, also of St. Andrews University, has given generously of his time and learning, and I have found his enthusiasm for theology an inspiration. I also want thank Walter Mead, Board President of the Polanyi Society, for reading an earlier draft of the text in its entirety and for his supportive criticism.

I am grateful to the staff of the Special Collections section of the University of Chicago Regenstein Library, the home of Michael Polanyi Papers, for their assistance during two research trips in 2003. I also want to thank Martin Moleski of Canisius College, Buffalo, and Phil Mullins of Missouri Western State University, St. Joseph, for their insightful help with a variety of issues relating to the Polanyi Papers and other matters of Polanyi scholarship.

Finally, thanks are due to my family. I am grateful to my parents, John and Enid Clark and also my mother-in-law, Magdalene Tatham, for their love and support. I am indebted to Tom, Jamie, and Hannah, my children, for providing many happy interruptions to the work which has helped me keep the project in a proper perspective. The greatest debt I owe is to my wife, Antonia. This book is dedicated to her, with my love.

Bibliographic Note

The Michael Polanyi Papers are lodged at the Special Collection Section of the Regenstein Library, University of Chicago. The collection comprises forty-six archival boxes and each box contains several folders. When a document from this collection is cited, it is identified firstly by box number and then by folder number.

All biblical references are from the New Revised Standard Version of the Holy Bible.

Foreword

THIS IS A work of considerable importance. Karl Barth and Michael Polanyi are each figures whose respective places in the intellectual history of the twentieth century remain to be fully charted, notwithstanding the considerable volume of ink already spilled on the task.

Barth in particular has been the subject of a veritable publishing industry in the English-speaking theological community over the last decade or so. And although fewer trees have been felled to aid the scholarly reception of Polanyi's thought, his name has been familiar to theologians since the publication in the 1960s of Lesslie Newbigin's *Honest Religion for Secular Man*. The list of theological works directly indebted to his thought is by now a long one, and one that continues to grow.

It is true of Barth's thought and Polanyi's, though, that the veins of insight and understanding buried within run far deeper than the quarrying skills of any individual or even school of interpretation can reach, and fresh, carefully conducted excavation is always welcome to bring their hidden resources to light. Anyone who has returned time and again to the same shafts sunk deep into the crust of *Church Dogmatics* or *Personal Knowledge* will know the experience of stumbling unexpectedly across some new and striking material which they could swear was not there the last time they passed the spot. Of course this has to do with refreshed eyes and newly sharpened tools as well as the rich resources of the texts themselves; but the fact remains that there is plenty still to be said and written with profit.

What Tony Clark offers us here, though, is much more than a fresh reading of two figures from the recent past. His deliberate exercise in intertextuality not only helps to clarify elements in Barth's theological epistemology, but pursues what T. F. Torrance (in an incisive but somewhat indigestible phrase) refers to as an appropriate "transformation and convergence in the frame of knowledge." In other words, by bringing insights from Polanyi's account of scientific knowing into conversation with Barth's Christian theology (a venture that Torrance himself pioneered), what emerges is an unexpected shift in which neither voice is left unmodified, but in which there is also an identifiable gain for the epistemic fields in which each habitually participates. A "convergence" of insights occurs that is transformative not just of the several elements that feed into it, but of our wider appreciation of the truth of things.

The particular outcome of this work is a deepened and more comprehensive account of what might be meant when Christians refer to "revelation," i.e. that event or series of events and phenomena in, with and through which God gives himself to be known. Barth's account of this is famously Christ-centered; but in its fullness it goes much farther than many accounts do in recognizing (insisting) that the revelation of God is an event which includes our human response and participation. Thus his account has a deliberate Trinitarian shape: that which begins with the Father and is made concrete in the incarnate Son comes to fulfillment and fruition through the work of the Holy Spirit in creating the obedience of faith in the Church and, thus, in the lives of particular men, women and children. While this acknowledgment belongs to the very structure of Barth's theology, though, it remains understated, and needs to be unpacked much more fully in concrete terms. By drawing on Polanyi's account of the structure and practical means of participatory knowing in the natural sciences, Dr. Clark offers us a modeling of various human practices entailed in our human participation in revelation. Keeping its sights firmly fixed on the divine origin and undergirding of our knowing of God from moment to moment, this is nonetheless an account which is able to take fully seriously the human manifestations of this knowing and their relationship to other epistemic circumstances. In particular, the place of creative and imaginative modes of engagement in our knowing of God (as in our knowing of most other things) is here taken fully on board in a manner which avoids fallacious misrepresentations of it as an essentially constructivist exercise.

This is a masterly study which attends skillfully and with great insight to some of the complex and contested claims of theological epistemology, but does so with its feet firmly planted on the ground of daily living in the church, and an eye to how our Christian knowing of God at this down to earth and practical level might be better understood and, perhaps, renewed and transformed by what intellectual giants such as Barth and Polanyi have to tell us, and what they might have to learn from one another.

Trevor Hart
Professor of Divinity
St. Mary's College
St. Andrews

Introduction

I FIRST MET WITH the thought of Michael Polanyi in the writings of Lesslie Newbigin in the late 1980s. Newbigin refers to Polanyi in many of his publications and makes extensive use of his ideas in the early chapters of *The Gospel in a Pluralist Society*. Newbigin prompted me to take a closer look at Polanyi's work and I became increasingly fascinated with the project with which he was engaged.

Many authors have written on the interrelationship of Christian beliefs and science. Polanyi was doing something different. He was not primarily interested in religion[1]; his "evangelical zeal" was for the life of science. Polanyi sought to articulate a theory of knowledge—and a philosophy of science—which authentically represented the *practice* of science.[2] One of Polanyi's startling conclusions is that scientific practice and progress are possible only when scientists embrace and participate in the "beliefs" which are intrinsic to the scientific community. What is more, these "beliefs" cannot be fully articulated, yet they are "known" and held through nurture and training within the scientific community. The life of science is, in this sense, a "life of faith" that is expressed and lived out within a community of "believers". Such language comes to the fore explicitly in the title of one of Polanyi's earlier philosophical writings, *Science, Faith and Society*.

What Polanyi has done is to expose the fiduciary nature of scientific work. While it is clear that Polanyi was not engaged in any kind of Christian apologetic, it occurred to me—as it had Newbigin and others before me—that Polanyi's work might have important insights for Christian thought and theology.

Just over a decade later, I was confronted for the first time (in a substantial way) by the work of Karl Barth. As had been the case with Polanyi, I was struck by the originality and rigor of Barth's thought. His doctrine of the Word of God, as it is expressed in the first three part volumes of *Church Dogmatics*, clarified for me some key issues about what it might mean for God to make himself known. Revelation, for Barth, is not the text of Holy Scripture, nor is it an "inner light" by which we can choose to know God. Revelation is not something that is, or can become, our possession but an "event" (as Barth would have it) in which God makes himself known by making himself present through the Spirit.

---

1. Although, as I shall demonstrate in the excursus, it is a significant secondary theme in his writings.

2. He felt that the philosophy of science, in modern times, had served to obscure rather than illuminate scientific practice.

Early on in my acquaintance with Barth's work, I started to puzzle over how his work stood in relation to Polanyi's. Polanyi had written on religious and theological themes, but those writings were, of all Polanyi's work, the most disappointing. He had described the life of science as participation in a "faith community" but had somehow missed—or substantially missed—the significance of this for religion. It seems that he lacked a sufficient grounding in religious and theological traditions. As a consequence the profound insights, evident in other aspects of his work, did not seem to flow into his treatment of religion. Barth's work represents something of a counterpoint to Polanyi's in that his theology is expressed out of a rich awareness of, and engagement within, the Christian tradition. However, despite the rigor with which Barth expresses his doctrine of the Word of God, and the effectiveness with which he differentiated his own position from the liberal tradition in which he had been nurtured, his discussion of how it is that we participate in this reality (by the grace of God) is significantly understated in his treatment of the doctrine.

As I reflected upon these things, it occurred to me that much might be gained by bringing some of the key ideas of these two intellectual giants into dialogue. Although Polanyi and Barth were contemporaries, it seems that they never met, nor is there any evidence that either of them was in any way influenced by the other.[3] However, the possibilities of such a conversation remain, and this work represents, as its major theme, an attempt to explore them.[4]

The chapters of this book are far from uniform in their approach, and a description of what I am attempting in each may be of assistance to the reader. The first chapter is expository in nature. It sets out Barth's doctrine of the Word of God on its own terms in an attempt to establish a point of departure for the doctrine of revelation that I seek to develop.

In the second chapter I ask some critical questions of Barth's doctrine, noting, among other things, that his acknowledgement of human participation in God's revelation is problematically understated. There are elements within his doctrine of the Word of God that threaten to eclipse the possibility of genuine human participation in revelation, and these must be confronted. Here I draw upon the work of several theologians, and Alan Torrance's book, *Persons in Communion*, in particular. Chapter 2 anticipates the significance of Polanyi's work but does not seek to establish or explore it.

---

3. It does appear that Polanyi knew of Barth. In a notebook made during a visit to Berlin: November 27—December 3, 1947, Polanyi mentions a meeting with the brother of Dietrich Bonhoeffer on the afternoon of Sunday November 30 during which they "Talk about Brunner and K. Barth." See "Polanyi Collection: Regenstein Library, University of Chicago." Box 44, Folder 5. No mention is made of the content of the discussion.

4. I am aware that some theologians have explored the possible interaction of the work of Barth and Polanyi along different lines. T. F. Torrance is, perhaps, the most outstanding example of a theologian who has engaged with Polanyi. His work is marked by, among other things, his engagement with Polanyi's ontology.

The third chapter is an exposition of Polanyi's work. Paralleling, in certain respects, the first chapter, it seeks to set out the various components of Polanyi's epistemology as an essential and somewhat extended preparation for articulating its significance for the main theme of the book. This is followed by an excursus that extends the exposition of Polanyi to his treatment of religion and theology. Although my evaluation of this aspect of Polanyi's work is a substantially negative one, it would seem inappropriate not to acknowledge his own contribution before going on to explore what *I* consider to be a more viable extension of his general epistemology in the general field of theological work—and the doctrine of revelation in particular.

Chapter 4 represents my first substantial attempt at a synthesis of the work of Barth and Polanyi. It takes the form of what I describe as a "Polanyian reading" of Barth's discussion of church confessions in *Church Dogmatics I.2*.[5] Here I attempt both to discern how some of the insights in Polanyi's work are already paralleled in Barth's method, and to suggest ways in which Polanyian insights might be adopted in order to develop and expand the kind of theological project in which Barth is engaged.

The fifth chapter extends the intentions of chapter 4 but adopts a significantly different trajectory. Here I refer back to Alan Torrance's critique of Barth and suggest several lines along which this might be extended. A significant element of Torrance's proposal is found in his discussion of "semantic participation." I suggest that to the semantic it is appropriate to add the epistemic, the bodily, and the hermeneutical, as further crucial (if not discrete) aspects that are integral to our participation in revelation.

The sixth and final chapter is an attempt to open up the question of imagination in relation for my main theme. The first half of this chapter is an exposition of Gordon Kaufman's treatment of imagination in theology. This functions as an example of how the relationship between theology and imagination can be seriously misconstrued. Out of my critique of Kaufman, the contours of an alternative approach are suggested in which, once again, I draw from the insights of Polanyi's work.

I believe that this work contains some important and original proposals for rearticulating a doctrine of revelation. It will be apparent that in bringing the work of Polanyi and Barth together, one significant purpose of the book is to make suggestions for further developments. Given this purpose, rather than drawing many threads together in a synthesizing conclusion, it is deliberately open ended, suggesting and provoking, I hope, further inquiry.

---

5. Barth, *Church Dogmatics I/2*, 621–60.

CHAPTER 1

An Exposition of Karl Barth's Doctrine of Revelation

Introduction

IN THE INTRODUCTION to his book *Christology*, Dietrich Bonhoeffer makes an observation that is indicative of some of the central themes that will unfold in this and the subsequent chapters. He writes:

> Teaching about Christ begins in silence. "Be still, for that is the absolute," writes Kierkegaard. That has nothing to do with the silence of the mystics, who in their dumbness chatter away secretly in their souls by themselves. The silence of the Church is silence before the Word. In so far as the Church proclaims the Word, it falls down silently in truth before the inexpressible: "In silence I worship before the unutterable" (Cyril of Alexandria).[1]

In making this comment, Bonhoeffer strikes at the heart of what ought properly to be said of revelation. We must begin with something that is given to us. We do not start with ourselves—with our religious views or spiritual experience—but with the Word that enters the sphere of our existence. This is an event that does not happen at our bidding, but in the freedom of God. The Word is God in person: the transcendent one.

This Word—the Logos—cannot be circumscribed, defined or captured in any human scheme of categorization (human "logoi") because it is a reality that transcends the human sphere in which these schemes are founded and established. Thus, to every human logos the Word is the "counterlogos," and as such, it calls all forms of human classification (and the forms of life in which they are established) into question.

Bonhoeffer goes on to point to the paradox that it is precisely this Word (which he calls "inexpressible") that must be proclaimed by the church. Even

---

1. Bonhoeffer, *Christology*, 27.

as the church proclaims this Word, Bonhoeffer claims, it remains inexpressible. The church can speak of the Word, but its words cannot encompass the reality of which it speaks. The presence of the Word in the church is an ineffable presence. It can transform the life and the speech of the congregation, but it cannot be assimilated, possessed, or demarcated.

Bonhoeffer writes: "to speak of Christ will be . . . to speak in the silent places of the Church. In the humble silence of the worshipping congregation we concern ourselves with christology."[2] Christology may be taught in the academy, but the reality of which the theologian speaks is the reality that confronts the church in its prayer and worship. On the one hand, we are concerned with the objectivity and inexpressibility of the Word that is given to the worshipping community of the church, and, on the other, with the church's commission to proclaim this Word. This is the paradox that must shape ecclesial life, practice, and self-understanding.

These themes will never be far from view in the following exposition of Karl Barth's understanding of the Word of God.

The Nature of the Word of God

"[T]he reality in which the New Testament sees God's revelation taking place is utterly *simple*, the simple reality of God."[3] It is Barth's belief that in revelation God is present, and is present in his freedom. In a statement reminiscent of Bonhoeffer's, Barth writes: "[W]e must first understand the reality of Jesus Christ as such, and then by reading from the tablet of this reality, understand the possibility involved in it, the freedom of God, established and maintained in it, to reveal Himself in precisely this reality and not otherwise, and so the unique possibility which we have to respect as divine necessity."[4]

The revelation of God is not God's answer to the religious questioning of humanity. In revelation humanity is confronted with the reality of God. This confrontation is God's decision and God's act, and there is no possibility of such a revelation for humanity apart from this decision and act of God. Nevertheless, "real revelation puts man in God's presence."[5] This is the gift of God's self-presentation to humanity; but because it is God's decision, in which a human decision has no part in it, it is a decision that God makes in freedom.

Consequently, Barth is able to say:

> When revelation takes place, it never does so by our insight and skill, but in the freedom of God to be free for us and to free us from ourselves, that is to say, to let His light shine in our darkness, which as such does not compre-

2. Ibid., 27.
3. Barth, *Church Dogmatics I/2*, 11; Barth's emphasis.
4. Ibid., 8.
5. Ibid., 237.

hend His light. In this miracle, which we can only acknowledge as having occurred, which we can only receive from the hand of God as it takes place by His hand, His kingdom comes for us, and this world passes for us.[6]

It is received "as it takes place." This is important for Barth. Revelation is not a commodity that passes from God to the person; it is the reality of God that becomes present to the person. It is an event. Barth says: "This is something God Himself must constantly tell us afresh."[7] He further asserts that "there is no human knowing that corresponds to this divine telling."[8] In this "divine telling," there is an encounter: there is a human-divine fellowship, but God does not give himself to humanity as a possession. Rather, there is a fresh divine telling. It is out of the encounter of these events that we must speak.

Because we are concerned with an event in which humanity is encountered, we *can* say what God's Word is, but we can only say this indirectly: "We must remember the forms in which it is real for us and learn from these forms *how* it is. This How is the attainable human reflection of the unattainable divine What. Our concern here must be with this reflection."[9]

The distinction here is a crucial one. Insofar as we are dealing with "this reflection," we are dealing with what can be said on the human side of the event of God actually speaking. The Word of God does, indeed, mean that God speaks. And, in view of this, Barth says: "For all its human inadequacy, for all the brokenness with which alone human statements can correspond to the nature of the Word of God, this statement does correspond to the possibility which God has chosen and actualised at all events in His Church."[10]

There is, in all forms of the Word of God, what Barth describes as an upper and lower aspect. First, there is the spiritual nature of the Word of God, as distinct from naturalness, or its nature as a physical event. Secondly, however, the Word of God is also natural and physical. Without this it would not be the Word of God that is directed to humanity. Were it not for this aspect, there would be no possibility of speaking of human participation in revelation.

God speaks to humanity because he *chooses* to, and not because he *needs* to. There is a distinction between what God says to himself and what he says to humanity. Barth states "What ... [God] says by Himself and to Himself from eternity to eternity would really be said just as well and even better without our being there, as speech that for us would be eternal silence. Only when we are clear about this can we estimate what it means that God has actually, though not necessarily,

---

6. Ibid., 65.
7. Barth, *Church Dogmatics I/1*, 132.
8. Ibid., 132.
9. Ibid., 132; Barth's emphasis.
10. Ibid., 133.

created a world and us, that His love actually, though not necessarily, applies to us, that His Word has actually, though not necessarily, been spoken to us."[11]

It is God's purpose to speak to us. He wills to speak to us, and his speech bears the weight of the one who encompasses our existence. The Word that is spoken to us by God is the Word of reconciliation. As we hear the Word of God, so we are reconciled by the Word of God. He promises himself as the content of humanity's future. He is the one who meets humanity on its way through time as at the end of time. Whatever God speaks to humanity, he does so as the basis of the renewal of humanity's relationship with him. "We can only cling to the fact—but we must cling to it—that when He spoke it was, and when He will speak it will be, the Word of the Lord, the Word of our Creator, our Reconciler, our Redeemer."[12]

It is possible to hear the words of Scripture—the human words—(which may or may not be understood) without there being an accompanying event. In this case, it is not the Word of God that has been heard. The Word of God is itself the act of God. In the Word is act: God's act is the Word. But this is out of God's freedom. When God's Word is heard and proclaimed, something occurs that—for all our hermeneutical skill—cannot be produced by our hermeneutical skill. This act, in the freedom of God, is not ours to command.

But when the words of Scripture *do* become for us the Word of God, when Jesus Christ becomes contemporaneous through the Scripture or proclamation, the hearer "comes under a lordship." This Word has a transforming power. Through it is created not only new light and a new situation, but a new person who did not exist before—the one who has heard the Word. But all this is *new*. Humanity is not claimed for God on the basis of a possibility latent in creation (which would imply that the fall had not been so radical in its consequences). It is not a matter of natural theology but of what Barth calls "supernatural" theology. However, as humanity "comes under a lordship," the significance of this event opens out to encompass every sphere of human existence.

> But such a [supernatural] theology, bearing in mind the power of God's Word, will have to claim the world, history, and society as the world, history and society in the midst of which Christ was born and died and rose again. Not in the light of nature but in the light of grace, there is no self-enclosed and protected secular sphere, but only one which is called in question by God's Word, by the Gospel, by God's claim, judgment and blessing, and which is only provisionally and restrictedly abandoned to its own legalism and its own gods. What the Word says stands whatever the world's attitude to it and whether it redound to it for salvation or perdition.[13]

---

11. Ibid., 140.
12. Ibid., 143.
13. Ibid., 155.

In the humanity of Christ, in the Bible, and in proclamation the Word of God is also a human act and, therefore, temporal event. Nevertheless, it is in the decision of God that God's Word is identical with the humanity of Christ, Holy Scripture, and proclamation and, thus, temporal event. But certain distinctions must be made. The first is that the Word of God is not a reality in the same way as the so-called "laws of nature." Indeed, it is not a reality in the way in which we would apply the term to other phenomena. This must be said despite the fact that it shares in this reality and that we can know the Word of God only in the context of this reality. This must be said because, as Barth puts it, "[T]he Word of God is a reality only in its own decision."[14] The second is that the Word of God—unlike created reality—is not universally ascertainable. It is God's decision made in relation to humanity. The Word of God retains power over its own self-disclosure like no other object. It is new in each new situation and it cannot be anticipated in advance of its reality.

In the Word of God a decision is made, but it is not the choice or the resolve of the individual. It is the decision of God in which judgment and acceptance are announced in relation to a particular person. There is, also, a decision made on the part of the particular person, but this can only be made within the decision of God. Barth says: "I am wholly and altogether the man I am in virtue of the divine decision. In virtue of the divine decision I am a believer or an unbeliever in my own decision."[15]

The Mystery of God

The speech of God is, in Barth's terminology, a mystery. Crucially, there is no possibility of proving the Word of God because there is no external basis upon which the Word of God can be judged. In this sense the mystery of God is the concealment of God. Here we touch again upon the paradoxical presence of God in the form of creaturely reality. When God speaks, he uses human words, and because he uses human words they *can* be understood as no more than just that. As Barth puts it, "Its form is not a suitable but an unsuitable medium for God's self-presentation. It does not correspond to the matter but contradicts it."[16] If God's revelation is really to come to us, it must come to us by way of a creaturely reality—even if this reality is opposed to God in its corruption and fallenness. If the Word of God is to come to us, it must come in creaturely form or it will not come to us at all.

---

14. Ibid., 159.
15. Ibid., 162.
16. Ibid., 166.

> Even our knowledge of the Word of God is not through reason that has somehow remained pure and can thus pierce the mystery of God in creaturely reality. It is wholly through our fallen reason. The place where God's Word is revealed is objectively and subjectively the cosmos in which sin reigns. The form of God's Word, then, is in fact the form of the cosmos which stands in contradiction to God. It has as little ability to reveal God to us as we have to see God in it. If God's Word is revealed in it, it is revealed "through it," of course, but in such a way that this "through it" means "in spite of it."[17]

Revelation means the incarnation of the Word of God. Implied in this is God's actual entry into secular reality. If God did not speak to us in this way, he would not speak to us at all. To evade or deny the secularity of the Word of God is to evade Christ. God's unveiling of himself in secularity is his grace towards us. The desire to know God in a direct way is, therefore, a desire for righteousness by works: "We . . . must cleave to the true and actual Christ as He lies in the crib and in the Virgin's lap."[18]

In relation to this paradox Barth introduces the conceptuality of "veiling" and "unveiling." When God's Word is spoken to us, it comes to us veiled or unveiled—not partly veiled and partly unveiled. We do not receive God's speech as partly God and partly human but as wholly God or wholly human—either veiled in its unveiling or unveiled in its veiling. This must always be the case as the secular form apart from the divine content cannot be the Word of God. But, equally, the divine content without the secular form cannot be the Word of God. The secular cannot suffice, but nor can it be left behind. The former would give us realistic theology, the latter idealistic. Both would be bad theology. The convergence of form and content is discernible to God, but not to us: "What is discernible by us is always form without content or content without form. Our thinking can be realistic or idealistic but it cannot be Christian. Obviously the concept of synthesis would be the least Christian of all, for it would mean no more and no less than trying to do God's miraculous act ourselves."[19] According to Barth, "believing means either hearing the divine content of God's Word even though nothing but the secular form is discernible by us or it means hearing the secular form of God's Word even though only its divine content is discernible by us."[20] It is only in the consummation of God's purposes for his creation that we will be relieved of this alternation. To abandon the indirectness of the knowledge of God is to abandon true faith.

---

17. Ibid., 166.
18. Ibid., 169.
19. Ibid., 175.
20. Ibid., 176.

The speech of God is and remains, for us, a mystery. Concluding his account of speech as the mystery of God, Barth draws attention to the person of the Holy Spirit. "To say Holy Spirit in preaching or theology is always to say a final word."[21] In Barth's view our hearing of the Word of God is a possibility only in and through the miracle that is the work of the Holy Spirit. To say that we can only hear the Word of God in faith is the same thing as to say we can only hear the Word of God by the Holy Spirit. There is no *method* whatsoever that can assure us of hearing the Word of God as it is not a possibility we have of ourselves. It is only by the Holy Spirit—by faith—that this is possible. We may speak only of how this event (our hearing of the Word of God) occurred after the event. In this way we may speak of "experiencing the Word of God," but, as Barth says, the only method of which we may speak is the "method of faith."

The Knowability of the Word of God

Barth prefers to speak of the "knowability of God" rather than the "knowledge of God." In so doing, he hopes to guard against any idea that there is a method that can be adopted in which the knowledge of God may be achieved. "We cannot produce this event and so we cannot give a basis for our reference; we could do so only by producing the event to which it points and letting it speak for itself."[22]

After the Event

The knowability of the Word of God is the presupposition of the church. If this were not so, both proclamation and dogmatics would be pointless and meaningless activities. So, when we ask about the "knowability" of God we "look back from the knowledge of God and . . . ask about the presuppositions and conditions on the basis of which it comes about that God is known."[23] Revelation is an event in the sphere of human experience, but it is always a movement from God, and all that we say of revelation must work from this "givenness." "God's revelation breaks through the emptiness of the movement of thought which we call our knowledge of God."[24]

It is inappropriate to speak in universal terms. We do not ask "How can *all* people know the Word of God?" because this is not a matter of universality. We do not speak of people in general, but rather we speak very concretely and specifically of people in the church. In the context of the church, the Word of God is

---

21. Ibid., 182.
22. Ibid., 228.
23. Barth, *Church Dogmatics II/1*, 63.
24. Ibid., 74.

known and therefore can be known. This being so, it must have been spoken and it must have come as a divine call to specific people.

If the Word of God is addressed to humanity it is because it is intended that the Word of God be known in the sphere of human existence. It is given to men and women in order that they may hear it and be transformed by it. Barth does not generalize the point, and insists that humankind in general has no capacity for receiving the Word of God. Barth explicitly rejects the suggestion that God's encounter with humanity is to be understood as a human religious experience that can be established historically and psychologically—an experience understood as the actualization of a general, demonstrable religious human capacity. Understood in this way, knowledge of the Word of God is the actualization of a specific possibility residing in human nature. Barth is fundamentally opposed to the idea that the knowledge of God is an anthropological possibility.

Barth does not deny that the Word of God may become an experience for humanity. What concerns him is how such an experience can come about. He writes:

> There can be no objection in principle to describing this event as "experience" and even as "religious experience." The quarrel is not with the term nor with the true and important thing the term might finally denote, namely, the supremely real and determinative entry of the Word of God into the reality of man. But the term is burdened—this is why we avoid it—with the underlying idea that man generally is capable of religious experience or that this capability has the critical significance of a norm.[25]

The issue at stake here is whether or not the event in which the Word of God is experienced can be placed alongside other events of human experience. Does it require a human potential that must be employed to make it an event? Is it bound up with some human property? Barth is clear that the human capacity to hear the Word of God cannot be attributed to humanity in general or any human being in particular. "God's Word is no longer grace, and grace itself no longer grace, if we ascribe to man a predisposition towards this Word, a possibility of knowledge regarding it that is intrinsically and independently native to him."[26] The Word that God speaks is one of reconciliation between God and humanity, and if this Word leans upon a human potential then we cannot speak of a radical renewal. Such a radical renewal is not possible unless men and women understand themselves as sinners living by grace and therefore as sinners closed up against God.

> [T]here can be no question of any ability to hear or understand or know on his part, of any capability that he the creature, the sinner, the one who waits, has to bring to this Word, but that the possibility of knowledge cor-

---

25. Barth, *Church Dogmatics I/1*, 193.
26. Ibid., 194.

responding to the real Word of God has come to him, that it represents an inconceivable *novum* compared to all his ability and capability, and that it is to be understood as a pure fact, in exactly the same way as the real Word of God itself.[27]

Barth discerns the ubiquitous influence of Renaissance philosopher Descartes in "modernist" theology. His proof of the existence of God derives from human self-certainty, but for Barth this will not do. He states emphatically that in theology it is impossible to think along Cartesian lines. "For we do not find the Word of God in the reality present to us. Rather—and this is something quite different—the Word of God finds us in the reality present to us. Again it cannot be produced again out of our direct experience. Whenever we know it, we are rather begotten by it according to Jas. 1:18."[28] The Word of God, because it is not a human possibility (deriving from a human capacity), is grounded and established in itself. We do not ask, therefore, of the will or intent of humanity with regard to the Word of God, but of the will and intent of God. "Men can know the Word of God because and in so far as God wills that they know it."[29]

In explicating his rejection of the "human possibility," Barth asserts that "We possess no analogy on the basis of which the nature and being of God as the Lord can be accessible to us."[30] But we do have a concept of lordship. Why should that not be extended "to the infinite and the absolute" of the lordship of God? Barth rejects this line of reasoning. *Our* ideas of lordship cannot help but rather hinder our understanding of the lordship of God. "For in the last resort they do not point us to God, but to ourselves, to our God-alienated souls, to our threatened life on this side of death, to a merely possible lordship set in the sphere of our choosing."[31] If we know of the lordship of God, it is through revelation alone, to which our understanding of human lordship cannot make any contribution. Barth extends this analysis to reject, in the same way, any continuity between our human concepts of creation and reconciliation, and what we know of God as creator and reconciler through revelation.

These observations, which we will take up in the next chapter, underline Barth's fundamental rejection of the supposition or speculation that "behind or above the fact of the real knowledge of God there is a kind of empty space which can be filled up by the assertions of an overlapping doctrine of being and knowledge in general."[32] The knowledge of God is known in the event of God making

---

27. Ibid.
28. Ibid., 195–96.
29. Ibid., 196.
30. Barth, *Church Dogmatics II/1*, 75.
31. Ibid., 76.
32. Ibid., 65.

himself known. Apart from this event, there is neither knowledge of God, nor knowledge that there is no knowledge of God.

The Fulfillment in Humanity

Barth affirms that God *is* known. Knowledge of God is a possibility for humanity because of God's grace and mercy. Barth refers to this as the "readiness of God."

If we are to inquire of the "readiness of humanity," as Barth does, it is necessary to affirm that this latter "readiness" is a possibility only insofar as it is encompassed by the former. Barth opposes natural theology because it attributes to the readiness of humanity an autonomous status. "In its own way all natural theology circles about the problem of the readiness of man to know God. It does so in its own way, i.e., by elevating the readiness of man into an independent factor, so that the readiness of God is not understood as the only one that comes under consideration, nor is the readiness of man regarded as included within it, and completely dependent upon it."[33] However, if in the readiness of God grace and mercy are bestowed upon humanity, the assertion of the readiness of humanity—*qua* autonomous humanity—is an assertion in defiance of God's grace and mercy. The person who makes such an assertion is one "who wants to carry everything, even—a very Atlas—the whole world. Under no circumstances will he let himself be carried. Therefore finally and at the deepest level he will always be an enemy of grace and a hater and denier of his real neediness."[34]

If there is no autonomous readiness, there must be, nevertheless, a readiness of humanity and as such a positive statement is to be made. To reach this positive statement, we must reach beyond our anthropology and ecclesiology to the readiness of humanity that is found in the one individual, Jesus Christ. "In Christian doctrine, and therefore in the doctrine of the knowledge and knowability of God, we have always to take in blind seriousness the basic Pauline perception of Colossians 3 which is that of all Scripture—that our life is hid with Christ in God."[35] Here the central christological aspect comes decisively into view. Barth explains, "Jesus Christ is the knowability of God on our side, as He is the grace of God itself, and therefore also the knowability of God on God's side."[36] In this it may seem that humanity is still left to "stand outside," but God in Jesus Christ is man, and as a consequence "In our flesh God knows himself. Therefore in Him it is a fact that our flesh knows God Himself."[37] In Jesus Christ, what is impossible for humanity is, nevertheless, fulfilled in humanity.

---

33. Ibid., 128–29.
34. Ibid., 136.
35. Ibid., 149.
36. Ibid., 150.
37. Ibid., 151.

We have only to speak ... the name of Jesus Christ, and in this name we say the one thing, but also the most positive thing, which is to be said about man's readiness for God. In Him the enmity of man against the grace of God is overcome, therefore man is no more outside, where God must be unknowable to him because he does not accept the grace in which God makes Himself knowable to him. He is inside, where God is knowable to Himself, the Father to the Son and the Son to the Father, where in the Son, therefore, God is also knowable to him, man."[38]

The question that now emerges is how humanity can participate in Jesus Christ. The answer that Barth gives is that not only has Jesus Christ participated in our humanity as an event in time and space and been revelation among us, he now—and for all eternity—stands before the Father as our representative. "Jesus Christ Himself sees to it that in Him and by Him we are not outside but inside. He Himself sees to it that His readiness is valid for us who are not identical with Him, and who in ourselves are not ready for God. He sees to it that what is true in Him in the height is and remains true in our depth."[39]

The readiness of humanity for God is in Jesus Christ. The participation of humanity in Jesus Christ is the work of the Holy Spirit. Here we must acknowledge the eschatological aspect of the work of the Holy Spirit in human lives: the outpouring of the Holy Spirit must be understood as anticipation rather than fulfillment. We walk by faith and not by sight. Barth writes: "Faith does not consist in an inward and immanent transformation of man, although there can be no faith without such a transformation. Basically, faith is more than all the transformation that follows it. As the work of the Holy Spirit it is man's new birth from God, on the basis of which man can already live here by what he is there in Jesus Christ and therefore in truth."[40]

If humanity knows God, there must be a readiness of humanity for God. We have established that this is the humanity of God in Jesus Christ. Having touched on the work of the Holy Spirit in the context of human participation in Christ, we must now offer a fuller exposition of the work of the Holy Spirit in God's revelation in Barth's work.

The Holy Spirit

As a further explication of what has already been said, Barth speaks of the Holy Spirit as the subjective reality of revelation. "The revelation of God in its subjective reality consists in the existence of men who have been led by God Himself to a certain conviction. They believe that the objective reality of revelation exists for

---

38. Ibid., 153.
39. Ibid., 156.
40. Ibid., 158.

them. They believe that it exists for them in such a way that they can no longer understand their own existence by itself, but only in the light of that reality: not apart from it, therefore, but only in relation to it."[41]

As christology must follow the fact of Jesus Christ, and has no other grounds, so it must be with the work of the Holy Spirit, in which the objective reality of revelation becomes a subjective reality. We cannot peer behind the event—we must accept it as the point from which we must make our departure. "All that we have to consider is that here the leap has already been made, the unheard-of and to us impossible leap from God to man."[42] If revelation is truly revelation, the gap is bridged. "If it really is revelation, if it does attain its goal, if there is in fact a revealedness of revelation, then necessarily it must be revealed—and previously was not revealed—both in the being and, in fact, as the being, of men."[43] Thus the objective reality of revelation becomes a subjective reality of human beings.

Barth's use of the terms "objective" and "subjective" is very particular to his own dogmatic development. Because of the givenness of the subjective reality of revelation, there is a kind of objectivity about this. Barth certainly rules out an interpretation in which the reality of revelation is the convergence of the "divine objective giving" and the "human subjective receiving" if the latter is understood as an autonomous act. It must be noted, also, that while in abstraction the "objective" and "subjective" of revelation may be considered separately, the distinction may not be made into a separation. Barth writes: "If we think of the subjective as something which has later to be added, then necessarily we have thought of the objective as an idol."[44] But Barth also insists that "the subjective reality of revelation can as such never be made into an independent theme."[45]

Barth starts with the subjective reality of revelation and moves on to the subjective possibility of revelation. Again Barth adopts an *a posteriori* method asking about the possibility in the light of the reality. "[I]t is possible as it is real."[46] It is possible not because it is a possibility for humanity, but because it is a possibility for God in the outpouring of the Holy Spirit. Barth identifies three ways in which revelation becomes a possibility for humanity in its freedom. Firstly, God's word is brought to the hearing of humanity. "The reason, and the only reason, why man can receive revelation in the Holy Spirit is that God's Word is brought to his hearing in the Holy Spirit. For the capacity of man to do this depends upon the fact, and only upon the fact, that it is God's Word which is brought to his hear-

---

41. Barth, *Church Dogmatics I/2*, 232.
42. Ibid., 234.
43. Ibid., 236.
44. Ibid., 238.
45. Ibid., 240.
46. Ibid., 246.

ing in revelation."[47] Secondly, God comes to be the Savior of humanity in person and does what humanity is incapable of doing. And thirdly, it is because in the outpouring of the Holy Spirit the Word of God becomes the master of humanity.

If the subjectivity as well as the objectivity of revelation is of God, what is the meaning of the participation of humanity in this possibility? Barth insists that we can never comprehend our participation, as something established on our side, but we can know that the possibility has been given to us. And it is genuinely *our* participation in the possibility given to us by God and not an eclipsing of our humanity. "Participation . . . does not signify an abolition of our identity with ourselves. It is a frightful misunderstanding to try to interpret it along the lines of a possession or trance. There are such states, but only when the consciousness of identity is removed."[48]

This leads us to a consideration of the theme of experience. Barth's hesitance about using the terms "experience" and "religious experience" has already been noted. His concern is that they are conceived in terms of an autonomous human capacity for God. Nevertheless, it is necessary to acknowledge that the Word of God is a reality, and one that can become determinative in human experience.

Religious Experience

According to Barth, the knowledge of God's Word becomes possible for humanity in the reality of God's Word. If the knowledge of God's Word is possible it follows from this that an experience of God's Word is possible. Barth affirms this explicitly:

> We have defined knowledge as the confirmation of human acquaintance with an object whereby its truth becomes a determination of the existence of the man who has the knowledge. This determination of the existence of the man who has the knowledge we call experience. Man does not exist abstractly but concretely, i.e., in experiences, in determinations of his existence by objects, by things outside him and distinct from him . . . If knowledge of God's Word can become possible for men, this must mean that they can have experience of God's Word, that they can be what they are as determined by God's Word.[49]

Barth affirms in the strongest possible way that the Word of God is grounded and established in itself, but this does not mean that (despite the radical distinction between God and humanity) it cannot be a reality in the lives of men and women. Barth believes that a person cannot know the revelation of God without

47. Ibid., 247.
48. Ibid., 266.
49. Barth, *Church Dogmatics I/1*, 198.

the Spirit's action (the Spirit being the subjective reality and the subjective possibility of revelation). Certainly, there is no capacity for God in humanity (there is no analogy of being), but there *is* a possibility for God in God's freedom to establish a point of contact with human beings (the "analogy of faith"). This is established in the event in which it becomes a reality. As a reality in the lives of men and women, the Word of God becomes a determination of their lives.

Barth reminds us that "If there is a such determination of human existence by God's Word, the primary point to be made is that this is not to be confused with a determination man can give his own existence."[50] He goes on to explain: "No determination man can give himself is as such determination by God's Word. Nor is there any place here for the view that this experience is a kind of cooperation between divine determining and human self-determining."[51]

Rather than placing revelation and experience in opposition, Barth affirms the necessity of experience. It is not an immanent human possibility but it is a possibility that can be established and made a reality by God. Barth explains: "If man lets himself be told by the Word of God that he has a Lord, that he is the creature of this Lord, that he is a lost sinner blessed by Him, that he awaits eternal redemption and is thus a stranger in this sphere of time, this specific content of the Word experienced by him will flatly prohibit him from ascribing the possibility of this experience to himself either wholly or in part or from dialectically equating the divine possibility actualised in this experience with a possibility of his own."[52]

Barth has no concern to set up experience and revelation in opposition (as he is sometimes accused of doing) or to present them as alternatives. He wishes only to establish with clarity that the human self-determination must itself be determined by God if in it we are to experience God's Word. "[M]en in their self-determination can be determined by God's Word: not just determined by any external factor that comes upon them, though naturally this can be true as well, but also determined by the Word of God."[53]

In his discussion of the experience of the Word of God, Barth warns against looking exclusively towards any one particular anthropological center or locus. What is at issue here is nothing less than the whole person. "We may quietly regard the will and the conscience and feeling and all other possible anthropological centres as possibilities of human self-determination and then understand them in their totality as determined by the Word of God which affects the whole man."[54] Barth quotes an illustration of Eduard Böhl to clarify the point:

50. Ibid., 199.
51. Ibid.
52. Ibid.
53. Ibid., 201.
54. Ibid., 202.

> "It is only in appearance that the rainbow stands on the earth, in reality it arches over the earth; true, it stoops down to the earth, yet it does not stand on our earth, but is only perceived from it. So it is with divine truth; this needs no human support, as the rainbow does not need the earth. True, it shines on man and he receives it; yet it is not dependent on man. It withdraws and man remains in darkness; it returns and man walks in light. But man is not its assistant; he cannot produce the light; similarly he cannot store it."[55]

Barth also deals with the issue of revelation and experience elsewhere. In his discussion, in §16, of the Holy Spirit as the subjective possibility of revelation Barth asks: "[W]hat is the significance of this miracle of Jesus Christ actualised in us in the outpouring of the Holy Spirit; what is the import of this encounter, *so that we can and must assert positively that it can confront us, that we do acquire a part in the divine possibility which is realised in it?*"[56] Responding to the question of engagement that he raises, Barth writes:

> [I]t is a question of our taking, receiving, laying hold of, appropriating the share in the divine possibility which is allotted to us. Moreover, we can and must realise that this participation is achieved in our own experience and activity, in that act of self-determination which we call our human existence. This participation has nothing whatever to do with a magical invasion of the inter-related totality of our physico-psychical human life by supernatural factors and forces. It does signify a limitation and interruption of our existence. Our existence is confronted by something outside and over against it, by which it is determined, and indeed totally determined. But it is determined as the act of our self-determination in the totality of its possibilities.[57]

For Barth the outpouring of the Holy Spirit of God is the event in which the whole person is confronted. It is not the infilling of a "God-shaped hole" or anything of the sort. "Man is confronted in the totality of his own possibilities, and therefore in all possible conditions and attitudes . . . In view of this totality of revelation to us we must not refer the revealedness in us to some obscure or even luminous place apart from our own experience and activity. We must not refer it to a place where we can exempt ourselves from all responsibility."[58] Revelation is not and cannot be a passing by or hovering above; it is the radical confrontation of the human being in its totality. It must be regarded as a miracle, for it is no human

---

55. Ibid., 223.
56. Barth, *Church Dogmatics I/2*, 265; my emphasis.
57. Ibid., 266.
58. Ibid., 267.

possibility, but as Barth says, "this does not mean that it is not we ourselves who are participators, we ourselves in our own experience and activity."[59]

In this confrontation there is what Barth describes as "acknowledgment." Acknowledgment entails the concept of knowledge. Barth believes that the Word of God is primarily and predominantly speech—communication from person to person. It expresses the fact that experience of God's Word involves the relation of a person to another person—the person of God. Acknowledgement is in the control of the person who acknowledges. This means not only subjection to a necessity, but adaptation to the meaningfulness of this necessity, approval of it and not just acquiescence. Here we refer to the purposiveness of God's Word and to its content as the Word of the Lord—the Word of humankind's Creator, Reconciler, and Redeemer. Barth says that the Word of God does not break people, but it does bend them in order to bring them into conformity with itself.

Human acknowledgement of the Word of God is human approval of the Word of God. However, the acknowledgement is not established on the basis of persuasion between equals. In this acknowledgement there is a yielding of the one who acknowledges before the one acknowledged. This is submission to authority. Barth insists that this does not contradict self-determination, but it does mean that the human self-determination takes place in a particular place in and at a particular point. It finds its beginning and its basis in another higher determination. He writes: "In the act of acknowledgement, the life of man, without ceasing to be the self-determining life of this man, has now its centre, its whence, the meaning of its attitude, and the criterion whether this attitude really has the corresponding meaning—it has all this outside itself, in the thing or person acknowledged. So far as it has all this, it has it from the thing or person acknowledged."[60] There is a human appropriation of the Word of God, but this is a possibility only as God gives it to be a possibility in the Holy Spirit: "Therewith we are . . . brought up against the frontier of what we can say about experience of God's Word as such. The final thing to be said is that while the attitude of acknowledgement *vis-à-vis* God's Word is really an attitude of man, an act of his self-determination, nevertheless it is the act of that self-determination of man whose meaning and basis, whose final seriousness and true content, whose truth and reality, cannot be ascribed to man himself but only to his determination by the Word of God."[61]

Barth is aware that many evangelicals will go along with him in his doctrine of revelation insofar as he affirms that there can be no faith unless God bestows it. But disagreement arises when Barth insists that faith must always come anew and can never become a possession:

---

59. Ibid.
60. Barth, *Church Dogmatics I/1*, 207–8.
61. Ibid., 208.

> Tell them . . . that for man generally, for man without faith or before faith, the epistemological order must . . . be from God to man, that without preceding revelation there can be no faith, and they will concede your point, not yet being affected themselves. But tell them that this epistemological order applies also and particularly to the religious man, that he also and particularly has no possibility, not even a received possibility, but can only receive the possibility of experience of God's Word, can use it only as it is conferred in the actuality of reception, tell them that this possibility is and remains God's possibility and does not pass out of His hands into any other hands, tell them this and at once bitter and irreconcilable controversy breaks out. When we tell them this, when we oppose to that thesis our counterthesis, which is separated from it only by a blade's breadth and yet by a chasm's depth, then an impressive majority among both the leaders and the led in the modern Evangelical Church is passionately against us.[62]

Barth calls this view "indirect Christian Cartesianism."[63] It is "indirect" in the sense that it does not look to itself but to the God who gives. But in the giving, there an "*influxus*" into the one to whom God speaks. Associated with the acknowledgement of the Word of God is also a possession: "revelation" passes from God to humanity. This is what Barth opposes.

If this "indirect Christian Cartesianism" was true to the reality of the Word of God, and we really were dealing with the possibility of knowledge of things that enter into the human sphere, it would be appropriate and reasonable to seek out the appropriate experts and specialists, as it would be in any other field. But with regard to the possibility of the knowledge of the Word of God, Barth insists that the situation is different. There are certainly experts—theologians and dogmaticians—who reflect upon the echo of its reality in the event of experiencing it. But if, in doing this, there is suggested an infusion, a problem immediately arises: "When we try to find the content of divine Spirit in the (pardoned) consciousness of man, are we not like the man who wanted to scoop out in a sieve the reflection of the beautiful silvery moon found in a pond?"[64]

This is an issue of central importance for Barth. He wishes to affirm that there *is* a human acknowledgement of what comes to humanity from God in his revelation. But if what comes *also remains* as a human possession, how will it be possible to sustain that this is God's free and sovereign activity in a fallen cosmos that is alienated from him? God retains power over his self-disclosure completely. Humanity cannot, by any means, come to know God if he does not give himself to be known.

Human acknowledgment of the Word of God may be regarded as part of the sphere of human religious history. As such, it is susceptible to being interpreted as

62. Ibid., 213.
63. Ibid., 214.
64. Ibid., 216.

an aspect of the cultural life of humanity and as an entirely this-worldly attempt to establish religious culture as an element of civilization. As such, it is human endeavor—human work. But human acknowledgement cannot be taken in this way. Barth warns: "If we cling to what we can affirm and investigate as the human acknowledgement of God's Word, to what can be experienced in Christian experience, where shall we find there the criterion by which to distinguish this experience from others, the authentic from the inauthentic? What is there here to stop us interpreting everything in terms of the religious, the cultural, the human generally, or finally indeed the biological?"[65] The point that Barth presses is that it is not what humanity can establish as such that distinguishes what must be said of the event in which the Word of God becomes the determination of human existence.

> As man knows God's Word, all that we have said about this act can be and is experienced. It becomes real and can be established psychologically. There takes place an understanding, a personal involvement, an acceptance, an assent, an approval, a making present of remote times, an obedience, a decision, a halting before the mystery, a stimulation by the inner life, the basing of man's whole life on this mystery that is beyond himself. All this takes place and has to do so ... But the fact that all this happens and must happen does not mean in the least that the possibility of experience of God's Word is to be seen and found in this event, that in it human self-determination becomes the opposite pole of the divine determination, that man becomes a "word-bound ego" in contemplation of which we must orientate ourselves in the question of the Word of God.[66]

God calls us in the totality of our human existence, but no response to this call can be conceived as being a counterpart to the event that God initiates. In this way the Word of God is a limit. It is not possible to look behind it and, insofar as human self-determination *does* happen in acknowledgement of God's Word—in the human experience of God's Word—it will not be able to understand itself, if it is real. As Barth puts it:

> It will just be true from God that human existence is engaged here in acknowledgement of the Word of God. For it will be true that God has spoken and man has heard. A new, regenerate man will arise in the act of this acknowledgement as the man whom God has addressed and who hears God, unknown, of course, to himself and others, in a newness that cannot be ascertained, for what can be ascertained in him will always be the old, not possessing himself, for to the extent that he possesses himself he certainly does not possess this regenerate man.[67]

65. Ibid., 217.
66. Ibid., 219–20.
67. Ibid., 222.

The knowability of God's Word is only to be found within God's Word. It can take place as an event, but it cannot be explained. We cannot anticipate it; but we can know it when it comes into view for us. "The knowability of the Word of God stands or falls . . . with the act of its real knowledge, which is not under our control."[68] In experiencing the Word of God, we turn away from ourselves because we are orientated towards the Word of God. God makes himself known to us and in this way we are moved. *This* is the knowability of the Word of God: recollection of the event in which it came into view, and expectation that God will again, in his self-manifestation, come into view.

> If a man, the Church, Church proclamation and dogmatics think they can handle the Word and faith like capital at their disposal, they simply prove thereby that they have neither the Word nor faith. When we have them, we do not regard them as a possession but strain after them, hungering and thirsting, and for that reason blessed. The same is true of the possibility of knowledge of God's Word. When we know it, we expect to know it. The assurance of its affirmation is thus the assurance of its expectation—the expectation which rests on its previous presence, on the apprehended promise, or, as we can already say here, on received and believed baptism—but still the expectation.[69]

In this way Barth shows that one must let go of the assurance that one brings oneself in order to be thrown back completely on God's grace. In this we see the dynamic of faith in assurance and expectation.

Faith

We must briefly consider Barth's treatment of the Word of God and faith. Faith is experience; a particular experience of a particular person at a particular time. Faith refers to the Word, Christ. Jesus Christ presents himself to faith as its object. Faith is faith by virtue of the fact that this object is given:

> [T]his object is the free God who is hidden from man because he is a sinner, who has, of course, put man in the new state of faith in which He can be known by him, but who in this very state—it is indeed that of faith—wills to be sought and found anew and then anew again. For Faith, He is and remains enclosed in objectivity, in the externality of the Word of God, in Jesus Christ. He must teach man to seek Him and He must show Himself to him in order that he may find Him. But it is by this external object that the Christian faith lives.[70]

---

68. Ibid., 224.
69. Ibid., 225.
70. Ibid., 231–32.

Barth explicitly rejects a symmetrical formulation in which faith is the human contribution to the knowledge of God—humanity's addition to the act of God. But Barth says: "What makes Him the true God is that one believes in Him in true faith. And the fact that the faith in which the true God is believed is true faith is not due in any way or in any sense to itself but to the fact that the true God has revealed Himself to it, i.e., it is due to the Word of God."[71] Barth insists that it is quite plain that faith has nothing to do with the shifting of the reality of faith from its object to the believing subject:

> [O]ne may say of the knowability of the Word of God given in the event of faith that it is not a possibility which man for his part brings to real knowledge, nor is it a possibility which in real knowledge accrues to man from some source as an enrichment of his existence. But as faith has its absolute and unconditional beginning in God's Word independently of the inborn or acquired characteristics and possibilities of man, and as it, as faith, never in any respect lives from or by anything other than the Word, so it is in every respect with the knowability of the Word of God into which we are now enquiring.[72]

We must not conceive of the knowability of the Word of God as some extraordinary art or skill. Its practice does not presuppose a special natural or supernatural facility or capacity. The Word of God comes as grace in God's freedom and it does not come according to the condition of the recipient. This is the scandal of the gospel:

> The believer is the same ungifted and idle or gifted and busy man he was as an unbeliever and may become again. He believes as the man he is, with the inventory corresponding to his condition. There is no question of an exalting or abasing of his existence; what is at issue is the grace or judgment of God on his existence . . . It is all highly extraordinary, of course, in so far as the Word of God becomes the truth here to this man and his knowledge. But whether extraordinary or not it is at least a possibility given to us, a possibility given for use, not for putting in an inventory or catalogue, not for storing on ice or placing in a museum.[73]

In faith there is a sense in which humanity conforms to God. This is not deification, but an adaptation of humanity to the Word of God. In faith a person really does receive the Word of God and has been made able to receive it. But this ability is not his or her own but is on loan from God. Again this is essential if there is to be *real* knowledge of the Word of God—if there is to be a point of contact between God and humanity. "There can be no receiving of God's Word

---

71. Ibid., 233.
72. Ibid., 236.
73. Ibid., 237.

unless there is something common to the speaking God and hearing man in this event, a similarity for all the dissimilarity implied by the distinction between God and man, a point of contact between God and man, if we may now adopt this term too."[74]

And so, despite rejecting the possibility of receiving the Word of God on the basis of an acquired or innate human capacity, Barth affirms that there is, indeed, a point of contact that God makes possible; he must make this possible if a person is to receive the Word of God. At this point in his argument, Barth makes reference to the image of God in humanity. Barth believes that the *imago Dei* in humanity is not merely distorted but totally annihilated. Humanity has totally lost its capacity for God. The possibility that comes through faith is not one that provides the basis for any common ground for discussion with philosophical and theological anthropology:

> The image of God in man of which we must speak here and which forms the real point of contact for God's Word is the *rectitudo* which through Christ is raised up from real death and thus restored or created anew, and which is real as man's possibility for the Word of God. The reconciliation of man with God in Christ also includes, or already begins with, the restitution of the lost point of contact. Hence this point of contact is not real outside faith; it is real only in faith. In faith man is created by the Word of God for the Word of God, existing in the Word of God and not in himself, not in virtue of his humanity and personality, not even on the basis of creation, for that which by creation was possible for man in relation to God has been lost by the fall. Hence one can only speak theologically and not both theologically and also philosophically of this point of contact, as of all else that is real in faith, i.e., through the grace of reconciliation."[75]

This new possibility that faith brings is a new person. Rom 6:3–4 suggests that this is to be understood in terms of "death" and "re-birth," and a new birth that is from God. But Barth is clear that this "re-birth" does not establish a permanent human state; it is not a received and established condition. "The statement about the indwelling of Christ that takes place in faith must not be turned into an anthropological statement."[76]

What happens in faith is a "capacity of the incapable." And, although the event of God's revelation can never become a human possession, the reality of it is not without its effect. Indeed, Barth claims, "The proof of the knowability of the Word consists in confessing it. In faith and confession the Word of God becomes a human thought and a human word, certainly in infinite dissimilarity and inadequacy, yet not in total alienation from its real prototype, but a true copy for all its

74. Ibid., 238.
75. Ibid., 239.
76. Ibid., 240.

human and sinful perversion, an unveiling of it even as its veiling."[77] Barth says of the believing person that they have not "come to faith"; rather "faith has come to them." The believer does not adopt faith; faith adopts them. The believer cannot be seen as the acting subject. However, although the Word is given to the believer, the believer's response is not passive. In faith we must in freedom become the people who apart from faith we were not free to be. We must participate in the revelation of God.

The Community of the Church and the Word of God

In the context of his discussion of the Holy Spirit as the subjective reality of revelation, Barth touches on the church as the community of the Word of God. This is a theme that is explored in surprisingly modest scope. However, what Barth has to say at this point is certainly of significance and the importance of the theme will be developed later.

It must be recognized that the church does not establish its members as the recipients of revelation. And because one is outside the church does not mean that one is excluded from receiving God's revelation. On the one hand, in the New Testament and in the Old Testament in particular, there are those who appear "at the given place" (in the church or as members of the Israelite nation) and yet appear not to be recipients of revelation. On the other hand, however, "in the Old Testament . . . figures are constantly turning up, who, quite away from the given place, outside the nation of Israel, seem nevertheless to have become genuine recipients of God's revelation."[78] Barth suggests that "this . . . appears more and more to have the significance of a corrective. Those who perhaps boast of their membership instead of boasting in God must be checked and shamed. Those who within its membership do not become recipients of revelation must be given a sign of judgment."[79]

In addition to this point, we must note an asymmetry in the relationship between God and the church. The church is bound to the Word of God in a way that must be distinguished radically from the way in which the Word is bound to the church. As Barth notes elsewhere, the Word is bound to the church "only so far as the Word, in once bestowing itself upon the Church, has bound itself to it as promise for the future."[80] Extending the theme of asymmetry, Barth writes:

---

77. Ibid., 241.
78. Barth, *Church Dogmatics I/2*, 210.
79. Ibid., 210.
80. Barth, *Church Dogmatics II/1*, 5.

> While God is as little bound to the Church as to the Synagogue, the recipients of His revelation are. They are what they are because the Church is what it is, and because they are in the Church and not apart from the Church and not outside the Church. And when we say "Church," we do not mean merely the inward and invisible coherence of those whom God in Christ calls His own, but also the outward and visible coherence of those who have heard in time, and have confessed to their hearing, that in Christ they are God's. The reception of revelation occurs within, not without, this twofold coherence.[81]

It is implicit in this that although God may choose to reveal himself outside the synagogue and the church (and that is, of course, God's business and not ours), the life of the community is of great importance. Barth makes this explicit in his comment that "Not secondarily, but primarily and radically, [the life of the children of God] . . . is the life of a community."[82] The church corresponds, on the human side, with the objective reality of revelation in Jesus Christ. The church, despite the fact that it is a human institution, cannot be regarded as the product of humanity. "Although it is in the world, it cannot be thought of as owing its existence to this world. Although we are in the Church, are indeed ourselves the Church, the Church cannot be thought of otherwise than as the reality of God's revelation for us, i.e., it is in strict relation to the revelation of God in us, it is in complete subordination to it, yet in that relation and subordination it is equally revelation, it is equally God's own act."[83]

The existence of the church cannot be understood apart from the outpouring of the Holy Spirit. This is the mystery of Pentecost: "the gift which men who themselves are not Christ now receive in their entire humanity for Christ's sake, the gift of existing from Christ's standpoint for Christ and unto Christ, 'the power to become the sons of God' (Jn. 1^{12})."[84] It is in the power of the Holy Spirit that the church proclaims the source of its life, and it is to the theme of the church's proclamation that we now turn.

Proclamation

Bonhoeffer spoke of the Word as the "inexpressible." But it is precisely this inexpressible Word that must be proclaimed by the church. This is Barth's understanding of the task of the church also, but what is "proclamation"? Barth answers: "Proclamation is human speech in and by which God Himself speaks like a king through the mouth of His herald, and which is meant to be heard and accepted as

81. Barth, *Church Dogmatics* I/2, 211.
82. Ibid., 217.
83. Ibid., 221.
84. Ibid., 221–22.

speech in and by which God Himself speaks."[85] The proclamation of the church, while remaining a creaturely voice, becomes the means by which God makes himself known. God makes himself real in the proclamation of the church.

As such, human talk about God must desire to serve the Word of God if it is to be proclamation, and it must point to a prior utterance by God himself. The proclamation cannot, as a human act, assume or presume that it is itself the Word of God; it can only take up the task. Creaturely utterance about God (intended as proclamation) is not itself grace, but it is placed in the service of grace. As a consequence, "[P]roclamation is not asked concerning its formal or material perfection, since even the highest possible perfection would not make human utterance proclamation, nor could the least imposing prevent it from being proclamation. It is simply asked whether it is service, whether it is commissioned."[86]

One can gain the impression that, for Barth, proclamation is to be exclusively identified with the preaching of the church. This might be reinforced by his trenchant criticism of the practice of the Roman Catholic Church in which he perceived an overemphasis on the Mass and insufficient emphasis on preaching. However, despite the priority that he attaches to oral proclamation, Barth does say that proclamation of the Word of God "is primarily and decisively preaching *and* the sacraments."[87] And, speaking of what is beyond what is "primary," Barth says, "The other, sacrificial and generally responsive elements in the Church's life may also be proclamation."[88] I will have much to say of these other elements later in the book.

It must be remembered that what Barth is attempting to articulate at this point in the *Church Dogmatics* is an understanding of the relation between proclamation and dogmatics. For Barth, the role of dogmatics is the humble questioning and testing of what the church intends as proclamation. To the extent that human words are intended as the means by which God will reveal himself to the church, they are to be considered as proclamation and the concern of the dogmatician. In this way the practical and pastoral theology of the church comes into view as do its liturgy and hymnody. Indeed, Barth makes the tart comment: "It is a strange thing that when there are revisions of books of order and hymn-books in the Evangelical churches every possible authority is usually consulted as a standard but not dogmatic science. The results naturally correspond."[89]

Of course, the church is not in a position to question its own proclamation in an absolute way, and therefore it cannot correct its proclamation in an absolute way. However, this does not preclude the possibility of a self-critical stance of

---

85. Barth, *Church Dogmatics I/1*, 52.
86. Ibid., 53.
87. Ibid., 80; my emphasis.
88. Ibid.
89. Ibid., 81.

church *vis-à-vis* its proclamation and this is the service that dogmatics has to offer to the church. We will give further consideration to Barth's understanding of the place of dogmatics at the end of this chapter.

God is not obliged to use what the church intends as proclamation, nor is God limited to using what the church intends as proclamation. The proclamation of the church is a means of grace, but the decision regarding its use resides in the sovereign freedom of God. God will do what God will do in his freedom: "God may speak to us through Russian Communism, a flute concerto, a blossoming shrub, or a dead dog. We do well to listen to Him if He really does."[90]

Barth criticizes "modernist" dogmatics for its lack of awareness that God must constantly say something to humanity that it is unable to say to itself. Barth sees in such dogmatics humanity speaking to itself. Here proclamation is conceived as an expression of the life of the community known as the church. It is an expression in which it draws from the treasures of those in the church and the interpretation of its own life. This is a view that Barth rejects. He comments: "Is it not plain that there is here a fateful confusion between the man of the present, the man of the *regnum gratiae*, and the man of eternal glory, who . . . neither needs nor will need any special talk about God, and consequently any being addressed by God, and consequently any Church? If we are not this man, whence does the Modernist doctrine get its legal ground?"[91]

We now turn to Barth's exposition of the forms in which God's revelation is mediated to humanity in terms of the scheme of his "threefold form." Barth begins this theme by taking up again the theme of the church's proclamation.

The Word of God in Its Threefold Form

In the event of revelation that which is creaturely becomes the means by which God reveals himself to humanity. In this way creaturely realities come to serve the purpose of God and achieve, in the grace of God, that which they have no power to do according to their own nature. As we have already noted, this is not only the way in which revelation *does* come to us, it is the way in which revelation *must* come if it is to reach us. God's revelation is mediated through creaturely realities.

It is appropriate to make a distinction between what God says to himself and what he says to humanity. In the former we are concerned with God's primary objectivity and in the latter, God's secondary objectivity. "In His triune life as such, objectivity, and with it knowledge, is divine reality before creaturely objectivity and knowledge exist. We call this the primary objectivity of God, and distinguish from it the secondary, i.e., the objectivity which He has for us too in His revela-

---

90. Ibid., 55. Barth does not hereby imply that these are the places in which we ordinarily *anticipate* that God will speak!

91. Ibid., 64.

tion, in which He gives Himself to be known by us as He knows Himself."[92] It is important to note that the former is to be differentiated from the latter "not by a lesser degree of truth, but by its particular form suitable for us, the creature."[93]

The Word of God Preached

Here Barth considers the relation between "real proclamation" and the church's preaching. Four points can be made:

Firstly, the church's proclamation is visible as the bread and wine of communion are visible. However, "They are not simply and visibly there . . . as that which they want to be and should be, as theologically relevant entities, as realities of revelation and faith. They have ever and again to come into being as this."[94] As proclamation *does* become "what it wants to be and should be," several things can be said of it. In the first place, it must be the Word of God that commissions the proclamation, rather than a scale of values immanent in human existence. There will be human motivations, but no proclamation is authentic unless over and above such motivations it rests on a commission that the church can only receive and have in the act of receiving.

Secondly, the Word of God must be the theme given to proclamation, if it is to be real proclamation. In this we are not saying that the Word of God is primarily the object of human perception, although it must become an object of human perception if it is to be proclaimed. Real proclamation does not rest in the fact that it is the object of human perception but in the fact that it is the Word of God—which can never be our possession.

Thirdly, the Word of God must judge the proclamation. There are no criteria by which we can ultimately substantiate the reality of proclamation. Its truth is given in itself as the act of God. The criterion is the Word of God. This may be both recollected and expected, but it is not at our disposal. We are not able to handle the criterion. The criterion must handle itself.

Finally, and crucially for Barth, the Word of God must be event: the event in which proclamation becomes real proclamation. This is the condition *sine qua non* if proclamation is to be true proclamation. Barth writes: "It is the miracle of revelation and faith when the misunderstanding does not constantly recur, when proclamation is for us not just human willing and doing characterised in some way but also and primarily and decisively God's own act, when human talk about God is for us not just that, but also and primarily and decisively God's own speech."[95]

---

92. Barth, *Church Dogmatics II/1*, 16.
93. Ibid.
94. Barth, *Church Dogmatics I/1*, 88.
95. Ibid., 93.

In his exposition of proclamation, Barth is careful to guard against docetism. If proclamation is real proclamation, it is speech that follows the speech of God—but it is concretely *human* speech that follows the divine speech:

> The miracle of real proclamation does not consist in the fact that the willing and doing of proclaiming man with all its conditioning and in all its problems is set aside, that in some way a disappearance takes place and a gap arises in the reality of nature, and that in some way there steps into this gap naked divine reality scarcely concealed by a mere remaining appearance of human reality . . . The willing and doing of proclaiming man . . . is not in any sense set aside in real proclamation. As Christ became true man and remains true man to all eternity, real proclamation becomes an event on the level of all other human events.[96]

The Word of God Written

Barth explains that proclamation must be ventured in recollection of previous revelation and in expectation of revelation in the future. In other words, church proclamation is based both upon the belief that revelation has already taken place, and that it will take place again. What kind of recollection is in mind here? Could it be the recollection of a revelation immanent in humanity's existence (a natural and original awareness of God)? Barth says that we cannot dismiss this possibility *a priori*. "The concept of divine freedom or potency provides no reason why this should be impossible."[97] However, Barth continues, "The real reason is that God did not make this specific use of His freedom and potency."[98] In support of his view, Barth points to the fact that the church does not appeal to itself as the source of the divine Word in support of the proclamation it seeks to make. It does not look to any hidden depths of its own. The church looks to itself only insofar as it looks to its own transcendent being—Jesus Christ—the one who establishes its existence. "He is immanent in it [the church] only as He is transcendent to it. This is the fact which makes the recollection of God's past revelation different from reflection on its own timeless ground of being. *It has pleased God to be its God in another way than that of pure immanence.*"[99]

The church is confronted by the Scripture and in this confrontation it is reminded that recollection of revelation relates not to a timeless truth immanent in the church but to the scriptural canon. Barth emphasizes that proclamation cannot be free floating. It does not start from scratch but recalls to memory a specific

---

96. Ibid., 94.
97. Ibid., 100.
98. Ibid.
99. Ibid., 100–101; my emphasis.

revelation in history that is quite distinct from the church, however important it may be for its genesis and its self-understanding.

> With its acknowledgement of the presence of the Canon the Church expresses the fact that it is not left to itself in its proclamation, that the commission on the ground of which it proclaims, the object which it proclaims, the judgment under which its proclamation stands and the event of real proclamation must all come from elsewhere, from without, and very concretely from without, in all the externality of the concrete Canon as a categorical imperative which is also historical, which speaks in time.[100]

It is not the words of Holy Scripture *per se* that are primary. These words are a deposit of the words of proclamation originally spoken by prophet and apostle. Barth quotes, with hearty approval, the words of Martin Luther: "'The Gospel simply means a preaching and crying out loud of God's grace and mercy merited and won by the Lord Jesus Christ with His death. And it is properly not what stands in books or is made up of letters, but rather an oral preaching and lively word and voice that rings out in the whole world and is publicly cried out loud that it may everywhere be heard.'"[101]

Barth distinguishes between canonical Scripture and the on-going proclamation of the church by pointing to the supremacy and "absolutely constitutive significance" of the former over the latter. He goes on to write, "if the Church is not alone in respect of its proclamation but finds itself in a concrete confrontation in which it is mindful of the past revelation of God, and if the concrete form of its opposite is really the biblical word of the prophets and apostles, then obviously the latter must have a fundamental distinction in relation to it."[102]

The thrust of Barth's argument here is not to give reasons for his positioning of the canon of Scripture in relation to the proclamation of the church so much as present it as an event that is to be described. To the question, "Why does the Canon, comprising the Old and New Testaments, have this authority?" Barth answers:

> It is the Canon because it imposed itself upon the Church as such, and continually does so. The Church's recollection of God's past revelation has the Bible specifically as its object because in fact this object and no other is the promise of future divine revelation which can make proclamation a duty for the Church and which can give it joy and courage for this duty. *If we thought we could say why this is so, we should again be acting as if we had in our hands a measure by which we could measure the Bible and on this basis assign it its distinctive position.* Our ultimate and decisive wisdom would

---

100. Ibid., 101.
101. Ibid., 102.
102. Ibid.

then be . . . the wisdom of a self-dialogue, even if a self-dialogue about the Bible. No, the Bible is the Canon just because it is so.¹⁰³

Canonical Scripture is, or becomes, the Word of God in exactly the same way that real proclamation is, or becomes, the Word of God. It is an event, and can be understood only as an event. But the fact that God's own address becomes the human Word of the Bible is God's concern and not ours. In this way, as in proclamation, the Bible is God's Word to the extent that God causes it to be his Word, to the extent that he speaks through it. *The point is not that we can grasp the words of the Bible, but the Bible grasps us by being the Word of God.*

The Word of God Revealed

In view of what has been said in the previous two sections about the Word proclaimed and written, it is clear that neither Scripture nor proclamation are in and of themselves revelation. The Bible is not God's past revelation, and church proclamation is not expected future revelation. The Bible is God's Word as it really bears witness to revelation, and proclamation is God's Word as it really promises revelation. Indeed, we dishonor the Bible if we equate it with revelation. It is only in the event of God's Word that revelation and the Bible become one. Barth writes:

> [T]he revelation to which the biblical witnesses direct their gaze as they look and point away from themselves is to be distinguished from the word of the witnesses in exactly the same way as an event itself is to be distinguished from even the best and most faithful account of it. But this distinction is trifling compared with the fact, for which there is no analogy, that in revelation our concern is with the coming Jesus Christ and finally, when the time was fulfilled, the Jesus Christ who has come."¹⁰⁴

The Bible attests to what has happened truly and once for all: the Word became flesh— our flesh. For Barth the Bible is a fallible human word, but it possesses "the most unheard-of authority"¹⁰⁵ because it bears witness to the supreme event in which God becomes one with alienated humanity in order to bring salvation.

Barth illuminates further the relationship between the first two categories (the Word proclaimed and written) and the third (the Word revealed) when he writes:

> If "written" and "preached" denote the twofold concrete relation in which the Word of God is spoken to us, revelation denotes the Word of God itself in the act of it being spoken in time. Above this act there is nothing other or higher on which it might be based or from which it might be

---

103. Ibid., 107; my emphasis.
104. Ibid., 113.
105. See ibid., 116.

derived unless it was from the transcendence of the eternal Word of God that it came forth in revelation. *It is the condition which conditions all things without itself being conditioned.*[106]

For Barth, revelation is not something different from Jesus Christ or the reconciliation that was accomplished in him. "To say revelation is to say 'The Word became flesh.'"[107] Jesus Christ speaks for himself. He requires no witness other than the witness of the Holy Spirit.

In concluding his discussion about the Word of God in its threefold form Barth suggests that the Word preached, written, and revealed corresponds to—or may be substituted by—the names of the divine persons: Father, Son and Holy Spirit. In this way Barth makes an early link between the doctrine of revelation and that of the trinity. This is an interesting suggestion, although one wonders whether this reading-off of a trinitarian doctrine from the exposition of revelation is substantially supplemented by the reading-in of a prior trinitarianism. The consistent and rigorous implementation of an *a posteriori* method is not easy to maintain, and it is uncertain, in my opinion, that Barth achieves it here.

The Task of Dogmatics

In answer to the question, "What is dogmatics?" Barth answers that it is reflection upon and examination of the distinctive talk about God in the context of the church. Dogmatics, in following and questioning the language of the church, has for its measure "its own source and object," by which Barth means the revelation of God. Dogmatics is not the revelation of God; indeed, it is always fallible human work. It must be conducted in the obedience of grace by the standard of what has been given to it by God. Its purpose is not to *anticipate* but to *respond*; it does not proceed *a priori*, but *a posteriori*.[108]

Is dogmatics a science? Barth suggests that dogmatics does not need to legitimate itself as a science at all, but it does describe itself as a science because it has no interest in segregating itself from other pursuits of human knowledge that bear this name. As a science, its object must be clearly stated: "Its scientific character consists in its orientation, in its conscious orientation, in what must always be its conscious orientation, to the question of dogma that is raised by the existence of the Church."[109] As such, dogmatics, like other sciences, is a human endeavor with its own definite object of knowledge. It follows its own definite path to knowledge and seeks to be self-consistent in doing so. Furthermore, it must be

---

106. Ibid., 118; my emphasis.
107. Ibid., 119.
108. This is, at least, a methodological ideal to which dogmatics ought to aspire.
109. Barth, *Church Dogmatics I/1*, 275.

able to give an account of that path—an account that is an authentic description of the actual method that it adopts.

Dogmatics may learn from the rigor practiced in other sciences but is not subject to their methods; it certainly must not justify itself on the basis of alien scientific method. Its object must determine its method. Indeed, the only way in which dogmatics can prove its own scientific character is by devoting itself to the task of knowledge as determined by its actual theme.

Barth suggests three practical (we might say pragmatic) reasons why theology ought to be considered a science. Firstly, as a human concern for truth, it recognizes its solidarity with disciplines that are concerned with other areas of thought, exploration, and discovery; secondly, so as not to "resign its title to others" (as Barth puts it)[110] and to remind the academy of the Christian church; and thirdly, to show that it does not take the supposedly secular nature of the other sciences seriously enough to place itself under a separate name.

Dogmatics is the science of dogma. Dogmatic inquiry presupposes that the true content of Christian talk about God can be known by human beings. It makes this assumption in and with the church's affirmation of Jesus Christ as the revealing and reconciling address of God to man. This is a point that is of crucial significance for Barth. Dogmatics is concerned with what is given to it in this revelation, and with this alone. Barth writes of the discipline of dogmatics: "[I]t does not have to begin by finding or inventing the standard by which it measures. It sees and recognises that this is given with the Church. It is given in its own peculiar way, as Jesus Christ is given, as God in His revelation gives Himself to faith. But it is given. It is complete in itself."[111]

God's revelation becomes an event in human life and existence. As this event is apprehended in faith, it may, and indeed must, be spoken of as a kind of echo of the event. But all Christian speech must be tested according to its conformity to Christ, and it must be said and understood that this conformity is never clear and unambiguous. This distinction between the event of God's revelation and human participation must be clearly grasped. The echo is a matter of human inquiry:

> It knows the light which is intrinsically perfect and reveals everything in a flash. Yet it knows it only in the prism of this act, which, however radically or existentially it may be understood, is still human act, which in itself is no kind of surety for the correctness of the appropriation in question, which is by nature fallible and therefore stands in need of criticism, of correction, of critical amendment and repetition. For this reason the creaturely form which the revealing action of God assumes in dogmatics is never that of knowledge attained in a flash, which it would have to be to correspond to

---

110. See ibid., 11.
111. Ibid., 12.

the divine gift, but a laborious movement from one partial human insight to another with the intention though with no guarantee of advance.[112]

Barth insists that the truth comes, but it is not a stable datum that we hold in our possession. It is necessary to start time and again. Therefore, the task of dogmatics is not to set out a number of truths of revelation already to hand that have been expressed once for all and the meanings of which are authentically defined. "The freely acting God Himself and alone is the truth of revelation."[113]

Two things follow from this. Firstly, the church is not the recipient of a fixed body of knowledge that is defined and delimited. As such, it does not ask what the apostles and prophets said, but what we must say on the basis of what they said. The authority of the tradition is not an infallible authority. Secondly, dogmatics is not possible apart from the act of faith. Without faith it would be irrelevant and meaningless because it is only in faith that the revelation of God is known.

Barth's understanding of the church's proclamation has already been expounded, and I have indicated the relationship between proclamation and dogmatics as he sees it. Four further things may be said for the purposes of reinforcement and closure.

Dogmatics Is Different from the Proclamation of the Church

The church must proclaim in obedience to the command of God. Dogmatics is required because this response to God's command is a human response and is therefore fallible. Given this relationship, it is clear that dogmatics is secondary, and, the proclamation of the church is primary. The proclamation of the church begins with God, revelation, and faith; dogmatics begins with the proclamation of the church. As such, it has its own peculiar function to fulfill. As has already been said, God, revelation, and faith are talked about in fallible human ways and yet the church has a responsibility to speak the truth in purity. As such, it cannot shirk the responsibility of questioning and correcting its own speech. It is in this way that dogmatics serves the preaching of the church.

Dogmatics Serves Church Proclamation

Dogmatics serves a different function to proclamation, but in no sense does it represent a higher knowledge of faith. Authentic proclamation of the truth is not to do with sophistication on the part of the hearer or the speaker, and dogmatics is not the technique of certain people with a particular spiritual skill. As it must serve the church, the role of dogmatics is never, primarily, the service of a particular form of critical thought or philosophy. "[W]e always need the insight

112. Ibid., 14.
113. Ibid., 15.

that critically reflective thought, even though it be that of human reason, and no matter what philosophical tints it has, must still be set in relation to the theme of the Church's proclamation, and its execution must be governed, not by its human origin and nature, but by its divine object."[114] Dogmatics is not an end in itself. God, revelation, and faith are given to proclamation; dogmatics takes them up from the church.

Dogmatics Informs the Content of Proclamation

It is the role of dogmatics to consider how, in the church's proclamation, we may best speak of God, revelation, and faith to the extent that human talk about these things is to count as church proclamation.[115] Barth explains: "[W]hat dogmatics has to give does not consist of contents but of guidelines, directions, insights, principles and limits for correct speech by human estimate. It can be called doctrinal law in this sense. But its presupposition is that preaching acquires its content elsewhere. For that reason it cannot be lord and judge . . . It can and should give counsel in all seriousness but it neither can nor should seek to give orders in the Church."[116] It is essential that the church's proclamation, even in view of what it might receive from dogmatics, remains free to receive afresh God's own free giving of himself in his revelation. "Church proclamation and not dogmatics is immediate to God in the Church. Proclamation is essential, dogmatics is needed only for the sake of it."[117]

Dogmatics Disturbs the Church

Dogmatics, in its own work, cannot be satisfied with merely repeating church proclamation. "Dogmatics cannot just be a historical account of the classical expression of the faith proclaimed by this or that period in the Church's past. Nor can it just be the clarification and presentation of the faith as the dogmatician concerned personally thinks it should be proclaimed. Nor again can it be just the phenomenology of a cross-section of the common faith proclaimed in a given present."[118] Dogmatics exists to unsettle rather than confirm the church's proclamation. This is its service to the church's proclamation, and one of things that it must always be prepared and ready to do. Its role must be to challenge and correct, and it will be thus as long as the church is a church of sinners. What the church

---

114. Ibid., 84.

115. Although dogmatics must not think that it can lay down what God, revelation, and faith are in themselves.

116. Barth, *Church Dogmatics I/1*, 86–87.

117. Ibid., 87.

118. Ibid., 281.

requires of dogmatics must be more vital and dynamic than bland affirmation if its problems are in any way to be confronted.

Barth suggests that the decisive point for dogmatics is that it is inquiring into the agreement of church proclamation with the revelation that is attested in Scripture:

> Dogmatic work stands or falls by whether the standard by which Church proclamation is measured is the revelation attested in Holy Scripture and not a philosophical, ethical, psychological or political theory. Now it is obvious that everyone who works at dogmatics works more or less with specific intellectual presuppositions. The only question is whether in addition to these he also knows the sign of the divine promise which is set up in the Church and whether he is able and willing, in a way that admits of no proof, to take this sign so seriously that in this context its direction takes absolute precedence over all the directions he might owe to the humanities."[119]

Dogmaticians belong to an age and culture and this will inevitably color their work. But what singles out dogmaticians is that they must give their unerring attention to the sign of canonical Scripture as it forms the church. Barth insists that the dogmatician has no right to disregard this: "If anyone resolutely refuses to accept this but insists on deriving the final standard in this field, too, from this or that logic, ontology, and psychology, or sociology, his attention must be kindly called to the fact that all the rest of the land is open to him but he should desist from working here, where he can only cause confusion with these other final standards."[120]

Dogmatics must be true to itself in being dogmatics. Barth underlines this by reinforcing his point about Scripture: "What finally counts is whether a dogmatics is scriptural. If it is not, then it will definitely be futile, for we shall definitely have to say regarding it that in it the Church is distracted, i.e., it is busy about other matters and is not doing justice to the scientific task set for it by the problematic nature of its proclamation."[121] He goes on to say, "The whole point of the correspondence between Holy Scripture and proclamation, and therefore the whole point of the path of knowledge in dogmatics, consists in the fact that in both Holy Scripture and Church dogmatics we are dealing with the Word of God."[122]

The question is not, of course, one of establishing an external basis, because one cannot be given. If a correspondence exists between the Bible and proclama-

---

119. Ibid., 283.

120. Ibid., 285. Barth's methodological rigor in the field of dogmatics is admirable, but it is somewhat curious that he implies that in other disciplines "anything goes" (methodologically). I think many scholars, working in a variety of areas, would want to contend what is implicit in Barth's comment.

121. Ibid., 287.

122. Ibid., 289.

tion, and if dogmatics is illuminated by this route, this is no accident and no result of general dialectic considerations; it must arise out of the matter itself, which is to say out of the fact that the Bible and proclamation *may become* God's Word. It is *as* the Word of God reveals itself that the Bible and proclamation *are* the Word of God. It is the concept of revelation that must give us the key to an understanding of the relations between the two and how we must approach them.

> We have to do with the concrete concept of revelation which the Bible attests to have taken place and proclamation promises will come, with the concrete bracket which embraces a specific past, the epiphany of Jesus Christ, and what is always a specific future, the moment when men will hear God's Word, in the Scripture that is adopted by the proclamation of the Church or in the proclamation of the Church which is set in motion by Scripture.[123]

The reality of revelation clearly stands beyond any concept of it. In this sense we cannot try to deal with the reality. We are, rather, dealing with the concept of the revelation of God, and according to Scripture and proclamation, this is the Father of Jesus Christ, Jesus Christ Himself, and the Spirit of the Father and the Son. Barth does not deny the possibility of investigating other revelations—nor even the possible development of a general concept of revelation. However, in embarking upon such as task, one inevitably abandons the task of church dogmatics.

Concluding Remark

The task of this chapter has been to offer an exposition of Karl Barth's doctrine of revelation, and it has attempted to do no more than that. Barth's contribution to the doctrine of revelation is—certainly in my own evaluation—of seminal importance for the contemporary church. The fact that the first chapter of this book is an exposition of his doctrine is indicative of the significance I attach to his achievement.

So far we have postponed any critical engagement with Barth's position, and so it is to this that we must now turn. The task of the next chapter and a significant proportion of the remainder of this work will be to criticize and develop Barth's doctrine of revelation as it has been expounded in this chapter.

---

123. Ibid., 290–91.

CHAPTER 2

Critical Engagement with Barth

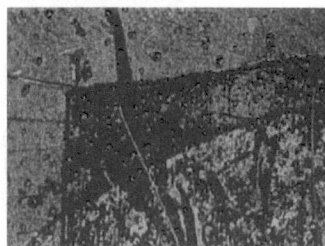

Introduction

IN THE FIRST chapter I offered an exposition of Barth's doctrine of revelation. In this chapter I proceed to engage in a critical evaluation of certain aspects of Barth's work. This chapter represents the first of a two-stage process in which I seek to revise and develop some aspects of the understanding of revelation as it is found in the early volumes of Barth's *Church Dogmatics*. The second stage will be pursued in the light of an exposition of the work of Michael Polanyi. In the course of this chapter, I will also suggest some similarities between the work of Barth and Polanyi that will serve as preparation for and anticipation of the themes that will be later developed.

I will introduce this chapter by making a few comments about the philosophical context in which Barth was working. It may be impossible to offer anything more than a highly generalized picture, but this modest portrait will be helpful in setting the scene both for an evaluation of Barth's doctrine of revelation, and for a provisional assessment of how Michael Polanyi's philosophical and epistemological insights might coherently expand Barth's vision.

The philosophers of the Enlightenment may not have spoken with one voice, but despite the distinctions that might be made between particular philosophers,[1] there are common themes that indicate the pervasive ethos of the movement. Enlightenment thinkers were united in the belief that the employment of reason and critical thought was a prerequisite for the pursuit of truth and the establishment of greater human freedom and dignity. The concomitant negative belief was a rejection of what was perceived to be an uncritical submission to authority in general and, in particular, to the "dogmatically" held beliefs and traditions of the

---

1. Distinctions might also be made on the basis of geography: the "Enlightenments" of the Continent, Scotland, England, or Russia, for example, may be regarded as distinguishable strands of a broader movement.

church. As such, *criticism* and *autonomy* represent two of the most significant principles of thought for the eighteenth century and the two centuries that followed.

There is insufficient space to trace the development of the doctrine of revelation as theologians sought to express it in these circumstances, but it will be apparent that—to the extent that the doctrine was conceived in terms of an uncritically received authority—it fared very poorly in the intellectual ethos in which the themes of criticism and autonomy were dominant. If philosophers set for themselves, in the name of truth and human freedom, the task of establishing rational justification for the knowledge they claimed, it is not surprising that theologians—in speaking of the knowledge of God—generally sought to produce similar forms of justification.

Insofar as this was the case, the theological task as may be conceived in terms of "faith seeking rational foundation." This carries with it the implicit assumption that faith, if it is to be authenticated, must be both received and commended on the basis of an extrinsic justification. In its turn, this implies that the rational justification of faith is, epistemically, more basic than the faith that it seeks to justify.[2]

In Barth's doctrine of revelation we may discern, among other things, an attempt to extricate theology from this kind of approach. It may not have been entirely successful for various reasons, but it does represent a substantial move away from epistemologies that have sought to establish an independent basis and justification for belief. *To the extent to which it is successful*, Barth's approach might be described as "post-Enlightenment."[3] It is, self-consciously, an approach in which faith seeks after understanding, as opposed to one in which faith seeks independent rational foundation.

At this early stage I want to suggest that there is an important parallel here between Barth's work and that of Michael Polanyi. The latter sought to establish a non foundational post-critical epistemology focusing initially upon the natural sciences and then proceeding to consider a wide range of questions outside science. Barth sought to establish a theology in which the absolute priority of God in his revelation is fully established and the epistemic priority of faith recognized.

It is ironic that Barth did not appear to see the significance of his approach[4] for areas outside theology[5] while Polanyi's attempt to apply his own post-critical

---

2. I do not intend to give an argument, at this point, for why I consider this to be problematic. This task will be postponed until we come to the exposition of the thought of Michael Polanyi. Polanyi's critique of "belief seeking justification" and his commendation of "faith seeking understanding" will be of particular interest because it is established primarily in the context of the natural sciences.

3. Although the term is, so far as I are aware, unknown to Barth, his theological method might also appropriately be called "post-critical"—in the sense in which it is adopted by Polanyi.

4. Methodologically *a posteriori*.

5. Indeed, it appears that Barth wished to affirm an essentially Kantian approach in spheres outside theology. This may have had, for Barth, the incidental or perhaps pragmatic value of emphasizing the distinctiveness of the knowledge of God with respect to other forms of human knowing.

approach in theology was lacking in the extreme.[6] I believe that there are important parallels in the work of Barth and Polanyi and, more than this, there is, a strong case to made that each might contribute significantly to that which is lacking in the other.[7]

In due course I will expand upon the terms and concepts that I have adopted here in the form of a rough sketch. At this point I only wish to indicate a particular kinship between the projects of Barth and Polanyi, and suggest thereby the potential for bringing their projects into conversation.

The Doctrine of Revelation in the Context of Modernity

In the modern era, questions about the ground and nature of human understanding have bulked large in philosophy, and this has had its impact upon the theological agenda. As Ronald Thiemann points out, "It would be misleading to say that Calvin offers an epistemology in the *Institutes*, because he has no interest in placing knowledge of God in a general theory of human knowing. He is interested in faith's particular knowledge of God and the fact that all such knowledge is a gift of God's grace."[8] But in the context of the Enlightenment, such an approach appears naive and calls for justification. Modern doctrines of revelation have responded to this call by developing such justifications for speaking about the knowledge of God. While this task might be conceived as an extension of the work of the reformers in a new context, in the pursuit of it a significant shift occurs whereby the assumptions made by a Calvin or a Luther are adjudged in need of external justification in this later period. In the atmosphere of modernity, it was no longer acceptable, as it was for the reformers, to *assume* knowledge of God as a background belief, and in such circumstances it was perhaps inevitable that the strategy of "faith seeking understanding" became "faith seeking foundation" or "faith seeking justification." Colin Gunton underlines this point when he comments that one of the key features of the modern tradition is "a deep-seated belief in the existence of an *intuitively* intellectual basis for all thought."[9]

But Barth's project neither calls for nor does it imply a return to pre-Enlightenment thinking. It is an attempt to move beyond it. While Gunton sees Barth's achievement in this regard as only a partial success he, nevertheless,

---

6. This assertion will be explicated and supported in the excursus that follows chapter 3.

7. The theology of Barth and the philosophy of Michael Polanyi both represent bold, expansive, and imaginative ventures along what might be called (in very general terms) "post-Enlightenment" or "post-critical" lines, and in very substantial discontinuity with the predominant modes of thought inhabited by their contemporaries.

8. Thiemann, *Revelation and Theology*, 10.

9. Gunton, *Theology through the Theologians*, 52; Gunton's emphasis.

considers it to be "something of a *tour de force*, plucked from the intellectual air by an act of intuitive genius."[10] In this there are parallels to be discerned between the projects of Barth and Polanyi. Some of these will be elucidated as we proceed.

Human Participation

A criticism that has been made of Barth's doctrine of revelation is that it leaves little room for human response or participation. Indeed, as we shall see in the criticism of Barth offered by Jürgen Moltmann, it has been questioned how far it is possible to speak of *human* knowledge of God at all within Barth's scheme of divine revelation. This is a serious criticism if it can be substantiated. It would certainly cut short any project that seeks to bring Barth's work into a meaningful conversation with Polanyi's post-critical philosophy. Personal participation and self-involvement are intrinsic to Polanyi's epistemology.

In his book on revelation, Ronald Thiemann writes, of Barth's *Epistle to the Romans*, "A position which stresses both God's sovereign transcendence and his knowability is hard pressed to give an account of how we can come to know such a God. Barth's solution . . . is to grant God's Spirit the mediating power to bring divine object and human subject together. The Spirit of God dwells within the believing interpreter and bestows the capacity to know the unknowable."[11] The difficulty is, of course, that the Spirit is not the human subject. Consequently, says Thiemann, "Human subjectivity . . . becomes nothing more than the vessel through which God knows himself. Whenever I contribute anything to the interpretation of God's being, it is the contribution of sin and falsity. True interpretation comes at the expense of the denial of the goodness of creaturely reality."[12]

If Thiemann makes this criticism of Barth in *Epistle to the Romans*, Moltmann makes a related complaint about Barth's doctrine of revelation in general.[13] Moltmann criticizes Barth for offering a false alternative between divine revelation and human experience of the Holy Spirit. If the Holy Spirit is the subjective reality and possibility of revelation, humanity is essentially bypassed in the revelatory event. If the "being revealedness" of revelation is the Spirit of God, can "revelation" be any more than an exclusively intra-Trinitarian event? He writes, "if God-consciousness only comes into being at all because the Wholly Other God reveals himself, then the Spirit of God is the being-revealed of this self-revelation of God in us; and it . . . [is] for us just as inexperiencable, hidden and 'other' as

---

10. Ibid., 53.
11. Thiemann, *Revelation and Theology*, 42.
12. Ibid.
13. Interestingly, in *Spirit of Life* (originally published in 1991) Moltmann chooses to draw on Barth's 1929 lecture, "The Holy Spirit and the Christian Life" rather than making reference to *Church Dogmatics* or other later works. It is clear, however, that Moltmann directs his criticism to Barth's work as a whole and not just to its earlier forms and expression.

God himself. In this case there is a permanent discontinuity between God's Spirit and the spirit of human beings."[14] Moltmann goes on to say, "I cannot see that there is any fundamental alternative between God's revelation to human beings, and human experience of God. How is a man or a woman supposed to be able to talk about God if God does not reveal himself? How are men and women supposed to be able to talk about a God of whom there is no human experience?"[15]

Moltmann interprets Barth's position as one in which revelation and experience are set in opposition to each other, and this is what Moltmann rejects. "Anyone who stylizes revelation and experiences into alternatives, ends up with revelations that cannot be experienced, and experiences without revelation."[16] This is the insoluble dilemma in which Barth finds himself, if Moltmann is correct. But does Barth set up revelation and experience as alternatives? It seems to me that Barth does not intend this. The exposition under the subheading "Religious Experience" in chapter 1 appears to make the point with some force. In consideration of *Church Dogmatics* § 6 "The Word of God and Experience" and the comments on it made in the first chapter, I would suggest that Barth has no interest in setting experience and revelation in opposition to each other or in presenting them as alternatives. Barth does not wish to establish that revelation and experience are incompatible (or alternatives), but that revelation, as it becomes an experience in the life of faith, does this on the basis of an event in which God makes himself known and not on the basis of a "natural" human religious capacity.

Moltmann's reading clearly goes against Barth's intentions. What might "knowledge of God" (of which Barth freely and frequently speaks) mean without a human experience through which the knowledge of God is mediated? It is basic to Barth's methodology that the question of the possibility of the Word of God is raised *a posteriori* in the actual knowledge of the Word of God. If there can be no knowledge of the Word of God apart from some mediate revelatory experience, it is clear that Barth is not setting up experience and revelation as mutually exclusive alternatives.

In the form in which he puts it, Moltmann's criticism of Barth can be answered. Barth's insistence that for a person to participate in the Word of God, that person must be given the capacity for the Word of God by God is, essentially, the insight of John 6:44.[17] To "come to Christ" cannot be conceived as a human choice since it is a possibility that can only be realized in the decision of God. Moltmann's criticism appears to be posited upon the assumption that such a state of affairs must exclude human participation in the event of revelation.[18] But why should

---

14. Moltmann, *Spirit of Life*, 5.
15. Ibid., 6.
16. Ibid., 7.
17. "No one can come to me unless drawn by the Father who sent me . . ."
18. Indeed, Moltmann seems to think such a conclusion is self-evident.

this be so? To say that a person can know the Word of God only if the capacity for this knowledge is given does not exclude the possibility that there might be a perichoretic relationship between the person and the Word of God that is established precisely in the bestowing of this capacity. Since Barth does wish to affirm knowledge of the Word of God as a *human* experience (God's gracious gift) and one in which human beings do participate *as* human beings, it is not only possible but more coherent to interpret Barth in this way.

Although Moltmann's criticism of Barth may be unsatisfactory, I think there is a problem with Barth's theology in this area that does require attention. Stated briefly, the difficulty is to be located in Barth's understatement of the place of subjective human participation in revelation.[19] It is not, as I intend to show, an absence, but this aspect of understatement has caused some interpreters of Barth (Moltmann is one) to miss the point. Gunton, who does not miss the point, observes: "For Barth, despite the frequent assertions or at least suggestions to the contrary in the secondary literature, human knowledge of God is not the conditioned reflex of the automaton. It is free personal action in relation, deriving from an indwelling in Christ and taking the form of thanksgiving, awe and the ordered employment of human concepts."[20]

Earlier in his argument Gunton asserts that "for Barth, the *fundamental* reality of our being is our indwelling in Christ."[21] The significance of this statement must not be overlooked. Here the relational aspect of human existence in Christ is established as primary. This does not exclude the possibility of propositional knowledge, but it does imply that such knowledge is derivative of knowledge gained through a personal participation or indwelling. Again it must be acknowledged that this is an understated theme in Barth, and yet we do find evidence of it as early as the first part volume of *Church Dogmatics*. In the context of a discussion of the *filioque*, Barth comments: "The intra-divine two-sided fellowship of the Spirit, which proceeds from the Father and the Son, is the basis of the fact that there is in revelation a fellowship in which not only is God there for man but in very truth—this is the *donum Spiritus sancti*—man is also there for God."[22] Barth acknowledges the intra-divine fellowship in the event of revelation but, over against Moltmann's interpretation of Barth, the communion of humanity with God is also involved—and explicitly so.

Barth insists, of course, that the fellowship established between humanity and God is established by the free initiative of God, but God wills to establish fellowship. "He wills to be ours, and He wills that we should be His. He wills to

---

19. This is more particularly the case in his explicit treatment of the Word of God in the early parts of *Church Dogmatics*. I will say about this later.
20. Gunton, *Theology through the Theologians*, 58–59.
21. Ibid., 54; my emphasis.
22. Barth, *Church Dogmatics I/1*, 480.

belong to us and He wills that we should belong to Him . . . His attitude and action is always that He seeks and creates fellowship between Himself and us."²³ This is so despite the darkness of human sinfulness. The human perspective of this fellowship is disturbed by sin, and Barth acknowledges that:

> For large stretches it may be *for us* doubtful, dark and incomprehensible. For large stretches it will seem *to us* like the very opposite of this relationship. It will reveal itself as such through judgment and grace, through dying and making alive, through veiling and unveiling . . . We shall have to learn ever and again what it really means to say that God seeks and creates fellowship between Himself and us.²⁴

Although our indwelling in Christ may be fundamental for Barth, this is articulated in the context of a theology in which the knowledge of God is radically tied to the decision and act of God in which he makes himself known. The sovereignty and freedom of God in his revelation, and the incapacity of an unassisted humanity to know God, are unmistakable and weighty emphases in Barth's doctrine of revelation. His description of revelation as "miracle," his insistence that humans have no capacity for revelation, and his designation of the Holy Spirit as the subjective reality and possibility of revelation, all place emphasis upon the initiative of God in his revelation rather than upon human participation. It is doubtless because of this emphasis that some critics of Barth's doctrine of revelation have accused his view as one in which human subjectivity is essentially bypassed. But does Barth's insistence on God's prior decision and continuing presence in revelation imply that human participation is excluded? Surely it implies only that human participation is contingent upon God's grace in establishing the relationship. As Gunton has noted, Barth *does* have things to say about human participation in revelation, and although this emphasis may be muted, it is not absent. In his discussion of the hiddenness of God, Barth makes an observation in which both the sovereignty of God and human participation in revelation are acknowledged in a particular relation:

> If we keep to the fact that God is known only by God, then whatever may be the function of our viewing and conceiving, and however necessary this function may be, it is fixed that we certainly do not know Him by these views and concepts of ours: that is to say, not by their inner power; not in virtue of their own capacity. i.e., of the capacity of human viewing and conceiving as such; not in virtue of a potentiality of our cognition which has perhaps to be actualised by revelation. We definitely cannot deny to this the character and function of an instrument in this event. In the act of the knowledge of God, as in any other cognitive act, we are definitely active as receivers of images and creators of counter-images. Yet while this is true, it

23. Barth, *Church Dogmatics II/1*, 274.
24. Ibid., 274–75; my emphasis.

must definitely be contested that our receiving and creating owes its truth to any capacity of our own to be truly recipients and creators in relation to God. It is indeed our own viewing and conceiving. But we ourselves have no capacity for fellowship with God.[25]

In this passage we see Barth's familiar denial of a human capacity for the knowledge of God, but we also see, circumscribed within the limits of what is made possible by God, not only the possibility but the necessity of an active human reception of and participation in God's revelation. There is no suggestion here of God bypassing our humanity in his revelation. Human participation has its designated role, and Barth recognizes this. What he denies is that that such a participation is a possibility apart from the decision and act of God in relation to a person. The relationship is an asymmetrical one: there is and can be no knowledge of God where God does not reveal himself. However, in God's revelation there is active, responsive human participation.

Gunton goes as far as to say that, in relation to this and a handful of other passages in the same volume of *Church Dogmatics*, "Barth uses language which is quite startling in its claims for the extent of the human side of the enterprise."[26] Gunton concludes that "Barth intends to set before us a conception of the knowledge of a personal God by free and thinking persons. The talk is of active human knowledge in the context of a relationship, one indeed in which there is a measure of reciprocity."[27]

While acknowledging that the theme of responsive participation in revelation is present in Barth's theology, it is clear that, in the context in which he found himself, his prior concern was to establish that the knowledge of God was not a natural or innate human capacity, but a possibility that is established in God's good pleasure.

In the light of this discussion I think that it is right to sustain the view that human participation in the Word of God is essential to Barth's general approach to the doctrine of revelation. Our indwelling of Christ is not to be conceived as a passive but an active, responsive relationship. In this way it is appropriate to speak of a relationship between humanity and God in which there is activity on both sides.

Human Capacity

In the above section, which was concerned with human participation in divine revelation, I spoke at various points about "human capacity" for God's revelation or more particularly, the lack of it. But if there is knowledge of God, isn't the denial of a human capacity a contradiction? It is the purpose of this section to

25. Ibid., 182.
26. Gunton, *Theology through the Theologians*, 59.
27. Ibid.

clarify what is and what is not implied in this denial, and in doing so I will draw on Trevor Hart's analytical exposition of this theme.[28]

Hart's discussion of "capacity" appears towards the end of his review and examination of the public disagreement between Karl Barth and Emil Brunner concerning the relationship between nature and grace, creation and redemption, and church and state. The particulars of this debate need not detain us, but his treatment of "capacity" is helpful in clarifying certain issues relating to the term and its implications for participation in particular.

"Capacity," as Hart points out, can carry both active and passive connotations.[29] Following the scheme that Hart devises, I will refer to the former as "capacity 1" and the latter "capacity 2." Borrowing Barth's illustration, Hart remarks that Mary, as a virgin, had no capacity 1 for childbearing. "Her womb did not, that is to say, apart from the conditions furnished by extrinsic factors—either coming together with a man, or else the direct creative action of the Holy Spirit—have the *active capacity* . . . to produce a fertile ovum. But passively, insofar as she was a woman and not a slab of granite, she might properly be said to have a passive capacity (capacity 2) for what happened to her to happen."[30] In the incarnation, God determines that it is from the womb of the Virgin Mary that Jesus is to be born. Although Mary has no capacity 1 for becoming the mother of Jesus, she has a capacity 2 for this in a way that other objects do not—or, at least, not in the same way. Mary's womanhood is not arbitrary or insignificant.

Extending his argument, Hart goes on to suggest that Jesus' body in the tomb has no capacity 1 for life while it does have the capacity 2 in a way that the stone that was rolled from the tomb does not. Here we note a differentiation within the category, capacity 2, because in this case the opposition of nature and grace is more clearly to the fore. What God must do in bringing Jesus' body back to life is to *oppose* natural propensities—which only bring physical decay—rather than rely upon them or seek their cooperation.

Similarly, humanity has no capacity 1 for revelation, but because God *does* reveal himself in a redemptive way to human beings, we may speak of a capacity 2. It is not impossible for God's redemptive Word to reach human beings (that would be to say that what is so is not possible). What *is* impossible is that this might happen as the realization of a "natural" human potential (i.e., that this should happen apart from the will and the act of God).

As will be apparent from the discussion in the first chapter, Barth's concern is not, and quite explicitly not, *a priori* speculation about what may be possible for God or for human beings. He is concerned to construct a theology on the basis of what God has done. This is the way in which we must understand the positing

---

28. See Hart, *Regarding Karl Barth*, 164–72.
29. See ibid., 166.
30. Ibid., 166–67; Hart's emphasis.

of a human capacity 2 for the reconciling knowledge of God. An *a posteriori* approach must attempt to work from the actual knowledge of the Word of God to a consideration of the possibility of such knowledge.

To establish that human beings can have a capacity 2 for God's Word (while maintaining that there can be no capacity 1) is, according to Hart, "vitally important"[31] because it enables us to see that "What is impossible for humanity as such is rendered possible by the God who calls new life into being out of nothing. God is capable of uniting us to himself. God is capable of revealing himself to us."[32] This is the "point of contact" between creature and creator—the bridging of the gap that exists because the creature is not like the creator—that is established when the creator comes to the creature in transforming grace. Without this point of contact, God would not be revealed to human beings and there would be no relationship in which humanity could be reconciled to God. Without a genuine point of contact, there could be no responsive human participation in the life of God. Hart writes, "The fact that the miracle of grace interrupts and is discontinuous with the normal pattern of nature does not make it any less a point of contact—it simply characterizes its shape."[33]

As we have seen in the exposition of Barth under the subheading "Religious Experience," the point of contact does not refer to a particular ("spiritual"? "mystic"?) aspect of our humanity but to the human subject in its totality. It is with *this* reality—in the rebellious and sinful nature in which God finds it—that God establishes the locus of contact.

Communication and Communion

In the second subsection I attempted to show that Barth's doctrine of revelation does not imply that human reception of revelation is the work of the Holy Spirit *in such a way* that we cannot, in any meaningful way, speak of "human participation." Barth *does* speak of human participation (even if it is judged that he does so in an unsatisfactory way), and he does speak, also, of experience of the Word of God. The third section of this chapter sought to show that such participation and experience is a possibility—but only as God, in his freedom, gives himself in revelation. In other words, it is a possibility only as God makes it a possibility. There is no possibility of a human knowledge of God apart from God's decision to make himself known in particular circumstances to particular people.

The misunderstanding of Barth's position in this regard may be, in part, located in a confusion of the issues raised in the respective subsections. Barth clearly rejects any idea that knowledge of God is a natural, autonomous human

---

31. See ibid., 171.
32. Ibid.
33. Ibid.

capacity. God is known in the event in which he gives himself to be known, and therefore it is not appropriate to think of the knowledge of God in terms of a possibility apart from divine revelation. Nevertheless, it is clearly appropriate to acknowledge that humans are the kind of beings to whom God can make himself known. In *this* sense human beings do have a capacity for revelation, and this is a receptive possibility whose actualization[34] rests in the decision of God. The task of theology is posited upon the belief that there *is* knowledge of God in the human sphere, and it is this that raises the question of *how* it is possible.

It may be Barth's insistence that the capacity is one that must be received from the grace of God that leads some of his critics to assume that in the event of revelation there is no responsive human participation. And because Barth's exposition of the human participatory element is muted, he does, in my opinion, leave himself exposed to such criticism. However, an insistence that the possibility of the knowledge of God must be given by God does not exclude the possibility of active human participation in the revelation that is given. Barth does not place sufficient emphasis upon active and responsive participation, but such an emphasis does not appear to be intrinsically inconsistent with his insistence on the sovereignty of God in his revelation.[35]

A further weakness in Barth's position (which, again, I would contend is a matter of understatement or underdevelopment rather than omission) is his failure to expand on the relationship in which God gives himself to be known to human persons. It may be that Barth believes that it is our indwelling of Christ that is the "fundamental reality of our being"[36] but in his exposition of the doctrine of revelation the emphasis upon relationship is insufficiently developed. It is my intention to develop an understanding of divine revelation in which the relational aspects of the knowledge of God, and the various contexts in which it is established, are more fully articulated. In order to achieve this I will draw on both critical and constructive comments on this theme expressed in Alan Torrance's *Persons in Communion*.

Much of the force of Torrance's argument in this book is indicated in the following introductory comment: "Although a doctrine of revelation is essential for Christian theology not only materially but also formally, divine communication cannot be separated from a proper theology of divine communion. Theologically interpreted, communication presupposes the category of communion and not the other way around."[37] Torrance's criticism of Barth is precisely that his tendency is

---

34. Both objectively and subjectively.

35. Without collapsing the distinctions, which must be acknowledged, between human knowledge of God and knowledge of other objects, it must be noted that a "self-involving" knowledge of any object is contingent upon the object being present to us "as object." In this sense there is continuity between knowledge of God and knowledge of other things.

36. See Gunton, *Theology through the Theologians*, 54, already quoted above.

37. Torrance, *Persons in Communion*, 3–4.

to invert the proper relationship between communion and communication, and that, as a result, the shape of his theology is distorted.

Torrance suggests that we must locate divine revelation, including divine self-communication, in the context of the intra-trinitarian communion of God and in acknowledgement of the openness of this divine communion to humanity. Torrance claims that apart from this acknowledgement it is not possible to understand the meaning of the revelation of God. Consequently Torrance criticizes what he calls Barth's "revelation model," as the source of theological distortions and commends, instead, a "worship model" in which the priority of relationality in communication is articulated. Torrance believes the latter will yield a theological construction that is more faithful to the self-presentation of God as this is attested to in Holy Scripture.

Some care must be taken in interpreting the terms "revelation model" and "worship model." What Torrance intends in developing a worship model is an articulation of the context in which God's revelation occurs. As such, Torrance is not opposing all the theological contours of Barth's conception of revelation, but he is criticizing and developing some of the detailed contours and some of the ways in which they are expressed. Although Torrance does not extend his argument along these lines, it seems appropriate to consider whether his worship model might be supplemented or extended by further "models," in which other aspects of the life of the church (as participations in the Spirit) are recognized as *loci* in which God makes himself known in his revelation.[38] Alternatively, a similar end might be achieved by making it clear that "worship" is not to be understood narrowly as private devotions and liturgical worship, but rather in terms of a person's self-offering of their life in the service of God.[39] In this way it becomes a much broader "umbrella-like" term.

Torrance concurs with Barth in his belief that the critical controls of dogmatics do not belong to dogmatics itself. It is the task of theology to serve the Word, and it is in this that dogmatics finds its point of reference. It is not entitled to look anywhere else for it. Torrance quotes Barth: "'In both its investigations and its conclusions it must keep in view that God is in heaven and not on earth, and that God, His revelation and faith always live their own free life over against all human talk, including that of the best dogmatics.'"[40] As such, both Barth and Torrance

---

38. Matt 25:31–46 might encourage us to think along such lines. The individuals depicted at the judgment at the coming of the "Son of Man" (whether commended or condemned) appear to be unaware of the divine presence in the hungry, the thirsty, the naked, and the outcast. However, one function of the pericope is to alert and inform the reader of that of which the figures at the judgment were ignorant. An implication of this would be that our activity in the service of those in need is a participation in the life of God. As such, it seems that what Torrance says of our doxological participation in the intra-divine communion in his "worship model" might be extended and paralleled in a "service model."

39. This is the meaning of worship adopted in Romans 12:1.

40. Quoted in Torrance, *Persons in Communion*, 47.

stress the importance of an *a posteriori* theological method. What Torrance is questioning is the degree to which Barth was successful in articulating a radically *a posteriori* definition of divine personhood through his modeling of revelation.

In this section we shall be concentrating upon Torrance's criticism of Barth, but it is important to recognize that this is intended not as a rejection but rather as an amendment of Barth's broader theological trajectory, as Torrance makes clear:

> [O]ur critique of Barth amounts essentially to a modification which seeks to support rather than repudiate his primary aims and central concerns. What we *would* suggest, however, is quite specific, namely that a) Barth's exposition of the Trinity as we have it in Volume One of his *Church Dogmatics*; b) the influence on it of what we have termed his 'revelation model' and, in particular, c) the outworking of this on the manner in which he explores the question of triune personhood require a degree of controlled reinterpretation.[41]

This "controlled reinterpretation" must take Barth's theology on from the limitations of the revelation model. Within the constraints of this model, his exposition of the Trinity and the Word of God are unsatisfactorily delimited, and this frustrates the development of a fuller understanding of ecclesial life as participation in revelation.

Torrance believes that a weakness in Barth that "haunts" the *Church Dogmatics* is that God's triple *reiteration of himself* is much more prominent than his *relation to himself*. Torrance claims in Barth "tritheism is sensed to be a greater threat than Sabellianism."[42] Torrance is troubled with what he suggests is Barth's "inordinate stress" on divine singularity. "Even if Barth may be defended against the charge of modalism . . . it is difficult to deny that there is at least a detrimental 'anhypostaticism' in his doctrine of revelation."[43] In this way the communion within God, into which humanity is taken by the Spirit in and through the vicarious humanity of the Word made flesh, becomes disturbingly marginal to revelation.[44] Torrance believes that Barth's emphasis on the singularity of the divine subject leads him to understate the importance of the notion of triune perichoresis. As

---

41. Ibid., 364–65; Torrance's emphasis.

42. Ibid., 103.

43. Ibid., 104.

44. Trevor Hart challenges Torrance's charge of "a detrimental anhypostaticism." He writes, "The doctrine of the *anhypostasia* as such is concerned to deny the independent subsistence of Jesus' humanity; it makes no prescription concerning its particular shape or content. The organs of human response and reciprocity belong to the category of 'nature' rather than 'hypostasis'. The affirmation of a fully human experience and relation to God, therefore is wholly compatible with 'anhypostaticism': the point of such a juxtaposition would simply be that in this particular case we have to do with *God's* fully human experience and relation to God. The suggestion that in Jesus we have to do with a human 'hypostasis' distinct from and independent of God's own hypostatically differentiated existence as Father, Son and Holy Spirit was one Barth was determined at all costs to avoid." See Hart's essay, "Revelation" in Webster, *Cambridge Companion to Karl Barth*, 56.

such, Barth has a tendency to interpret unity in terms of singular identity rather than divine communion.

Related to this is Barth's decision, in referring to the Trinity, to reject the term "persons" in favor of "*Seinsweisen*." His reason for doing this is to avoid the danger of projecting an anthropologically rooted concept onto the being of God. But Barth's alternative has its own problems. Torrance points out, "The metaphor does not imply that the category of communion is appropriate to conceiving of the relationship between these eternal 'repetitions', indeed, rather the opposite."[45] Barth's "threefold repetition" similarly offers little promise of opening up for us the dynamic communion within God. Torrance believes that if the metaphor of repetition is to be used to establish the singularity of the divine identity in the threeness, it must be qualified by a much more profound doctrine of perichoresis than Barth offers in this context. Torrance believes that Barth's adoption of the term *Seinsweisen* effectively obscures the concept of communion in God, and this is problematic, as the New Testament suggests, at its heart, that there is indeed communion between the Father, the Son, and the Holy Spirit. Can there be communion between *Seinsweisen*? The answer to this question is less than clear.

A further justification for adopting the term *Seinsweisen* was Barth's conviction that the term was more neutral than "persons." But Torrance believes that this was mistaken. I agree with Torrance that, far from being neutral, the term has a strong tendency to undermine notions of mutuality and relation within the divine identity. Torrance asks whether there is not an *a priori* element here, stemming from his analysis of the logical structure of revelation, that threatens to shape his doctrine of God. Torrance conceives the danger of this move as the separation of the priestly and prophetic offices of Christ, by which he means that it risks separating worship and proclamation; *koinonia* and the divine address; and the sacraments and preaching. Torrance concludes:

> In this light it may be justifiable to argue that for Barth the revelation model received prominence . . . at the cost of other models. It is, indeed, our view that a 'worship' or 'communion' model is preferable to the extent that this would offer, on the one hand, a more integrative conception of the theological programme as a whole and, on the other, a profound exposition of the one *Anknüpfungspunkt*, the point of contact (at–one–ment) between the divine and human, which is not simply an event of divine address but the whole humanity of Christ in his life of communion with the Father, as we are brought not merely to 'connect with' it but to participate in it by the Spirit.[46]

As we established in the first chapter in our exposition of Barth and reaffirm now, when humankind meets (or is met by) God in his revelation, it meets

---

45. Torrance, *Persons in Communion*, 115.
46. Ibid., 118–19.

not with a part of God, or with an instantiation of God or with some other "thing" that is distinct from God and humanity. Rather, we meet with God in person: he is relationally present to us. In this revelatory event, God is what he is eternally and antecedently in himself. Torrance's question is whether Barth has established and sufficiently elaborated the relations within the divine Trinity. This is an important question because it has consequences that extend beyond the doctrine of revelation.

Barth refers to the Trinity as the name of a single being, and Torrance suggests that this comes closer than is helpful to using the term "single" in a manner that threatens to subsume God within a class of "single beings," where singularity is conceived with reference to its application within our own sphere of existence. Barth says, "The wonder of God's inner trinitarian life is that the numerically single personal 'I' of the one being that God is . . . has his being only in the true community of a personal 'we' . . . The basic meaning of the begetting of the Son is that God posits community in himself."[47] But, responding to this, Torrance comments:

> What Barth's conception of unity fails to take due cognisance of is the extent to which the New Testament accounts make it difficult to avoid affirming that God is a Thou to himself and an I in relation to himself, and that this eternal mutuality is opened to the world so that we are brought into communion *within* the union not of *a* 'we' but of *the* one, eternal and primordial We—'The Father and I (i.e. "we") are one.' There is, after all, a substantial grammatical difference between a) 'The Father and I are one', and b) 'The Father and I are single'—or, indeed, as Barth's conception of identity would suggest might be said, 'The Father and I is/am one.'[48]

Torrance moves towards a crucial part of his thesis when he writes:

> When the Son reveals the Father to a person this revealing is considerably more than the heuristic bridging of an epistemic gap by way of a 'revealedness' which is identified with the Spirit. The event requires to be explained in more radically personal categories. We are taken to share in the Son's personal communion with the Father in and through the personal agency of the Spirit. Theologically this should be interpreted as an ecclesial event in which the eucharist is inseparable from the proclamation of the Word.[49]

What Torrance is saying here is that in his revelation God is drawing human persons into what he calls "provisional, participatory communion with the intra-divine communion."[50] This is the element that Torrance believes is lacking in Barth's exposition in the first volume of *Church Dogmatics*.

---

47. Quoted in Ibid., 219–20.
48. Ibid., 220; Torrance's emphasis.
49. Ibid., 223.
50. Ibid., 224.

Torrance complains of an "Aristotelian tinge" to Barth's categorical way of posing the question. He points out that it is not necessarily the case that the term "person" must apply to the Father in the same way that it applies to the Son and the Holy Spirit. Barth's choice of the term *Seinsweise* is essentially a negative move that he makes in order to defend himself from perceived dangers.[51] As we have already intimated, his choice may not be as safe as he appears to think. Torrance warns:

> Barth underestimates the extent to which the language of *Seinsweise* risks sterilising rather than communicating an appreciation of the dynamic, perichoretic and participative presence of the Triunity. It is inappropriate, not least in theology, to dissociate the meaning of the word from its ('performative') effect, its conditioning of the apperception of the theological community. A false conditioning is a false communication and thus a semantic distortion. Polluting language which communicates divine 'communing' into that which communicates mere 'being' can have that effect![52]

Torrance acknowledges that Barth is correct in guarding against a literalism or a nominalism that implies non allegorical parallelisms between human and the divine that are not commandeered[53] by the revelation event and the participative life of the church. This fails to adopt an appropriate open-endedness of theological conceptuality. But Torrance does not see that these considerations warrant the exclusion of the term "person" any more than the terms "Father," "Son," and "Holy Spirit" (or, indeed, "*Seinsweise*"). Torrance believes that it is not at all clear that Barth's decision at this point is driven by *a posteriori* considerations of the inner triune relations, and he suggests that "it seems at this point that Barth risks failing to be true to the *content* of biblical revelation through his concern with the biblical *concept* of revelation."[54]

Torrance is unhappy about the lack of dynamic mutuality in the "interconnections" of the *Seinsweisen* and believes that it is a failing that leaves Barth too close to modalism—closer than Barth himself considered himself to be. Certainly, for Barth, none of the modes of being would be what it is if it were not in coexistence with the others. No one mode exists as a single individual—this is Barth's understanding of perichoresis. But Torrance says: "The question we are left with is whether it should be conceived dialectically or, rather, dynamically in terms of the category of communion. Despite Barth's occasional association of the notions of *perichoresis*, communion and modes of being, he fails to ground his exposi-

---

51. It is interesting to note that the terms "Father," "Son," and "Spirit" are not questioned by Barth in the way that he questions the term "person." Although these terms (unlike the term "person"), find expression in the biblical witness, this fact alone is no guarantee that the anthropologically conceived meanings of these terms will not be mapped on to theological terms that are linguistically co-terminus with them.

52. Torrance, *Persons in Communion*, 232.

53. We shall consider the meaning of the "commandeering" of language below.

54. Torrance, *Persons in Communion*, 239; Torrance's emphasis.

tion in Volume One in anything like as dynamic a conception of the perichoretic communion of the Trinity as is to be found, for example, in the writings of John Zizioulas and others from the Eastern tradition."[55]

Torrance regrets that Barth did not establish a more adequately integrated concept of *koinonia* and "being." He believes that Barth's weakness at this point leads him into a concomitant failing in his concept of divine economy and the integration of communion and communication. Torrance thinks that such problems could have been effectively avoided by the employment of a worship model rather than a revelation model. He suggests: "A doctrine of the Trinity which takes seriously the mutuality of loving communion opened up for humanity in Christ by the Spirit suggests the ultimate identification of the source of being and the communion of the Triunity."[56]

Torrance and Zizioulas

John Zizioulas has made a considerable contribution to our understanding and conceptualization of the term "person."[57] And it is clear that, in Torrance's evaluation, his work represents a substantial corrective to Barth's weaknesses in the areas we have discussed.

Zizioulas finds it necessary to reject any rigid or static definition of "person" because the person is not for him (as so often is the case) defined in terms of internal features or qualities but in terms of relationships. Persons are in relationship: that is what they are. Any concept of the person apart from relationship is either distorting or, more probably, meaningless. The person is not a static entity, but one that establishes its existence and being *in relation*.

The Roman conception of personhood failed adequately to progress beyond the original concept of *persona*, in which the theatrical nuances of the word, and its associations with theatrical masks and the roles of actors in plays, were in view. In this way the ontology of personhood was not taken on board in the West. The radical development of the Greek Fathers was to develop the concept of the person with absolute and ontological content.[58] The consequences of this move were considerable, as Torrance explains: "The result was the admission of a relational term (*prosopon*) into ontology and the drawing of an ontological category (*hypostasis*) into the relational categories of existence. The culmination of this process was the identification of being and communion. 'To be and to be in relation become

---

55. Ibid., 256.
56. Ibid., 258.
57. See Zizioulas, *Being as Communion*; and Torrance, *Persons in Communion*, 283–306.
58. This is the source of Zizioulas' inspiration in the development of his understanding of the term "person."

identical."⁵⁹ Torrance quotes Zizioulas' own summary, "'In other words from an adjunct to a being (a kind of mask) the person becomes the being itself and is simultaneously—a most significant point—*the constitutive element* (the 'principle' or 'cause') of beings.'"⁶⁰

The first thing to be said in the light of Zizioulas' understanding of person is that Jesus Christ must be conceived of as "savior" not only because of his teaching and example but because he realizes in history the reality of the person (true person) and provides the possibility and the hypostasis for all people. Torrance affirms that "In doing this Zizioulas does a great deal to take theology beyond the obsession with epistemological concerns which has characterised so much theology since the Enlightenment—even, as Colin Gunton suggests, Karl Barth's theology."⁶¹

It is clear that Zizioulas' contribution is of considerable importance to Torrance in establishing an understanding of both intra-trinitarian relations and human participation in God but, nevertheless, Torrance has some concerns that Zizioulas has overdrawn the distinction between persons in communion with God and persons not in communion with God and he asks whether this approach is open to a charge of operating an ontological "positivism of communion" or "personalist foundationalism." What is the meaning of the gospel of grace for those who reside on the outside of the "circle of revelation"—outside the church? Torrance points out:

> The story of Jesus' life and death testifies to a divine immanence which is much more than an ek-static participation with people whose personhood is thus realised in an event of communion. An adequate account of the grace of God must speak of that "unheard-of immanence: God's presence, incarnate and unseen, in that godless world, among its criminals and cripples, its villains and victims, beside whom and as whom Jesus lived and died and was interred."⁶²

Jesus' death is more than a preliminary to his exaltation, and his resurrection more than a gloss on his crucifixion and death on the cross. Torrance complains that the suffering of Jesus appears to bear little significance for God's being, in the thought of Zizioulas. In his rigorous focus upon the function of the "person" within the context of the church and the eucharist the distinction that Zizioulas makes between those within and those without the church is very clearly drawn, and in Torrance's view, overdrawn.

---

59. Torrance, *Persons in Communion*, 286.
60. Quoted in ibid.
61. Ibid., 299–300. I would suggest that rather than taking theology "beyond" epistemological concerns, it substantially transforms the way in which those concerns are understood and expressed.
62. Ibid., 301–2.

Torrance wonders whether Zizioulas' theological ontology takes on an *a priori* role in the way that parallels the function of Barth's revelation model. But, despite these concerns, Torrance is able to say that Zizioulas' contribution remains "very substantial indeed."[63] More specifically Torrance suggests that "Supremely important is his establishing the primacy of communion over revelation and affirmation of the integral relationship between truth and communion—'the essential thing about a person lies precisely in his being a revelation of truth, not as "substance" or "nature" but as "mode of existence".'"[64] The relationship between truth and communion, albeit cast in the form of different terminology, is one that will be explored in considerable detail when we come to the exposition of the epistemology of Michael Polanyi.

From a "Revelation Model" to a "Worship Model"

Torrance believes that Barth's decision to reject the concept of "person" *vis-à-vis* the Trinitarian life was driven by his model of divine revelation. What Barth lacks, in Torrance's evaluation, is a sufficiently profound concept of the "person" on the one hand and of the intra-divine communion on the other.

Torrance refers to the work of Jürgen Moltmann who (as a committed social Trinitarian theologian) argues for an essential connection between theological knowing, theological participation, and, also, doxology. But Torrance believes that there are weaknesses in Moltmann's discussion, the most significant of which is that he assumes that worship is something that *we* do and that *we* initiate, albeit by the Spirit and in the fellowship of Jesus. This fails to recognize, according to Torrance, the mediatorial priesthood of Christ. Over against Moltmann's view Torrance asserts that our worship is, "*the gift of participating, through the Spirit, in what Christ has done and is doing for us in his intercessions and communion with the Father.*"[65]

Torrance wishes to establish that worship is human participation in the transcendent life of the trinitarian God: "Doxological participation is an event of *grace*."[66] Understood as such, worship cannot be conceived as something for which human beings have a "natural" capacity. Here we must refer back to our discussion and conclusions under the subheading "Human Capacity." What was said of revelation must now be said of worship. We cannot speak of an active capacity to worship God, if by that we mean that we can participate in worship out of an ability that is native to us as creatures, and regardless of God's decision to be

---

63. Ibid., 304.
64. Ibid.
65. Ibid., 311; Torrance's emphasis.
66. Ibid., 313.

present to us as we come before him. But as God makes himself present to us we do participate and enter into communion with the trinitarian life of God.

Torrance wishes to avoid a Pelagianism in which worship is conceived in terms of the creature's approach to God. He insists that, on the contrary, worship is the "free participation by the Spirit in something that God perfects on our behalf."[67] It is "a mediated gift of participating in the intra-divine communion wherein it is the one High Priest *alone* who offers that worship and 'worthship' that the unconditional grace of God unconditionally requires of us."[68] Later he writes, "Communion is not something into which we 'enter' so much as something into which we are drawn by the Spirit. It is, moreover, neither a form of 'praxis' nor a mode of *doing*, but a dynamic in which we find ourselves. It is a mode of *being* . . . but one which is discovered *a posteriori* in and through the event of our participation within it."[69]

Torrance speculates that it may be appropriate to speak of a *vestigium trinitatis* insofar as "the Father is the author of worship, the Son is the worshipper and the Spirit is the agent of worship."[70] Indeed, he suggests that it is more appropriate to speak of a *vestigium* here than in relation to the structure of revelation—as Barth does in Volume One of *Church Dogmatics*.[71] Torrance justifies this by claiming that the worship model (conceived in terms of the inclusive economy of the Trinity *ad intra*) meets three criteria in relation to which, by comparison, Barth's revelation model falls short. Firstly, it indicates more fully the openness and inclusiveness of the communion of the Trinity with respect to human beings. Secondly, it affirms more effectively the communal or personal nature of the intra-trinitarian relations and, finally, it offers a fuller explication of the agency of the Holy Spirit that moves beyond the tendency in Barth to reduce the role of the Spirit to providing for persons the condition for the reception of revelation. Torrance goes on to explain that the event of grace does not stop at the beginning of the human response; the human response is included in the act of grace to the extent that the human response is completed on our behalf in Christ. The human creature desires to worship and serve the living God when the desire is given by the living God and this desire is given in our indwelling of Christ.

> [A]s we are brought to participate in *his* human life and live 'out of' the vicarious worship (as this includes the totality of human 'worthship') provided in him by the Spirit *on our behalf*—and where we are thereby

---

67. Ibid., 314.

68. Ibid., 313; Torrance's emphasis.

69. Ibid., 320; Torrance's emphasis. Although there *is* a "mode of doing" and a "praxis," and these are far from insignificant. These are the forms of activity in which we are incorporated into the intra-trinitarian communion in worship. The point is that it is by the free act of God that in this activity we are drawn into worship.

70. Ibid., 314.

71. See Barth, *Church Dogmatics* I/1, 295–347.

recreated to live *out of* this event of grace in all its *objectivity*. It is as we find ourselves (*post factum*) subjectively caught up in this event of participation that the implications of God's covenant commitment to humanity are *subjectively* (and subliminally) realised in us such that there may be brought about, by grace, a reforming and transforming of our lives and apperceptions—where this is rooted in subjective desire, that is, a desiring that is given, a 'desire' that is not 'desired' in advance of its being realised in us.[72]

The apostle Paul insists that it is not the Christian who lives, but Christ. The Christian does not pray, it is the Spirit who intercedes. The Christian does not understand, but is brought into participation in the understanding that is Christ's. This does not mean that our humanity is overshadowed, or that our will is withdrawn and replaced. Rather I take this to mean that the "shape" of our humanity is transformed and enabled, by the Spirit, to participate in the life of Christ. It is a participation in the life, prayer, and knowledge that is complete in Christ and that is offered by Christ to the Father on behalf of humanity.

Torrance's position might be summed up in three affirmations: that the trinitarian relations *ad intra* are to be conceived as open to humanity; that the "human-Godward" (or "enhypostatic") movement is achieved and made complete in the Son (the true worship of the Father); and that this is the communion into which we are drawn—as human creatures—by the Spirit.

> [T]he strength of the doxological approach—a 'worship orientated paradigm' as opposed to a 'revelation-oriented paradigm'—is its capacity to direct us to that event of triune communion which is conceived not as a 'mode of being' to be appropriated or taken on by the human subject, but as the gift of sharing in the life of the Second Adam as it is constitutive of the New Humanity—of sharing in and living out of *his* life lived in place of ours (his worthship), *his* continuing and vicarious priesthood (his worship) and in *his* union and communion with the Father in the Spirit.[73]

What Torrance's worship model cannot do—and in this there is an equivalence with Barth's revelation model—is resolve the difficulties felt by those who see in such views a privileged access to God for those who have been caught up in what has been derogatorily described as the "magic circle." Torrance makes several responses to those entertaining such concerns[74] and suggests that the most coherent response in defense of Barth, and, by extension, his own position, points to the fact that "possession"[75] of such knowledge bears no concomitant sense of moral commendation, nor does the lack of it imply moral condemnation.

---

72. Torrance, *Persons in Communion*, 319; Torrance's emphases.
73. Ibid., 324; Torrance's emphasis.
74. See ibid., 93–94.
75. I would prefer to adopt the word "participation" in this context.

Torrance writes: "the self-authenticating event of Self-disclosure is simply an *event* and never an *accomplishment* at the human level."[76]

It is my contention that Torrance's modification—or "controlled reinterpretation"—of Barth's revelation model contains important insights and correctives. His particular strategy for reintroduction of the term "person" into the articulation of the trinitarian life guards against a tendency towards modalism and is more faithful to the New Testament witness from which it is drawn. It is clear that Torrance's method is not the projection of an anthropologically conditioned understanding of "persons" onto the "Father," the "Son," and the "Holy Spirit." Rather, he adopts the term and adapts it in the light of the way in which God has made himself known.[77] Also, and significantly for our project, in elucidating a dynamic and open model of the Trinity, Torrance is able to articulate with greater clarity than Barth, by way of his "doxological model," the form and the possibility of human participation in the intra-trinitarian communion.

Concepts, Words, and Revelation

According to Barth, there is a sphere in which human beings may know God. Human beings participate in this sphere as God gives himself to them. Apart from the event in which God gives himself to be known, knowledge of God is not possible. But *in* this event there is, according to Barth, a linguistic participation. But how can we conceive the function of language in this sphere of revelatory knowledge? We must return, briefly, to Barth's *Church Dogmatics* in order to consider his response to this problem.

Can human language be brought into correspondence with revelation? Barth characteristically reminds his readers that, insofar as this is a possibility, it is a possibility given to us by God. "To the question how we come to know God by means of our thinking and language, we must give the answer that of ourselves we do not come to know Him, that, on the contrary, this happens only as the grace of the revelation of God comes to us and therefore to the means of our thinking and language, adopting us and them, pardoning, saving, protecting and making good."[78] But, given that Barth believes that this is a possibility that is indeed given by God, what is the relationship between our language and concepts and the God who gives himself as object? Barth claims, "this relationship is to be regarded as a positive relationship, i.e., one in which there exists a real fellowship between knower and his knowing on the one hand and the known on the other."[79]

---

76. Torrance, *Persons in Communion*, 94; Torrance's emphasis.

77. In the next section I will consider in some depth the way in which language is used in relation to God.

78. Barth, *Church Dogmatics* II/1, 223.

79. Ibid., 224.

If we are to affirm this relationship, we do not, according to Barth, suppose that there is parity between the way in which we apply our words and concepts to God and the way in which we apply them to creaturely reality. "For this would mean a denial of God's hiddenness, and His revelation would no longer be understood as an unveiling in veiling."[80] If there were parity it would be because God was no longer God, or because humanity had become God. However, although Barth refuses the possibility of total parity, he also refuses the possibility of total disparity. If there were disparity, it would mean that there was no knowledge of God. Barth wishes to affirm that there *is* knowledge of God. He claims: "The fact that we know Him must mean that, with our views, concepts and words, we do not describe and express something quite different from Himself, but that in and by these means of ours—the only ones we have—we describe and express God Himself. Otherwise, without this relationship, under the presupposition of a simple disparity, there cannot possibly be any question of the veracity of our knowledge of God."[81] As such Barth resists the description of the relationship as one of simple parity or disparity. He suggests, "We have stumbled again on the co-existence and co-inherence of veiling and unveiling in God's revelation. That God also veils Himself in His revelation certainly excludes the concept of parity as a designation of the relationship between our word and God's being. And that God also unveils Himself in His revelation excludes the concepts of disparity."[82]

If this is so, how does the *partial* correspondence arise? It is, in Barth's view, the result of an active human response to God's revelation. Human concepts can be adapted by us to apply to God.[83] Barth claims that "Our views, concepts and words, grounded on God's revelation, can be legitimately applied to God, and genuinely describe Him even in this sphere of ours and within its limits."[84] This task is according to Barth "authorized" and "commanded" by God. "[I]t is not the case that when He authorises and commands us in His revelation to make use of our views, concepts and words God is doing something, so to speak, inappropriate, because if they are to be applied to Him, our views, concepts and words have to be alienated from their proper and original sense and usage. No, He takes to himself something that already belongs originally and properly to Him."[85] Because God is creator he has an appropriate claim on our words and concepts, and claims them precisely in his revelation. "And disposing of them as His property, He

---

80. Ibid.

81. Ibid., 225.

82. Ibid., 235–36.

83. Although it is not a theme pursued by Barth in this context it is clear that this process of adaptation is to be understood as a task of the church. As a task of the ecclesial community it is executed under the guidance of Holy Scriptures and in conversation with creedal formulations and broader theological expressions of its various traditions.

84. Barth, *Church Dogmatics II/1*, 227.

85. Ibid., 228.

places them at our disposal—at the disposal of our grateful obedience—when He allows and commands us to make use of them in this relationship too."[86] But we must take careful note of the way in which our words and concepts are adopted in this relationship:

> For example, the words "father" and "son" do not first and properly have their truth at the point of reference to the underlying views and concepts in our thought and language, i.e., in their application to the two nearest male members in the succession of physical generations of man or of animal creation generally. They have it first and properly at a point to which, as our words, they cannot refer at all, but to which, on the basis of the grace of the revelation of God, they may refer, and on the basis of the lawful claim of God the Creator they even must refer, and therefore, on the basis of this permission and compulsion, they can actually refer—in their application to God, in the doctrine of the Trinity.[87]

Another example, offered by Barth, is the word "patience." He insists that the meaning with which we should be *primarily* concerned is not the virtue as it is (or is not) practiced by us, "but the incomprehensible being and attitude of God which is shown in the fact that He gives us time to believe in Him."[88] Barth makes the more general point that "Their proper use obviously consists in the fact that they point away and beyond themselves, taking on a new pregnancy, referring to that to which they cannot refer at all as our views and concepts."[89]

It is the error of natural theology to imagine that we can say things of God that we say of things in the creaturely realm. But, in his revelation, a new possibility arises for us with regard to our use of language. The point is not that there are analogies that we know but that there are analogies of which God knows. "Analogy of truth between Him and us is present in His knowing, which comprehends ours, but not in ours which does not comprehend His."[90] It is in God's movement towards humanity in the decision of his grace and in our encounter that the analogous meaning of our words and concepts can be discerned. It is because God *does* make this movement that "the relationship between the knower and the known on the basis of revelation is to be understood as a positive one."[91]

The correspondence between our words and concepts and God is perceived in relational terms. We cannot think of the relationship between our words and concepts apart from the relationship in which humanity is confronted by God. "[A person] is drawn into the light that is given with the fact that God has entered

---

86. Ibid., 229.
87. Ibid.
88. Ibid., 230.
89. Ibid.
90. Ibid.
91. Ibid., 233.

into relationship with him."[92] Because humanity is confronted by God in this relationship (and because God veils himself in his unveiling and unveils himself in his veiling), we must not only say that the correspondence is partial, but, also, that it is not possible to say *how* it is partial.

> Because God is always God in this relationship, He is (in His entirety, in the quantitatively as well as qualitatively quite unlimited truth of His being) the object of the views, concepts and words which He places at man's disposal in His revelation, which in His revelation He allows and commands him to use to designate Him. He is this in so far as He is gracious to man and actually accepts him in grace. But because God is always God, He is also in His revelation (again in His entirety and therefore without deduction of a part of His being, of which something else might be said) the hidden God, who is definitely not the object of the views, concepts and words which we may apply to Him, and who has certainly not given Himself by His permission and command even into the sphere of our apprehension and disposal, much less into our hands.[93]

In knowing God in his revelation, we know him in his gracious movement towards us. We do not and cannot know him apart from this and therefore should not seek to know him apart from this. "[W]e must not and will not leave the grace of His revelation. We must not dispense with it. Nor will it become superfluous to us. Each step that we take as we come from the hiddenness of God must, and will, consist in a new reception of grace of revelation."[94]

In this brief revisitation of Barth's *Church Dogmatics* we can see, with some clarity, the relational aspect of his thinking. While, for Barth, there is no possibility of a correspondence between our concepts and words and God independently of his revelation, *in* God's revelation—which Barth conceives in relational terms—the task is a genuine human task *in relationship*.

In Moltmann's criticism of Barth, which was noted earlier in this chapter, he complains that revelation bypasses genuine human experience. And yet Barth, as we have seen, wishes to affirm that God's revelation *can* be experienced. Although we are entirely dependent upon God to make himself known to us, this does not mean that in the event in which he does make himself known to us we have no active part to play in response. In this related issue, in which we consider the correspondence of our words and thoughts with the being of God, it must again be acknowledged that there is no possibility of our establishing such a correspondence apart from the relationship in which God, by his grace, confronts us and makes himself known. But, similarly, this does not mean that *in* God's gracious confrontation of humanity our human capacities are bypassed and our participa-

92. Ibid., 234.
93. Ibid., 235.
94. Ibid.

tion reduced to zero. On the contrary, Barth affirms that in this relationship the establishment of such a correlation is not only possible but is "commanded" of us by God. Our response, in this regard, is required, and we may be either obedient or disobedient to this command. This is *our* work and *our* participation.

The confusion to which I have made reference at several points in this chapter stems from the assumption that what God achieves in his revelation is—and must be—opposed to human participation. I suggest that revelation ought to be understood very differently. What God achieves in his revelation ought properly to be conceived as the establishing of a *possibility* for human beings. This is, of course, a possibility that would not be present apart from God's grace, but it opens up, nevertheless, a new *human* possibility. This possibility (which is intrinsically relational in nature) is one in which genuine human participation is both possible and required.

As this point is developed, we will consider the transformative aspect of this participation.

Semantics, Human Transformation, and Indwelling

Following on from this exposition of Barth's understanding of the relationship between human concepts and God's being, I will now take up Alan Torrance's discussion of "semantic participation."[95] Having established a positive relationship between human words (and concepts) and the revelation of God it is necessary to consider the dynamic nature of this relationship and its part in human transformation. Torrance's comments represent an extension of Barth's position and draw on insights in the linguistic philosophy of Ludwig Wittgenstein.

Torrance believes that theologians have generally been too ready to adopt naive referential and uncritically realist conceptions of the meaning of terms. It is too often assumed that the meaning of a term is simply to be understood as that to which it refers. It is also too often assumed that there are things that are known "pre-linguistically" by "pure thought," to which terms are subsequently attached in the mental act of referring. Augustine, for example, adopts this sort of position. Torrance quotes Wittgenstein: "'Augustine describes the learning of human language as if the child came into a strange country and it did not understand the language of the country; that is, as if it already had a language, only not this one. Or again: as if the child could already *think*, only not yet speak. And 'think' would here mean something like 'talk to 'itself.'"[96]

---

95. See Torrance, *Persons in Communion*, 325–55.
96. Quoted in ibid., 328; emphasis in the original.

But this is an inadequate description of the way things are. Children do not have another language and do not "speak to themselves." The use of language is a skill that is learned by children as they are nurtured in a particular life context. Language helps us to make distinctions but, although these distinctions are certainly not arbitrary (in that they are grounded in the structure of reality), the way in which they are made bears an intrinsic relation to the particular life context (or, better, contexts) in which the child participates.[97] Torrance says, "Despite the extensive commonalities which characterise humanity as a whole and which are reflected in the fact that we can translate one language into another—a factor with which the relativism of 'post-modern' theology has failed to come to grips—there are differences to be found between different societies and the manner in which they distinguish objects and 'divide up' reality."[98] The learning of a language is less a process in which we learn to attach particular terms to particular things[99] and more like learning to participate in a game.

The significance of these observations for Torrance's broader argument now emerges. If we use the term "person" of the members of the Trinity *and* use it of human beings, this does not necessarily imply that in each case the meaning of the term must be the same. It may be that there are indeed "family resemblances," not between the referents, but between the ways in which the term functions. The rules by which such connections are made are open and not closed. There are "fuzzy boundaries" between terms, and this openness of meaning must be taken into account if we want to avoid misconstruing the nature of the work that is being done in theological description and affirmation. Torrance suggests that "Allowing for this stands to *serve* a proper theology of communion rather than the opposite. It reminds us when using the term 'person,' for example, not to suppose that the whole 'family' of its rules of use in the human context applies appropriately when it is used of the intra-divine communion and that the degree of continuity between the two sets of rules of use must be determined reverently."[100]

In this context we must now consider Torrance's use of the phrase "commandeering of language."[101] In a position that parallels Barth's, Torrance explains that theology, which is bound to work out of the context in which God's revelation is known, takes up terms that are meaningful in public discourse and allows them

---

97. It is worth noting in parenthesis that this analysis corresponds closely to Michael Polanyi's concept of "calling." For Polanyi's this concept denotes our "placement"—both historically and geographically—and our rootedness in the linguistic and cultural life of the context or contexts in which we are nurtured. Although we are profoundly shaped by this participation, our knowledge of this context is largely tacit. This is a theme which we will explore in more detail later.

98. Torrance, *Persons in Communion*, 328–29.

99. Although this is clearly part of the process.

100. Torrance, *Persons in Communion*, 332–33; Torrance's emphasis. In speaking of "reverent" use we may take Torrance to mean "*a posteriori*"—in the light of revelation.

101. What is in view here is akin to Barth's discussion of the way in which words and terms are adopted and adapted in the event of God's revelation.

to be adapted in the light of revelation. We have considered in some detail Barth's view that human words and concepts are able, in the event of revelation, to correspond to it. Torrance wishes to proceed beyond this affirmation to consider the nature of the transformative process in which this may be so.

With regard to the use of the term "person"—which might appropriately be regarded as a paradigm case—Torrance suggests that "the whole conceptuality of personhood is *semper reformanda* and must not, without collapsing theology into anthropomorphism, be conceived in terms of the subliminal operation of categories which are anthropologically or ethically predetermined."[102] Theological construction will inevitably be distorted if its categories are not sufficiently commandeered in the event of God's self-presentation. Torrance concedes that there have been times when this has indeed been the case with theological terms being significantly shaped by metaphysical systems, such as Aristotelianism. However, Torrance believes, in contradistinction to Barth, that the use of the term "person" (as it is adopted and adapted to denote the triune God), should not be considered *intrinsically* problematic. Its meaning may be appropriately extended as it is commandeered in the event of revelation.[103]

One aspect of Torrance's exposition of this theme, which is not emphasized by Barth, is the *ecclesial* aspect of the revelation event. The commandeering of words and concepts is not to be understood as a private matter or in terms of a private language (which, arguably, has no meaning). It is a process that happens in the context in which God makes himself known and the primary identification that Torrance makes in this regard is the church community. The church is a worshipping community, and in its worship it participates in the life of the God it worships. This is the mode of existence of the church community and it is as *this* community that it develops and establishes a mode of language and discourse that is consonant with its life.[104] The task of "language shaping" is a human task—it is the task of establishing appropriate forms of theological articulation—but it is contingent upon a participation in the trinitarian life of God. Torrance draws several strands of his argument together when he writes:

> [T]he use of a theological term presupposes a community which provides the context of its use, that is, the rules of the use of the term. Terms are used in the context of social participation with respect to which certain rules of use apply. This adds support . . . to the insistence (implicit in the *analogia*

---

102. Torrance, *Persons in Communion*, 333.

103. It is important to note that it is not the case that the term "person" *must* be adopted. The obligation under which we fall in faithfulness to God's self-presentation is to ensure that the language-games function as effectively as possible in reflecting the triune life as it is ecclesially known. It is the question of faithfulness that is the key to determining the appropriateness of theological description.

104. As noted above, there are other aspects of the church's life that might appropriately be distinguished from its worship. Such aspects, alongside the worship of the church, combine to establish the form of the community's life.

fidei) that the commandeering of terms for theological usage takes place within the Church, that is, within the community of Christ. There is no unilateral, esoteric or inner transformation of meaning, there is simply the language-game which is constituted, which 'takes place' within the body of Christ by the Spirit and which we are brought to indwell as the means of the communion which stems from the triune life.[105]

An implication of the relationship between the language of the church and the life of the church is that the words and terms that are established within the community will not coincide with the meanings that are associated with the same terms outside the community. This is not unique since dissonance (with regard to the meaning of terms) will arise in differing ways and to differing degrees between all sorts of different communities, or social groupings. But the particular form of semantic formation that is established in the church is unique (and must be distinguished as such) in that its possibility is only a possibility insofar as God draws the church, in the various aspects of its life, into communion with himself. As such, it is a "language-game" that cannot arise apart from the decision and act of God.

One important dynamic aspect of the church's "language-game" is that it is established in the event in which God confronts people in reconciling grace. Human transformation is a possibility as we are drawn into participation in the life of God by the Spirit of God. Such an encounter requires human transformation—one in which the transformation of language is also implied. The significance of the distinctiveness of the language-game should not be underplayed. Baptism into the Body of Christ means the sharing of a *metanoia* that necessitates the taking up of language-games appropriate to the ecclesial context. If we assume more continuity than is actually the case with regard to the use of language, this will only serve to subvert a proper appreciation of the discontinuity between life in and outside the church and understate the distinctions that ought appropriately to be made. Torrance writes:

> A coherent exposition of revelation . . . requires . . . an 'in-depth' exposition of human, semantic participation as it is created by the bestowal of communion and as it involves the creation of human participation in new forms and levels of (ecclesial) language-games as these are constituted by the Logos in and through the Body of Christ and by the *creative* presence of the Holy Spirit working a *meta-noia* with respect to our *noiein*, *logein* and *semainein* such that they may be brought into full participation with the one *Semeion* who is the incarnate *Logos*.[106]

---

105. Torrance, *Persons in Communion*, 336.

106. Ibid., 342; Torrance's emphasis. As I shall note below, Torrance's interests are very much focused on the "*semainein*."

One might reflect upon the way in which Jesus, in what he taught and what he did, undermined the assumptions of the scribes and the Pharisees. The parables of Jesus represent a radical method for calling people to reconsider the form of life that they inhabit, and the use of language associated with it, and introducing them to another form of life—life in the Spirit. This implies human transformation, or *metanoia*, in which life and language are radically re-shaped. The reconfiguring of language is not, of course, peculiar to the church. Torrance points out that the commandeering of language is an important element quite generally in human discovery. Language functions in such a way as to extend knowledge, and this is particularly true of metaphors. As such, language is an agent of discovery. In this connection Torrance quotes Janet Soskice: "'New knowledge is a product of the formation of new relationships between ourselves, our language and the rest of reality.'"[107]

Extending his understanding of the significance of the community, Torrance offers a criticism of Kant that strongly echoes that of Michael Polanyi:

> Kant saw that perceptions without conceptual categories of understanding are "blind" events. The transcendental condition of understanding he interpreted in subjective terms. Consequently, his *Critique of Pure Reason* did not succeed in breaking adequately with the Cartesianism that had shaped European thought before him—and its interpretation of semantics. Wittgenstein, however, shows the extent to which our conceptual processes of interpretation belong to the public domain and take the form of obeying rules—a form of obedience that we do not choose but are born into.[108]

By "obeying rules," Torrance means not so much "obeying laws" as "playing in accord with the spirit of the game."[109] The categories by which we interpret things are not just given but are rooted in particular life contexts. The categories that we use are established in our participation in such contexts.[110] Torrance makes the point that implied in "playing the game" (participation in the "life-forms" of a community) is the development of skills, and this is only meaningful in

---

107. Quoted in Ibid., 347. Although Torrance does not pursue the matter, it is, nevertheless, interesting to reflect on the ways in which scientific discoveries have led to the commandeering of terms and language. It might also be interesting to explore the role of language in the facilitation of scientific discoveries.

108. Ibid., 338.

109. Although there are aspects of language that are tighter and more specific than this metaphor might imply.

110. By way of clarification, it should be noted that our knowledge of the life contexts in which we participate is largely tacit. This is to say that although we may be skilled in "playing according to the spirit of the game" (and, indeed, a variety of "games"), we may be able to articulate only a small part of what we know. Here we anticipate Polanyi's distinction between explicit and tacit knowledge and his aphorism "we know more than we can tell."

terms of "public practice." Torrance also claims that the participation is "blind":[111] participation precedes interpretation. As a consequence, Torrance acknowledges that "To a significant degree we are socially 'created' at the cognitive level prior to any decision to acquire these skills."[112] This latter observation has important consequences for the way in which we think about participation in the ecclesial community. Torrance writes:

> The stress on the priority of participation over interpretation and understanding is paralleled in the ecclesial context in various ways. The 'performative' logic of grace as held forth in infant baptism is irreducibly bound up with its purpose of training a child (in and through its being brought up to understand what its baptism means) in the "skill" of interpreting the world from the perspective of the paradigms associated with the ontological and existential realities held forth in baptism.[113]

Torrance is not saying that as human beings we are socially determined; just that we are social beings. To attempt to understand human being apart from human sociality can only lead to distortions and misconceptions. The semantic aspect of the social contexts in which we participate is clearly an important one in relation to this sociality.[114] As Torrance points out, "There is no Archimedean point outside of language from which we can speak or state or describe the relationship between language and the world. We cannot step outside of language in order to articulate either to ourselves or to others the way language 'connects' with 'the world.'"[115] It is certainly the case that from within the context of our semantic participation we are able to isolate and reflect upon particular aspects of our practice, but we may only do this as part of our continued participation in some or other language-game. It is, therefore, our participation—and primarily our uncritical participation—that has a logical priority over any possible critical internal evaluation. Dogmatics cannot afford to overlook this state of affairs. The point that Torrance makes here (one that has particular prominence in Michael Polanyi's work, as we shall see) is that language is something that, primarily, we *indwell*.

> We indwell the world by means of words and by the use of language as much as we 'indwell' the world by means of visual, audial and tactile means. To this extent, language becomes essential to our being as persons. To put it in other words, to the extent that our 'indwelling' the world is a

111. See Torrance, *Persons in Communion*, 339.

112. Ibid.

113. Ibid.

114. I agree with Torrance but feel that his emphasis upon the semantic is inadequately supplemented with emphases upon other aspects of our participation in a context of life. I will expand upon this concern, and offer what I believe is a corrective, later in the book.

115. Torrance, *Persons in Communion*, 340.

formal condition of our being persons, language, which is the ground of the 'immediacy' of this indwelling, becomes a (socially mediated) 'given' constitutive of our personhood.[116]

Here we recall one of the crucial emphases of Zizioulas' work: we cannot think of a person as somehow existing and then, out of this existence, proceeding to "relate." As we have already seen, relating is intrinsic to our existence. This point is significant for understanding the way in which language functions. Torrance insists "It is not the case . . . that we exist as persons, conceptualise, think and analyse and *then* attach words to our thoughts and express or communicate our conceptualising in language . . . [O]ur very thinking and analysing presupposes our obedience to social rules, that is, *participation within the community*."[117]

Torrance insists that this does not lead us into the slough of relativism. Indeed, it is our indwelling in which our claim to objectivity is rooted. Once again, this analysis resonates strongly with the ideas of Michael Polanyi, who conceives of indwelling as the only way in which it is possible to move towards "objective" knowledge. Again it must be said that there is no Archimedean point from which we are able evaluate our indwelling. Any evaluation of that which we indwell can be made only from within that which we indwell. Torrance explains:

> The (Cartesian) fear that the failure to be able to indwell our 'indwelling' in certain objectivistic ways may lead to relativism and uncertainty is as foolish as believing that if we cannot visually see that our seeing is veridical while seeing something then our visual capacities may not be trusted. The very quest amounts essentially to a failure to appreciate the irreducible given-ness of our there-being or *Da-sein* (Heidegger). In other words, the self is not a detached thinking 'I' who attaches terms to thoughts about God and the world and infallibly checks out all one's stepping-stones to the 'outside world' before standing on them.[118]

The conclusion that we must draw is that theological criticism issues forth from ecclesial being and not vice versa. This is certainly in harmony with Barth's position in that he asserts that "there is no possibility of dogmatics at all outside the Church."[119] We must begin by standing within the Body of Christ. Therefore it is relative in the sense that it is relational rather than self-sustaining. It is also relative in the sense that it must be provisional, before God. But, again, we must insist that this is not relativism. It is what Michael Polanyi calls post-critical realism, and a post-critical realist view is able to sustain the integration of subject and object, language and world. Torrance writes:

---

116. Ibid., 343.
117. Ibid., 344; Torrance's emphasis.
118. Ibid., 346.
119. Barth, *Church Dogmatics I/1*, 17. Barth's dogmatics is, after all, a *church* dogmatics.

Post-critical realism conceives of the world as giving itself to be known—taking hold of our language, revising and extending our terminology and conceptualities, and compelling us to use semantically incremental metaphors in such a way that they receive a new and *a posteriori* propriety from the given structure of the world. The way in which these things *are* is seen, therefore, as epistemically invasive, instituting heuristic leaps in our processes of understanding—an invasiveness that is, again, conceptually mediated by our language and language-games (as these include the grammar of scientific models).[120]

Without denying our own participation (which is, in fact, essential), we may conceive nature as imposing, albeit in an incremental way, its form upon our language-games. Insofar as this is true, a deeper engagement with reality is made possible. This conceptuality is extended in a profound way by Michael Polanyi through his concept of the tacit dimension. Through this it becomes clear that our knowledge is not limited to that which can be rendered explicit. The tacit dimension is the *sine qua non* of heuristic leaps of discovery. It is this that provides Polanyi with his novel resolution to the problem posed by Plato's *Meno Paradox*.[121]

According to Polanyi, our awareness of the techniques of using the "tools" by which we indwell the world, of which language is one, is substantially subliminal, so that we do not attend *to* such things but *from* them. Taking as an example a blind man with a stick, we would say that he does not attend *to* the stick but attends *from* it. Hence Polanyi makes the case that meaning tends to be displaced away from ourselves. When we indwell language (that is, when we *use* a language), we do not attend *to* it, but *from* it.[122]

In his analysis Torrance brings together insights from both Polanyi and Wittgenstein. The significance of these two influences for his own theological task are further illuminated when he writes: "Semantic participation, as it includes—and, indeed, constitutes—our epistemic 'indwelling', is an essential *coefficient* of doxological participation in communion to the extent that worship is cognitive, conceptual and social (ecclesial), and thus grounded in the creative reconstitution in Christ, by the Spirit, of the language-games that constitute our 'capacity' for communion."[123]

---

120. Torrance, *Persons in Communion*, 349; Torrance's emphasis.

121. See Polanyi, *Tacit Dimension*, 22. I will give further consideration to Polanyi's treatment of the *Meno* in chapter 3.

122. This is ordinarily the situation. We can desist from using that which we indwell in order to attend directly to it (as we do, for example, when we think about how we have used a word or how we have constructed a sentence) but this inevitably interrupts the satisfactory performance of the activity. I will offer a more detailed explanation of this phenomenon in my exposition of Polanyi in the following chapter.

123. Torrance, *Persons in Communion*, 356; Torrance's emphasis.

As I seek to develop the doctrine of revelation, I will affirm Torrance's emphasis upon semantic participation and transformation, while suggesting that such an emphasis must be supplemented in recognition of other aspects of our participation that are not adequately developed in Torrance's work.

Analogy

Torrance believes that there is an *analogia entis* but that this must be conceived in eschatological terms. It will be only in the eschaton that human participation will be complete and where God will be all in all. As we have seen, we can make no claims that our own words circumscribe God. The claim is, in the terminology adopted by Bonhoeffer, that the human *logos* is confronted by the "counterlogos"—the *Logos*. And so "Our language only becomes 'God-talk' . . . *given* the creation and redefinition of our language-games instituted in and through the Word and which take place within the ecclesial community as the reconciled Body of the Word."[124]

But a parallel is suggested between the intra-divine communion (a communion that is opened to us in Christ) and the communion of human persons in the Body of Christ. But what of an analogy beyond the community of the church? What of human interrelationships on a wider scale? Torrance thinks that the answer to this question depends upon "the extent to which we can interpret obedience to social rules, which is the ground of semantic interaction, as a form of unconditional, 'covenantal' commitment to others, that is, as a form of communion in itself."[125] He is clearly hesitant about this. He writes: "It would appear to be difficult to argue for an easy identification between 'sociality' and 'communion' that does not commit us to a generic concept of *koinonia*."[126] Nevertheless, he does note that "The interesting feature of semantic sociality is that it *would* seem to repose on a degree of unconditional commitment at the subliminal level—although one which may only manifest in a 'marriage of convenience' rather than an intentional covenant commitment!"[127] One might suggest that instead of invoking generic concepts of *koinonia*, it might be appropriate to speak of "family resemblances" in the use of "community" inside and outside the church. Torrance is trying to avoid the position adopted by Zizioulas in which communion is regarded as possible only for those who are located within the ecclesial community; a position that implies a strong discontinuity with all other forms of social interrelatedness. Torrance makes the comment:

---

124. Ibid., 357; Torrance's emphasis.
125. Ibid., 358.
126. Ibid.
127. Ibid., 358–59; Torrance's emphasis.

Only an over-realised eschatology (and the resulting isolationist ecclesiology) combined with a grossly inadequate doctrine of creation will suppose that the boundaries between semantic sociality within the secular context and the semantic participation within the Church can or should be clearly drawn. Continuities between ecclesial communion and created sociality beyond the Body of Christ are the *sine qua non* of communicating with and hence loving—and hence hearing and speaking to—our neighbour. As such they are divinely intended.[128]

Affirming the appropriateness of a stronger doctrine of creation than we find in Zizioulas, and with the essential qualification that "created sociality" is to be interpreted in the light of the ecclesial community, Torrance ventures that it is appropriate to speak of an analogy between the intra-trinitarian communion (which, in Christ, is open to human participation) and forms of sociality we find beyond the ecclesial context.

The Significance of the Historical Jesus

In this chapter I have acknowledged that Barth has been criticized for failing to give due weight and recognition to responsive human participation in revelation. My suggestion is that this problem is, essentially, one of understatement. My hope is that I have been able to show that human participation in revelation is both consistent with Barth's theological scheme and, to a modest degree, acknowledged within it. I do not think that we need concern ourselves unduly with the reasons for this limitation in Barth's doctrine of the Word of God beyond pointing to the particular theological challenges of his time and the energetic and radical way in which he confronted them. By way of a corrective, I have sought to place greater emphasis upon human participation in the event of divine revelation in a variety of ways. As I come to the final section of this chapter, I wish to turn my attention to a further theme within the doctrine of revelation in which it is possible to discern another understatement in Barth's account: the significance, for revelation, of the "historical Jesus."

In the first three part volumes of *Church Dogmatics* Barth strives to articulate an account of revelation as relationship. Revelation occurs in the relationship that God establishes with humanity in his sovereignty and freedom. Revelation is, to refer again to Barth's phrase, "the simple reality of God."[129] The church's intention, in its proclamation, is revelation, but this is not in the church's gift. Proclamation is revelation because God is present in it and makes it so. The biblical testimony witnesses to the revelation of God and may become the locus of revelation, but it is not revelation in and of itself. Both that to which it witnesses and that to which

---

128. Ibid., 359.
129. Barth, *Church Dogmatics I/2*, 11.

it may become, was and will be revelation in the decision of God. Furthermore, Jesus of Nazareth is not revelation by virtue of being God "in the flesh." Jesus becomes revelation in the decision of God.[130]

The things of this world become the mediators of God's revelation. Church proclamation, Holy Scripture, and the person of Jesus are not in themselves revelation, but they become revelation in the free decision of God. Mediation is necessary in revelation, and there is no revelation without it, but as these things become the mediators of revelation, they become what they are not "in themselves": they are taken up by God as he accommodates himself to their fleshy reality. This is Barth's doctrine of the two natures.

Barth's theological reasons for adopting this position have already been discussed, but it may be helpful at this point to identify a particular problem that emerges in the way in which he sustains this position in the first three part volumes of *Church Dogmatics*. The problem, briefly stated, is that if what is required for revelation to occur is that some fleshy reality is taken up by God for the purpose of making himself known, the significance of the *particular* fleshy substance that is taken up by God in his revelation is not immediately clear. It was noted in the first chapter that Barth does reflect upon the possibility that "God may speak to us through Russian Communism, a flute concerto, a blossoming shrub, or a dead dog."[131] So, given the theological structure of revelation that Barth gives us, can we attribute any particular significance to church proclamation, Holy Scripture, and, in particular, Jesus of Nazareth that might not (in principle) be attributed to a decaying canine, given that God *may* choose to speak to us through any one of them?

This is the problem that Trevor Hart addresses in his essay "Was God in Christ?"[132] Hart expresses the problem in this way: "If Barth's *Logos* becomes *sarx*, the particular way in which the 'becoming' or the union between the two is consistently construed in his theology nonetheless risks reducing it to the point where it loses all purchase in the real world, thereby robbing it of any genuine redemptive and revelatory force, and finally robbing theology of both its theme and its form as talk about God."[133] What is the significance of the historical figure, Jesus of Nazareth, beyond the fact that he may be the locus of an event in which God makes himself known at some particular point in time to some particular person?

---

130. This point is made with some clarity in Matthew's Gospel in the account of Peter's confession, at Caesarea Philippi, that Jesus is the Christ (Matt 16:13–17). Note, in particular, the words of Jesus: "Blessed are you, Simon son of Jonah! For flesh and blood has not revealed this to you, but my Father in heaven."

131. Barth, *Church Dogmatics I/1*, 55.

132. Hart, *Regarding Karl Barth*, 1–27.

133. Ibid., 4.

Hart suggests, "This . . . is where the two-natures doctrine is vulnerable if it is to be adopted as a satisfactory christological framework in and of itself."[134] This is because "In itself it does not offer any clear framework for identifying and evaluating what in positive terms it might mean for the flesh that God is in it."[135] While it may be claimed that this is not the purpose of the two-natures doctrine,[136] it is, nevertheless, the case that "its interest in the humanity of Jesus tends ever towards the general and the shared, that 'humanity' which all humans indwell rather than the particular character of the man from Nazareth."[137] Although Barth is, of course, very much concerned about the incarnate Christ as the one in which the "readiness for God" is established, this concern does not lead in the direction of a consideration of the way in which this is established in the life of a particular man. Hart comments that "in its constant careful segregation of Jesus' 'human' from his 'divine' predicates this doctrine shifts attention away from the role of the humanity of Jesus in revealing God to us."[138]

The difficulty is that if everything that might be said of Jesus of Nazareth equates only to his human nature, what basis can we have for claiming that this historical figure points us in the direction of the character of God? Whatever might be said of Jesus' life must be subject to the qualification that while this is true of his human nature, it does not pertain to his divine nature. Hart comments that "This . . . taken alone, rather short-circuits the revelatory role of his humanity as such."[139] But is the particular flesh and blood that Christ put on merely arbitrary? Hart believes that there are elements of what Barth has to say in this regard that incline him in such a direction.[140]

Despite these emphases in Barth, it is, in fact, clear that the life of Jesus is important for his theology. Hart maintains that he "eschewed any form of docetic lack of interest in Jesus, his character, teaching, actions and passion."[141] The point for Barth is not that the particular form in which revelation comes to humanity is arbitrary or irrelevant, but that it is not, and cannot be, *in itself* revelatory as "its creaturely and phenomenal vehicle."[142] The positive significance of Jesus of Nazareth for Barth is indicated in the first part of the second volume of *Church Dogmatics*:

134. Ibid., 18.
135. Ibid.
136. Its purpose was to expand upon the doctrine of the hypostatic union.
137. Hart, *Regarding Karl Barth*, 18.
138. Ibid.
139. Ibid., 19.
140. Hart points out, for example, that for Barth the form of revelation is not just *distinguishable* from its content, but is a *contradiction* of its content; see ibid.
141. Ibid., 20.
142. Ibid., 21.

> In becoming the same as we are, the Son of God is the same in quite a different way from us; in other words, in our human being what we do is omitted, and what we omit is done. This Man would not be God's revelation to us, God's reconciliation with us, if He were not, as true Man, the true, unchangeable, perfect God Himself... How can God sin, deny Himself to Himself, be against Himself as God?... Therefore in our state and condition He does not do what underlies and produces that state and condition, or what we in that state and condition continually do. Our unholy human existence, assumed and adopted by the Word of God, is a hallowed and therefore a sinless human existence.[143]

But in saying this, Barth is precisely *not* saying that in the humanity of Christ we have a miniaturized God present to us or, as Hart puts it, "a representation or icon of the divine *ousia* under the form of the human *ousia*."[144] What we have is God's hypostatic presence within the sphere of created things as a human being. "[T]he Word who becomes, precisely, not-God, and not 'micro-God.'"[145]

This particular hypostasis, far from being arbitrary or irrelevant, is charged with significance because in it—in the human flesh with which Christ is clothed—a form of humanity is established that corresponds to God in a way that is proper to its "nature." The primary distinction to be made between the humanity of Christ and our humanity is not that in the former we see what God is like and in the latter we do not, but that in the former we see what true humanity is like whereas in the latter we do not.[146] In Christ we have the first fruits of a humanity brought into proper relationship with its God. As such, Hart suggests that "When God speaks his Word into the realm of flesh... it results not in an echo, but precisely in a reply, a response from the side of the creature to the Creator's call."[147] As a consequence, if we are to inquire into the proper relationship between human creature and creator, our warrant is not to engage in *a priori* reasoning and generalizations but to consider the particularity of Jesus' life in the context in which we find it in the gospels and the broader contours of the biblical narrative.[148]

This is an emphasis that ought not be understated and in Barth—particularly in the earlier volumes of the *Church Dogmatics*—it is. Here Hart's criticisms echo those made by Alan Torrance: "It must be admitted that Barth's christology suf-

---

143. Quoted in ibid.

144. Ibid., 22.

145. Ibid.

146. This is an important theme for Barth, clearly anticipated in the above quote and worked out in great detail in his anthropology in the *Church Dogmatics III.2*. It is, of course, a theme which is intrinsically connected to Barth's understanding of "the readiness of man," expounded in the first chapter.

147. Hart, *Regarding Karl Barth*, 22.

148. In this exposition of Barth, Hart emphasizes the *humanity* of Christ in order to guard against docetic tendencies. It must be acknowledged, however, that in his doing so, his acknowledgement of the *divinity* of Christ becomes somewhat muted. Jesus may show us true humanity, but there is more to be said: he also shows us something of God. ("Whoever has seen me has seen the Father," John 14:9.)

fers from a relative lack of development in this respect. For reasons having to do largely with his absolute determination to avoid all forms of subordinationism he fails to develop the model of divine self-communication as inherently relational. A relationality that embraces humanity into the network of its own rich dynamics, and witnesses God not just as human *speaker* of the Word, but also as its *hearer* and *respondent* from the human side."[149]

In emphasizing this, however, Barth's fundamental insights into the nature of revelation must not now be lost. We must not say that Jesus of Nazareth is the revelation of God on the basis of the hypostatic union in which Christ's humanity and divinity are co-terminus. Jesus becomes the revelation of God through the activity of the Spirit: a person is given the ability to see that in this person the purposes of God for humanity are fulfilled.[150] We must follow Barth in his insistence: *finitum non capax infiniti* but, on the basis of the humanity of Christ, we must also acknowledge: *infinitum capax finiti*. Hart explains that we may take the characteristics that we find in the person of Jesus to be indicative of who and what God is like—although they do not do this *directly*. "[T]hey point beyond themselves to the reality of God, and the nature of this 'pointing beyond', and the precise points at which it does and does not occur, are not knowable in isolation from the relationship of faith in which we are properly related to God himself."[151]

This brings us back to Barth's insight that revelation must be conceived in terms of a relationship between God and human being; and if this is to mean anything to us, it must be known to us in particular life-contexts. In this relationship God is present to persons and, through the Spirit, they are enabled to respond to their creator. The point that I have tried to establish in this section of the chapter is that insofar as the historical Jesus, as he is presented to us in the gospels, is the locus of revelation, his character, teaching, and example—far from being marginal or even irrelevant—are of crucial importance. Jesus does not only represent the one authentic human response to God[152] but also provides for us the pattern for true human existence as it is sustained in relationship with God in the power of the Spirit.

Concluding Remark

This chapter represents a critical engagement with Karl Barth's doctrine of the Word of God and his understanding of revelation. It also hints at certain parallels between the work of Barth and Michael Polanyi. In chapters 4 and 5 I will

---

149. Hart, *Regarding Karl Barth*, 23.

150. Here we may remind ourselves again of this point as it is expressed in Matt 16:13–17.

151. Hart, *Regarding Karl Barth*, 24.

152. Representing, thereby, the one human being who fulfills the covenant on the human side and, as a brother, does this vicariously on behalf of all others.

focus on the ways in which Polanyi's thought can be utilized to expand upon the understanding of revelation that I have been developing in this chapter. By way of preparation for this, it is necessary, in the chapter that follows, to offer a substantial exposition of the themes in Polanyi's work that will be employed when I turn my attention to this task.

CHAPTER 3

Michael Polanyi's Theory of Knowledge

Introduction

MICHAEL POLANYI'S DISTINCTIVE theory of knowledge was the fruit of his career as a philosopher. But philosophy was not Polanyi's first career; having trained as a medical doctor, he switched focus to become a research scientist in the field of physical chemistry. It was only after a distinguished career in scientific research that he turned his full attentions to philosophical questions. Polanyi's grounding in science and passion for scientific research proved to be crucial both in his turn to philosophy and in the shape of his philosophizing. In his philosophical work he constantly refers back to his science, and, as the philosopher, he does not cease to think as a scientist. It is clear enough from his writings that his insights are frequently quarried from his wealth of experience as an experimental physical chemist. Polanyi is a *practitioner*, and it is inconceivable that his unique insights in the field of epistemology would have come to fruition had he not been so.

Marjorie Grene, a philosopher and close associate of Polanyi's, in her assessment of his contribution to epistemology, distinguishes his approach from those of others in the field. Grene writes:

> [H]e came to the problem, raised it and grappled with it from within the life of science. It was knowledge in the concrete context of existence, the existence of science and scientists, that he was concerned to vindicate. What resulted was often obscure, sometimes mistaken, and couched in a rhetoric that most professional philosophers find hard to tolerate; but it was a philosophy rooted in reality, neither the clever gymnastics of analysis, nor the prophylactic debate of a philosophy of science based on a

grave misconception of, and almost entirely out of contact with its alleged subject matter.¹

Polanyi's turn to philosophy was made in response to what he regarded as a significant philosophical threat to the freedom of science.

> I first met questions of philosophy when I came up against Soviet ideology under Stalin which denied justification to the pursuit of science. I remember a conversation I had with Bukharin in Moscow in 1935. Though he was heading towards his fall and execution three years later, he was still a leading theoretician of the Communist party. When I asked him about the pursuit of pure science in Soviet Russia, he said that pure science was a morbid symptom of a class society; under socialism the conception of science pursued for its own sake would disappear, for the interests of scientists would spontaneously turn to problems of the current Five-Year Plan.²

This encounter is mentioned on many occasions in Polanyi's writings and appears to have a defining significance for him. As Drusilla Scott has noted, "Polanyi was challenged in his whole outlook by this attitude, and astonished that a socialist theory which claimed to be scientific could so misunderstand science, denying the reality of independent scientific thought."³ It was out of a concern to confront this threat to pure science (already established in Soviet ideology but attracting interest in Britain during the 1930s) and to defend the freedom of scientists from the hegemony of the social planners that Polanyi turned his attentions from scientific research to philosophy. He left his career as a scientist in order to construct a robust philosophical critique of the view that Bukharin had articulated, among various other views that he thought were deeply mistaken. In his studies he sought to develop a theory of knowledge that would authentically reflect the practice of science.

It is not possible, given the limitations of space, to describe the development of this work.⁴ It is important to acknowledge, however, that Polanyi's epistemology developed out of this project, and that all of his philosophical writings are profoundly influenced by the issue that caused him to turn from science to philosophy.

In his published work in the field of philosophy, Polanyi sustains a substantially consistent position, although there are some changes in emphasis. The most significant of these is the shift from a stress on the "fiduciary" component in *Personal Knowledge*, published in 1958, to that of the "tacit" in *The Tacit*

---

1. Grene, "Tacit Knowing," 166–67.
2. Polanyi, *Tacit Dimension*, 3.
3. Scott, *Michael Polanyi*, 5.
4. For a thorough presentation of Polanyi's early defense of liberty and freedom in science, see Polanyi, *Logic of Liberty*.

Dimension, published in 1966. In the introduction to *The Tacit Dimension*, Polanyi writes: "Viewing the content of these pages from the position reached in *Personal Knowledge* and *The Study of Man* eight years ago, I see that my reliance on the necessity of commitment has been reduced by working out the structure of tacit knowing."[5] If, as Polanyi claims in *Personal Knowledge*, "It is the act of commitment in its full structure that saves personal knowledge from being merely subjective,"[6] we can understand Martin Moleski's comment that "The shift in emphasis is somewhat disquieting."[7] However, as Moleski notes, when "commitment" does appear in *The Tacit Dimension*, "Polanyi continues to use the concept very much as he had in *Personal Knowledge*."[8] Indeed, in concluding his own introduction to *The Tacit Dimension*, Polanyi asserts that "any attempt to avoid the responsibility for shaping the beliefs which we accept as true is absurd . . . Thought can live only on grounds which we adopt in the service of a reality to which we submit."[9] There can be little doubt that this echoes the concept of "commitment" we find in *Personal Knowledge*.[10]

So, to trace the succession of emphases that we find in Polanyi's major publications (in broad-brush style), we may say that in *Science, Faith and Society*, a short and early statement of his epistemology, and in *Personal Knowledge*, Polanyi's *magnum opus* based on his Gifford Lectures at the University of Aberdeen (1951–52), the "fiduciary" component is to the fore, while in *The Tacit Dimension* and in *Knowing and Being*, "the structure of tacit knowledge" is more dominant. In *Meaning*[11] (written with Harry Prosch towards the end of his life) there is a development of the structure of tacit knowledge in which a sub-theme of "integration of incompatibles" comes into focus. As these emphases are *substantially* consistent in their inter-relations, this exposition of Polanyi's epistemology will attempt to illuminate various themes within his work as a whole rather than suggest a significant progression or development of thought.

5. Polanyi, *Tacit Dimension*, x.
6. Polanyi, *Personal Knowledge*, 65.
7. Moleski, *Personal Catholicism*, 57.
8. Ibid.
9. Polanyi, *Tacit Dimension*, xi.
10. There are clearly strong linkages between the themes of commitment and tacit knowledge. Perhaps we can say that Polanyi somewhat overstates what is certainly a change in emphasis. Polanyi is not saying, for instance, that one can only be committed to that which is explicit.
11. This is the last book that Polanyi published. Due to his advancing years and waning powers of concentration, the work was co-authored by philosopher Harry Prosch. In the preface Prosch insists that "Substantively . . . this is Michael Polanyi's work. These are his ideas, expressed for the greater part in his own language. In the work I have done on his lectures I have not consciously altered any of the ideas he has expressed in his numerous published and unpublished works." Polanyi and Prosch, *Meaning*, x. This being the case the text of the book cannot be attributed to Polanyi's hand without this qualification. In the excursus which follows the present chapter I will consider the extent to which Prosch's evaluation of his own role in the writing of *Meaning* might be questioned.

In view of the fact that our reading of Polanyi will be deployed, in the present work, in the further development and explication of the doctrine of revelation, the exposition of the themes to be found in Polanyi's writings will be shaped by this concern. As such, it is necessary to forfeit any claim to a general and comprehensive presentation of Polanyi's thought. To offer just a couple of examples: his extensive analysis of totalitarian regimes and his theory of hierarchy (a crucial component of his ontology) will not be dealt with here despite the importance of these themes in Polanyi's work.

I must now turn my attention to the various themes that comprise Polanyi's theory of knowledge. This represents the groundwork for my assessment of how Polanyi's work might further illuminate and contribute to the further development of the doctrine of revelation. Before coming to this, I will also, in a short excursus, expound Polanyi's own work on the theme of religion. As I have already intimated, Polanyi's treatment of religion is disappointing, but it is important to acknowledge his religious writings as they emerge from his epistemological concerns. The theme was one that Polanyi regarded as significant, and he did pay considerable attention to it. As I shall deal with this aspect of his work in the excursus, I will postpone comment on Polanyi's discussion of religious until then.[12]

Polanyi's work is not presented and ordered according to a structured systematic development. While, for the purposes of exposition, I have separated out a number of themes these are not clearly delineated and distinct. There is an interweaving of many strands in Polanyi's epistemology and it is both inevitable and appropriate that these interconnections are represented in an exposition of his work.

Against "Objectivism"

Polanyi's scientific and philosophical work were both conducted within a context significantly influenced and shaped by logical positivism, a philosophy that sought to free itself from all metaphysical concerns and to found itself upon two sources: empirical experience and the reasoning of logic. This was but a particular manifestation of the forms of Enlightenment thought noted in the previous chapter but one that, because of its particular concentration upon explicit operations, was often to the fore in Polanyi's critique of philosophy. But Polanyi's particular interest in logical positivism must be seen in the broader context of (rather than in abstraction from) the strands of epistemology that were associated with the Enlightenment—the philosophy of "modernity." The kind of epistemological approach to which Polanyi was opposed—and that he sought to replace with his post-critical philosophy—I shall refer to as "objectivism."

---

12. Polanyi tends to place his discussion of religion and theology in the midst of his exposition of other themes.

Jerry Gill explains the situation succinctly when he writes: "The chief epistemological dilemma of modernism is that it forces us to choose between an indubitable grounding and open-ended relativism, between objectivity and subjectivity. Unfortunately the former is impossible, and the latter yields no knowledge."[13] What we find in Polanyi's work, among other things, is a substantial proposal for resolving this dilemma.

If Barth sought to establish a "post-Enlightenment," "confessional" theology, it is not far from the mark to say that Polanyi sought to do something broadly parallel in his "post-critical" philosophy.[14] He saw himself as one reacting against a broad philosophical tradition (as well as more specific developments within it—such as logical positivism), illuminating its distortions, and offering a renewed vision of human knowing. Polanyi's intentions are best expressed in his own words toward the end of *Personal Knowledge*:

> [My] aim is to re-equip men with the faculties which centuries of critical thought have taught them to distrust. The reader has been invited to use these faculties and contemplate thus a picture of things restored to their fairly obvious nature. This is all the book was meant to do. For once men have been made to realize the crippling mutilations imposed by an objectivist framework—once the veil of ambiguities covering up these mutilations has been definitively dissolved—many fresh minds will turn to the task of reinterpreting the world as it is, and as it then once more will be seen to be.[15]

The first theme to be considered in this chapter is Polanyi's critique of "objectivism."[16] The dominant position that he sought to refute entailed a belief that in scientific knowledge all "subjective" elements should be purged in the pursuit of "objectivity." Polanyi sets the scene in a passage towards the beginning of *Personal Knowledge*:

> [T]he prevailing conception of science, based on the disjunction of subjectivity and objectivity, seeks—and must seek at all costs—to eliminate

---

13. Gill, *Tacit Mode*, 29.

14. See, for example, Grant, "Michael Polanyi: The Augustinian Component," 462. Grant follows up Polanyi's suggestion that Augustine was the author of the first "post-critical" philosophy and that Polanyi's philosophy is, in significant respects, a similar movement. Grant claims that the "strong Augustinian component" of Polanyi's work reflects his study of Augustine over many years.

15. Polanyi, *Personal Knowledge*, 381.

16. It is important to note that Polanyi's use of "objective" and "subjective" (and cognates) can be idiosyncratic and has the potential to mislead. In reading him, one must be careful to attend to the author's meaning as it emerges from the context of the argument. His use of the term "objective" may hold negative or positive connotations depending upon whether, in context, it is associated with objectivist claims to impersonal knowledge or with "personal contact with reality." For Polanyi, the term "subjective" is not to be equated with "personal" (which has entirely positive connotations) as it denotes individualistic or idiosyncratic perceptions or conceptions that reflect inadequate personal epistemic participation.

from science . . . passionate, personal, human appraisals of theories, or at least to minimize their function to that of a negligible by-play. For modern man has set up as the ideal of knowledge the conception of natural science as a set of statements which is 'objective' in the sense that its substance is entirely determined by observation, even while its presentation may be shaped by conventions.[17]

The philosophy against which Polanyi was reacting placed exclusive emphasis upon empirical observation and logic. It denied that the theories of physics could have any *inherent* rationality and held that such theories had no jurisdiction beyond that which could be established by observation. Objectivism placed an embargo on theories running ahead of the facts. If there is more to a theory than the facts a "contribution" to the theory is being made by the scientist. For the objectivist this is fundamentally unacceptable: it compromises objectivity by admitting subjective elements into scientific theory. Polanyi, in contradistinction, regards such "personal" contributions as intrinsic to the way in which things are known. For him the desire to purge personal participation is nonsensical, and an epistemology that upholds such an approach as capturing the ideal of knowledge can only serve to distort our understanding.

Positivists believe that a theory should be abandoned as soon as an observation is made that contradicts it. But do we always get our observations right? Even the most hard-bitten logical positivist would recognize the potential for observational error. This problem cannot easily be swept aside. Polanyi points out that "there is no rule—*and can be no rule*—on which we can rely for deciding whether the discrepancies between theory and observation should be shrugged aside as observational errors or be recognized, on the contrary, as actual deviations from the theory. The assessment in each case is a *personal* judgment."[18]

Polanyi insists that the scientist has a responsible role both in the construction of a theory and in the accreditation of observational data. The scientist is not just a fact gatherer who allows "facts" to speak for themselves. Nothing that the scientist can investigate has a label "fact" placed upon it. *Concepts* such as "simplicity," "economy," and "symmetry" must guide the scientist in the development of a theory. "[T]he act of knowing includes an appraisal; and this personal co-efficient, which shapes all factual knowledge, bridges in doing so the disjunction between subjectivity and objectivity. It implies the claim that man can transcend his own subjectivity by striving passionately to fulfil his personal obligations to universal

---

17. Polanyi, *Personal Knowledge*, 15–16.

18. Polanyi and Prosch, *Meaning*, 30. First emphasis Polanyi's, second emphasis mine. In such judgment there is a significant—perhaps predominant—tacit component. The significance of tacit knowledge will be explored later in the chapter.

standards."[19] For Polanyi, the objectivist view of the scientist as a disinterested fact gatherer is a profound misrepresentation of the role of the scientist.

The disjunction between objective and subjective—central to the objectivist outlook that has permeated Western culture in many ways—is, according to Polanyi, untrue to the way in which science does and must proceed. The scientist *must* make choices about what to look at and which experiments to do. Which facts are going to be regarded as significant? Science *per se* cannot direct how this should be done; the scientist must make a choice. Before the observations and the collecting of data can start, the significance of the personal co-efficient is already clearly apparent and operative. The factors that actually determine which observations will be made and which data will be collected are many: the interests of the scientific community (influenced by inherited traditions and currents of contemporary concerns) will inevitably have a bearing on the matter, as will a particular scientist's interests, experience, aspirations, and abilities. But the fact is—and this is what has already been established—there is no sense in which this process can be understood as purely "objective," if by that we mean: "no personal involvement."

In this brief discussion of "factual knowledge" and empirical observation, we see the thrust of Polanyi's critique of various forms of objectivism, cast in the form of a powerful argument for the presence of an active personal co-efficient in processes that were held by those he opposed to be *impersonal*. This is a crucial component of Polanyi's epistemology: *all knowledge is personal knowledge* and cannot be conceived in impersonal terms without distortion.

It may also be noted at this point that the personal participation of which I have spoken is *skillful* participation. Polanyi has much to say about such skillful participation and this point will emerge more fully as we proceed. It is sufficient here to note that scientific knowledge and all other knowledge is a human achievement—the product of training, practice, and ingenuity that is predominantly tacit in its operation. Clearly there is a great range of levels of achievement, but Polanyi believes that whether we speak of a modest achievement, such as the recognition of a face, or of a profound scientific discovery, such as that of the theory of relativity, it is not only appropriate but *necessary* to speak of a human achievement facilitated by the skills—the *tacit* skills—of the knower.

Problems and Discoveries

For Polanyi the personal co-efficient in knowledge is a vital force of great consequence. Polanyi points to a fundamental urge that takes hold of humanity and all "fully awake" animals: to make sense of their situation. This is to be understood both intellectually and practically. It is within this urge that Polanyi locates the capacity for discovery, and this is a theme of quintessential significance for him.

19. Polanyi, *Personal Knowledge*, 17.

To recognize a problem is, in itself, an addition to knowledge. "To recognize a problem which can be solved and is worth solving is in fact a discovery in its own right."[20] Polanyi points out that even an animal will not start solving a problem, finding its way in a maze, for example, unless it is aware of the fact that there *may* be a way through, and a way through to something that would represent a reward. A problem or discovery does not exist "in itself" but only if it presents itself to someone as something that needs to be solved. Once conceived as a puzzle, or a problem, it commands the attention of the one who noticed it and draws them into a period of wrestling with it and reflecting upon it: "An extensive preoccupation with a problem imposes an emotional strain, and a discovery which releases from it is a great joy. The story of Archimedes rushing out from his bath into the streets of Syracuse shouting 'Eureka' is a witness to this."[21]

There is, of course, nothing inevitable about a discovery. A search for the solution to a problem may end in failure. It is impossible to know at the outset whether or not an intuition will prove fruitful. Even if a genuine discovery is made, the path to it may be long and difficult, and there may be many detours and wrong turns *en route*. And yet discoveries *are* made. In an attempt to illuminate further the stages of the process, Polanyi draws attention to Henri Poincaré's schema for discovery in mathematics that, Polanyi believes, is of significance in other areas in which discoveries are made. The sequence is as follows: "preparation" (evaluation of the problem that has been discerned); "incubation" (a time when nothing appears to happen and the "work" is being done by the unconscious mind); "illumination" (the dawning awareness of a solution); and "verification" (by which the validity of what appears to be a solution is tested).[22] Once a solution to the problem is seen and realized, the puzzlement evaporates and the urge is satisfied. A discovery has been made. And this represents, on the part of the discoverer (be it an animal or a human), a new intellectual power; for once the discovery is made, the problem ceases to exist. No matter how difficult or long the process toward making the breakthrough, once made it can no longer be the source of puzzlement. "Heuristic progress is irreversible."[23] Polanyi expands this point: "The irreversible character of discovery suggests that no solution of a problem can be accredited as a discovery if it is achieved by a procedure following definite rules. For such a procedure would be reversible in the sense that it could be traced back stepwise to its beginning and repeated at will any number of times, like any arithmetical computation. Accordingly, any strictly formalized procedure would also be excluded as a means of achieving discovery."[24] Discovery cannot be

---

20. Ibid., 120.
21. Ibid., 122.
22. See ibid., 121–22.
23. Ibid., 123.
24. Ibid.

understood as a strictly logical performance, because it can be achieved only by crossing over what Polanyi calls a "logical gap." "'Illumination' is then the leap by which the logical gap is crossed. It is the plunge by which we gain a foothold at another shore of reality. On such plunges the scientist has to stake bit by bit his entire professional life."[25]

As noted already, one motivation that sustains the would-be discoverer is the sense that there is a solution to the problem. Polanyi explains: "We are looking for it as if it were pre-existent."[26] This is part of the process in which we are trying to make sense of things, and this is posited upon the belief that things do make sense. Polanyi describes a problem as "an intellectual desire."[27] He writes: "[L]ike every desire it postulates the existence of something that can satisfy it; in the case of a problem its satisfier is its solution. As all desire stimulates the imagination to dwell on the means of satisfying it, and is stirred up in its turn by the play of the imagination it has fostered, so also by taking interest in a problem we start speculating about its possible solution and in doing so become further engrossed in the problem."[28]

Although discovery is an intrinsic part of the sciences and is understood to be the goal of much scientific work, it has been considered a much more problematic category among philosophers. It will be apparent that the objectivist philosophy, detailed above, cannot accept the description of discovery that Polanyi offers. At the heart of Polanyi's analysis is the recognition that the process is unspecifiable, and it affirms the existence of a reality that we only partially comprehend, or that we comprehend in such a way that we are left dissatisfied with our understanding. If the phenomenon of scientific discovery plays an important part in Polanyi's epistemology, it is unsurprising since while its importance in the history of science is of great consequence, it is at the same time "a most striking concrete example of an experience that cannot possibly be represented by any exact theory."[29] In *The Tacit Dimension*, Polanyi expands these ideas about discovery in the context of a discussion of his theory of tacit knowledge. I will revisit the theme of discovery when I come to consider that theory later in the chapter.

Polanyi states that it is a commonplace that good science requires good problems. "[T]o see a problem is to see something that is hidden. It is to have

---

25. Ibid. Polanyi does not deny the importance of the use of logical operations in certain circumstances whether in mathematics, science or elsewhere. What he is concerned to demonstrate is that there are many situations in which explicit logical operations will prove either incapable or insufficient in the pursuit of the solution to a problem. We shall see in the final chapter that for Polanyi illumination must be coupled with imagination.

26. Ibid., 126.

27. See ibid., 127.

28. Ibid.

29. Polanyi, *Tacit Dimension*, 21.

an intimation of the coherence of hitherto not comprehended particulars."[30] To identify a problem that will lead to an important discovery is not only to see something that is hidden "but to see something of which the rest of humanity cannot have even an inkling."[31] But how is it possible to identify a good problem? Indeed, how is it possible to identify any problem at all? This was the question that Plato considered in the *Meno*. Polanyi summarizes the paradox of the *Meno* by stating "that to search for the solution of a problem is an absurdity; for either you know what you are looking for, and then there is no problem; or you do not know what you are looking for, and then you cannot expect to find anything."[32] Polanyi notes that Plato's solution to the paradox (the remembering of past lives) has not generally proved acceptable, but alternative explanations have not been forthcoming. To conclude that the *Meno* cannot be resolved appears to render the problem-solving and discoveries of over two thousand years of human history "either meaningless or impossible."[33] Polanyi thinks that such a conclusion is unnecessary if we are prepared to acknowledge the tacit dimension of knowing. He suggests: "[T]he *Meno* shows conclusively that if all knowledge is explicit, i.e., capable of being clearly stated, then we cannot know a problem or look for its solution. And the *Meno* also shows, therefore, that if problems nevertheless exist, and discoveries can be made by solving them, we can know things, and important things, that we cannot tell."[34]

This is a substantial response to the problem that Plato raises, but Michael Bradie has objected that Polanyi's formulation of the *Meno* is in part false,[35] and Bradie gains support for his criticism from Herbert Simon.[36] Bradie says, "Suppose a mathematician is trying to refute Goldbach's conjecture that claims that every even number is representable as the sum of two primes. Then he knows that *what he is looking for is a number that is not the sum of two primes*."[37] In other words,

30. Ibid.
31. Ibid., 22.
32. Ibid.
33. Ibid.
34. Ibid. Polanyi later came to see this formulation as inadequate. Although his subsequent reflections upon the *Meno* were never published, they are revealed in a letter to Marjorie Grene dated 26th April 1965. See "Polanyi Collection: Regenstein Library, University of Chicago." Box 16: Folder 1. Polanyi states that his resolution of the *Meno* in the Terry Lectures of 1962 (and published in *The Tacit Dimension*) is lacking because it is "purely verbal, rashly identifying [the] unspecifiability of tacit knowing with indeterminacy . . . " Polanyi describes to Grene how he came to see his earlier account as inadequate: "It came to me when I identified James's description of voluntary action with the effects of the imagination in producing the erection of the penis, and Hefferline's observation that the sight of the galvanometer's deflections greatly assists the production of conditioned subliminal twitches. I saw then the full solution to the problem." In other words, the tacit knowledge which brings resolution to the *Meno* paradox must not be limited to that of indeterminate articulation but be located much more broadly in our bodily indwelling.
35. Bradie, "Polanyi on the Meno Paradox," 203.
36. Simon, "Bradie on Polanyi on the Meno Paradox," 147–50.
37. Bradie, "Polanyi on the Meno Paradox," 147; Bradie's emphasis.

the mathematician knows what he or she is looking for, but there is still a problem. This criticism, though formally correct, seems to miss the force of Polanyi's case. Polanyi is not offering an *a priori* analytical argument but an *a posteriori* observation. Polanyi is interested in exposing the inadequacy of a philosophy of science, which holds that all knowledge is explicit in order to explain the phenomenon of scientific discovery. As such, the formal correctness of the criticism of Bradie and Simon does not seriously detract from the force of Polanyi's answer to Plato *insofar as Polanyi's purpose in the endeavor is kept in mind*.

Great scientific discovery will be marked by its fruitfulness. But how can such fruitfulness be recognized? If we hold to the view that all knowledge must be explicit, it is meaningless to speak of fruitfulness if, by it, we mean to refer to things that are as yet undiscovered. But it *can* make sense if we believe that we can have what Polanyi calls "foreknowledge" of as yet undiscovered things. Polanyi suggests that "to know that a statement is true is to know more than we can tell and that hence, when a discovery solves a problem, it is itself fraught with further intimations of an indeterminate range, and that furthermore, when we accept a discovery as true, we commit ourselves to a belief in all these as yet undisclosed, perhaps as yet unthinkable, consequences."[38]

It will be apparent that implied in Polanyi's epistemological convictions are certain ontological convictions. "[A]s we can know a problem, and feel sure that it is pointing to something hidden behind it, we can be aware also of the hidden implications of a scientific discovery, and feel confident that they will prove right. We feel sure of this, because in contemplating the discovery we are looking at it not only in itself but, more significantly, as a clue to a reality of which it is a manifestation."[39] In making a discovery, we claim to have made contact with reality, "a reality which, being real, may yet reveal itself to future eyes in an indefinite range of unexpected manifestations."[40] We will only make significant discoveries if we are "deeply committed to the conviction that there is something there to be discovered."[41]

Intellectual Passions[42]

We have now considered a number of ways in which Polanyi has shown the inadequacies of the objectivist understanding of science. In his discussion of

38. Polanyi, *Tacit Dimension*, 23.
39. Ibid., 23–24.
40. Ibid., 24.
41. Ibid., 25.

42. As with "objective" and "subjective," Polanyi's use of the word "passions" is somewhat idiosyncratic and must be understood within the context in which it is used. It must be said, however, that part of the problem here stems from the popular misconception that scientific work is "dispassionate" and "detached."

intellectual passions, he seeks to expound a more authentic description of the dynamics of science.

The notion of the scientist, central to the objectivist philosophy and of considerable influence in our own day, is that of the detached, dispassionate researcher resisting any temptation to allow his or her own personal concerns or interests to influence—and thereby sully—the purity of the scientific work in which they are engaged. Over against this, Polanyi believes that the passions of the scientist are an intrinsic element of scientific endeavor.

> The function which I attribute ... to scientific passion is that of distinguishing between demonstrable facts which are of scientific interest, and those which are not. Only a tiny fraction of all knowable facts are of interest to scientists, and scientific passion serves also as a guide in the assessment of what is of higher and what is of lesser interest; what is great in science, and what is relatively slight. I want to show that this appreciation depends ultimately on a sense of intellectual beauty; that it is an emotional response which can never be dispassionately defined, any more than we can dispassionately define the beauty of a work of art or the excellence of a noble action.[43]

A scientific discovery represents the advent of new knowledge. This knowledge is accompanied by a vision that is not knowledge.[44] In one sense it is *less* than knowledge in that it is a "guess," but in another sense it is *more* than knowledge in that it is an anticipation or "fore-grasping" of things as yet unknown or even inconceivable. "Our vision of the general nature of things is our guide for the interpretation of all future experience. Such guidance is indispensable."[45] Any attempt to establish scientific truth by formal, objective criteria must fail as "Any process of enquiry unguided by intellectual passions would inevitably spread out into a desert of trivialities."[46] Commenting on the practice of scientists to ignore evidence incompatible with current scientific theory, Polanyi says: "The wise neglect of such evidence prevents scientific laboratories from being plunged for ever into a turmoil of incoherent and futile efforts to verify false allegations. But there is, unfortunately, no rule by which to avoid the risk of occasionally disregarding thereby true evidence which conflicts (or seems to conflict) with the current teachings of science."[47]

---

43. Polanyi, *Personal Knowledge*, 135. Although Polanyi uses the definite article here this is one of the several functions of "scientific passion," as shall see.

44. Polanyi illustrates this point by tracing the developments which followed on from the "vision" established in Copernicus' heliocentric view of the universe. See Polanyi, "Science and Reality."

45. Polanyi, *Personal Knowledge*, 135.

46. Ibid.

47. Ibid., 138.

The vision of which Polanyi speaks is of fundamental significance because "[W]ithout a scale of interest and plausibility based on a vision of reality, nothing can be discovered that is of value to science; and only our grasp of scientific beauty, responding to the evidence of our senses, can evoke this vision."[48] This analysis flows from Polanyi's belief that the scientist must be able to distinguish that which is trivial from that which is not, as well as being able to distinguish between that which is true and that which is false. The ability flows from the scientist's knowledge of science, but it also implies the scientist's antecedent interest in the subject matter. Polanyi makes the simple point that animals were not discovered by zoologists, nor plants by botanists. The scientific study of animals and plants represents an extension of a pre-scientific interest, and in the absence of such a pre-scientific interest it is inconceivable that a scientific interest would have emerged.

Polanyi, as a seasoned scientific researcher, draws attention to the fact that the pursuit of a discovery will often place heavy demands upon a scientist and may do so for long periods of time. What sustains the scientist in such protracted and exacting pursuits? The dedicated pursuit of a solution to a problem over extended periods of time can only be sustained by the intellectual passion evoked by the intimation of a discovery: the prospect of uncovering something that is hidden. The intimation may prove to be right, or it may prove to be wrong; this is a risk that is intrinsic to the work of the scientist in pursuit of discovery. Polanyi comments: "Intellectual passions do not merely affirm the existence of harmonies which foreshadow an indeterminate range of future discoveries, but can also evoke intimations of specific discoveries and sustain their persistent pursuit through years of labour. The appreciation of scientific value merges here into the capacity for discovering it; even as the artist's sensibility merges into his creative powers. Such is the *heuristic* function of scientific passion."[49]

The scientist is, to use Polanyi's phrase, "trying to guess right." The accomplishment of this end is sustained by a "heuristic passion." This work is creative in that in its attainment it changes the world as we see it. As a result of it, our understanding of the world is deepened. As has already been stated, an act of discovery is irreversible, and once it is made, the world is forever seen as with different eyes. A heuristic gap, which stands between the formulation of a problem and a discovery, is crossed. Polanyi re-emphasizes the passionate and personal roots of the advancement of scientific principles:

> Major discoveries change our interpretive framework. Hence it is logically impossible to arrive at these by the continued application of our previous interpretive framework. So we see once more that discovery is creative, in the sense that it is not to be achieved by the diligent performance of any previously known and specifiable procedure. This strengthens our concep-

---

48. Ibid., 135.
49. Ibid., 143; Polanyi's emphasis.

tion of originality. The application of existing rules can produce valuable surveys, but does not advance the principles of science. We have to cross the logical gap between a problem and its solution by relying on the unspecifiable impulse of our heuristic passion, and must undergo as we do so a change of our intellectual personality. Like all ventures in which we comprehensively dispose of ourselves, such an intentional change of our personality requires a passionate motive to accomplish it. Originality must be passionate.[50]

What emerges from this—and most emphatically so—is the *personal* nature of discovery. The passions and the beliefs that lead scientists to discovery are passions and beliefs that are *personally* held. Does this imply that science, and the pursuit of discovery in science, is "subjective," as the objectivist would fear? Polanyi says not. The reason for this is that the scientist is constrained by the nature of that which is being explored. This is the external pole of truth that the discoverer wishes to establish. There is always the possibility that the discoverer may be mistaken; nevertheless, discovery is never presented as private opinion, it is commended by the discoverer as the truth. It is held with what Polanyi terms "universal intent."[51] A further reason for rejecting the accusation of subjectivity is that the scientist works within the discipline of a tradition in a community of explorers that provides both peer support and criticism.

An implication of this is that the scientist who propounds the truth of his or her theory is making a demand that it be accepted as such by others. This demand will not always be met, as Polanyi knew from his own experiences in science, and this can be a perplexing matter. It is doubtless because of his own experiences that he describes the situation of the discoverer in impassioned terms: "In order to be satisfied, our intellectual passions must find response. The universal intent creates a tension: we suffer when a vision of reality to which we have committed ourselves is contemptuously ignored by others. For a general unbelief imperils our own convictions by evoking an echo in us. Our vision must conquer or die."[52] Hence, in addition to the function of scientific passion in *selection* and the *heuristic* passion in moving to a discovery, there is the *persuasive* passion in calling others to become fellow participants in a new vision. The processes involved in discovery are not only *personal* but, in this significant sense, *inter-personal*.

The divide between two systems of thought bears some similarities to the gap that exists between a problem and its solution. "Formal operations relying on *one* framework of interpretation cannot demonstrate a proposition to persons who rely on *another* framework."[53] The proponents of a new system of thought,

---

50. Ibid., 143.
51. This is a concept to which I will return later in the chapter.
52. Polanyi, *Personal Knowledge*, 150.
53. Ibid., 151; Polanyi's emphasis.

in order to defend their own credibility and gain the support of others, must win the intellectual sympathy of their opponents. Those who listen sympathetically may gain what they would never have gained for themselves, and this is what Polanyi variously describes as a "self-modifying act," a "heuristic process," and a "conversion." It is not difficult to see why such a process might fail, or imagine circumstances in which those on either side of a divide are reduced to an engagement in which the wholesale discrediting of one another becomes the *modus operandi*. It is not difficult to see why such conflicts are sometimes described as "personal attacks." All this is indicative of the personal nature of the way in which views are held by both sides, and of the passions that attend them. This is why science cannot be free from controversy and conflict. In an article dealing with passions in science, he writes: "Not that I like to see a scientist trying to bring an opponent into intellectual contempt, but I acknowledge that such means of controversy may be tragically inevitable. I certainly affirm that passion, and controversy moved by passion, must continue in science and that a comprehensive revision of our philosophy of science is needed to give due weight to this essential aspect of scientific truth."[54]

Polanyi points to the example of extra-sensory perception (ESP) in order to illustrate his point. At the time of writing *Personal Knowledge*, Polanyi believed the credibility of ESP to be an open question, but he was aware that the great majority of scientists rejected the phenomenon. Polanyi observes that "The evidence for it is ignored today by scientists in the hope that it will one day find some trivial explanation. In this they may be right, but I respect those too who think they may be wrong; and no profitable discussion is possible between the two sides at this stage."[55]

The Narrative of the Scientific Community

Science grows and expands. New theories are advanced, and the possibilities of old visions are explored. There is also the "telling of the story" of what has gone before. Polanyi writes, "[I]n the history of science, as in that of all other human activities, it falls finally to him who tells their story, to endorse or revise all previous assessments of their outcome—while simultaneously responding to contemporary issues unthought of before. Traditions are transmitted to us from the past, but they are our own interpretations of the past, at which we have arrived within the context of our own immediate problems."[56]

Polanyi recognizes that the context and the flow of the scientific tradition is of great importance. Issues of procedure and beliefs in science are mutually

---

54. Polanyi, "Passions and Controversy in Science," 119.
55. Polanyi, *Personal Knowledge*, 158.
56. Ibid., 160.

determined. Our expectations determine how we proceed, and our anticipations are shaped in response to the results that have been achieved by the procedures that we have adopted. Polanyi reminds us that, by and large, the concerns of science are shaped by, among other things, the concerns of common experience. "The methods by which we establish facts in everyday life are . . . logically anterior to the special premisses of science, and should be included in a full statement of these premisses."[57] Of course, the standards adopted in dealing with the subject matter in science will differ from those used in the context of everyday experience. However, our belief about the nature of things, as it is expressed in the realm of common experience, can certainly not be excluded from our account of science.

In connection with this, Polanyi notes the significance of common experience for establishing which facts are significant for science: "The logical premisses of factuality are not known to us or believed by us *before* we start establishing facts, but are recognized on the contrary *by reflecting on the way we establish facts*."[58] He continues:

> Our acceptance of facts which make sense of the clues offered by experience to our eyes and ears must be presupposed first, and the premisses underlying this process of making sense must be deduced from this afterwards. Since the process of discovering the logical antecedent from an analysis of its logical derivative cannot fail to introduce a measure of uncertainty, the knowledge of this antecedent will always be less certain than that of its consequent. We do not believe in the existence of facts because of our anterior and securer belief in any explicit logical presuppositions of such a belief; but on the contrary, we believe in certain explicit presuppositions of factuality only because we have discovered that they are implied in our belief in the existence of facts.[59]

Polanyi shows that this point is illustrated in the performance of skills. We perform a skill—making a golf shot, for example—without any antecedent focal knowledge of how it is that we do it. But we do, and must, have a subsidiary knowledge as part of our competence in performing the skill. It is possible to reflect upon the accomplishment after the event even if during the performance of it we were "focally ignorant." It is in the reflection upon the event that it is possible to develop maxims—"keep your head still"; "do not look up too soon"; "do not try to hit the ball too hard," etc.—which may prove helpful as self-reminders or in giving advice to others who wish to develop the skill. Nevertheless it is quite impossible to perform any skill on the basis of explicit rules alone, or to articulate a "total set of rules" on the basis of which we are able to perform the skill. In applying this observation to the realm of science, Polanyi explains: "The logical antecedents of

---

57. Ibid., 161.
58. Ibid., 162; Polanyi's emphasis.
59. Ibid.

an informal mental process like fact-finding, or more particularly, the finding of a fact of science, come to be known subsidiarily in the very act of their application; but they can become known focally only later, from an analysis of their application, and, once focally known, they can be applied by re-integration to guide subsidiarily improved performances of the process."[60] So, referring back to the example of golf, it must be acknowledged that various maxims and other words of advice do, at least on occasion, contribute to the proficiency of the aspiring golfer.

The breadth and complexity of the body of scientific knowledge is such that no one scientist can understand any more than a small fraction of the totality in any depth. Each member of the scientific community is competent to judge the work of colleagues working in the same or closely related fields, and in this way, Polanyi believes, the self-regulating structure is established and maintained. Hence, there is a consensus across the scientific disciplines, and within the confines of this consensus it is possible to say whether a new contribution is "scientific" or not. In this way the more radical scientific debates are cast in the form of a conflict between established authority and a challenger to that authority; the one challenging may not be credited with the status of scientist—at least with regard to the issue in dispute. It is important to realize that challengers do not attack the authority of scientific opinion in general but only in respect of a particular detail. Paradoxically "[E]very thoughtful submission to authority is qualified by some, however slight, opposition to it."[61] Hence the advancement of the body of scientific knowledge is dependent upon challenges being made to it, while its stability is dependent upon a recognition, on the part of both scientists, and to some degree society as a whole, of the authority of the scientific tradition. Anyone who rejects the authority of the tradition *in a general way* would find no basis on which to resolve their disagreement with those who accept it.

When challenges are made to the consensus how are they resolved? Polanyi is aware that this is a question to which no complete and final answer can be given—in part because things have, in fact, been resolved in various ways on different occasions. A simple appeal to the "facts" is entirely inadequate. In a scientific dispute there may well be disagreement on what the facts are, and there is yet more likelihood of disagreement of what is admissible as evidence. Also, as Polanyi sees so clearly, "good science" is not a fact-collecting exercise. By way of illustration Polanyi writes: "Take Mach's principle of 'mental economy,' according to which science is the simplest description or the most convenient summary of the facts. Imagine the puzzled examiners of de Broglie's doctoral thesis having recourse to this criterion as to the scientific value of the work. How could they? Most of the facts which the theory was eventually found to describe were yet undiscovered."[62]

60. Ibid., 163.
61. Ibid., 164.
62. Ibid., 166.

De Broglie's wave theory was founded not upon "facts," but upon speculation that was guided by criteria of internal rationality and a deep familiarity with many relevant phenomena.

The question arises, "how, given all these circumstances pertaining to the practice of science, could scientists fail to see the inadequacies of a philosophy of science in which the scientist has no substantive role to play?" Polanyi offers two responses. The first relates to the ideological power of the dominant philosophy. He suggests, "The decisive reason why such obviously inadequate formulations of the principles of science were accepted by men of great intellectual distinction lies in a desperate craving to represent scientific knowledge as impersonal."[63] But Polanyi also offers an explanation of *how* scientists can hold such views: "We owe this immense power for self-deception to the operation of the ubiquitous tacit co-efficient by which alone we can apply any articulate terms to a subject matter described by them. These powers enable us to evoke our conception of a complex ineffable subject matter with which we are familiar, by even the roughest sketch of any of its specifiable features."[64] Put simply, an established scientist *may* be able to accept as true an inadequate description of his or her work by tacitly supplementing and creatively interpreting that description. This is a process that can certainly be extended beyond the realm of science and is akin to the phenomenon, well known to psychologists, that we have a considerable propensity to "see" what we expect to see in a particular circumstance rather than what is actually "there."

Indwelling

Polanyi ought not to be misunderstood: he is not opposed to the formulization of science. What he claims is that the formulization of science can never adequately represent scientific theory and practice. However instructive and valuable the explicit representations of science may be, they can never be a substitute for a genuine indwelling of the disciplines and skills that comprise the life of the scientific community. In a confessional statement Polanyi says:

> The discoveries of science have been achieved by the passionately sustained efforts of succeeding generations of great men, who overwhelmed the whole of modern humanity by the power of their convictions. Thus has our scientific outlook been moulded, of which these logical rules [the formulizations of science] give a highly attenuated summary. If we ask why we accept the summary, the answer lies in the body of knowledge of which they are the summary. We must reply by recalling the way each of us has come to accept that knowledge and the reasons for which we continue to do so. Science will appear then as a vast system of beliefs, deeply rooted

63. Ibid., 168–69.
64. Ibid., 169.

in our history and cultivated today by a specially organized part of our society. We shall see that science is not established by the acceptance of a formula, but is part of our mental life, shared out for cultivation among many thousands of specialized scientists throughout the world, and shared receptively, at second-hand, by many millions. And we shall realize that any sincere account of the reasons for which we too share in this mental life must necessarily be given as part of this life.[65]

Polanyi makes the point that the tradition of science as we know it is "of recent origin and its tradition is rooted in a limited area."[66] He notes that many other civilizations of equal richness and antiquity failed to produce a systematic natural science. From the perspective of the twenty-frist century, the credentials and stability of science may appear unassailable, but this appearance may be deceptive. Science grows within a society of fellow practitioners whose skills are predominantly unspecifiable. Because of the unspecifiability of the body of scientific knowledge (in Polanyi's terms, the "tacit component"), the safe passage of the tradition from one generation to the next is by no means assured. For the same reason it is difficult for science to take root in cultures and societies where it has not previously been practiced. Polanyi claims: "Rarely, if ever, was the final acclimatization of science outside Europe achieved, until the government of a country succeeded in inducing a few scientists from some traditional centre to settle down in their territory and to develop there a new home for scientific life, moulded on their own traditional standards."[67]

For Polanyi, science is not a body of knowledge that can be abstracted from the life, community, and beliefs that sustain it. It is an example of what Polanyi calls an "articulate system." This is an important term in Polanyi's philosophy, and it will receive some attention in this chapter. But two particular difficulties attend it. Firstly, to call a system (such as science) "articulate" might well lead one to assume that it is a system that is "articulated," i.e., that it can be described. But this is not Polanyi's intention. There is much in science that can be and is articulated, as we have seen, but the innovation of Polanyi's philosophy is to show that such systems cannot be fully articulated. Consequently the term "articulate" is potentially misleading. A second difficulty is the sheer range of phenomena to which Polanyi attaches the term. He cites science, technology, mathematics,[68] works of art,[69] mo-

---

65. Ibid., 171.
66. Ibid., 181.
67. Ibid., 182.
68. Ibid., 203.
69. Ibid., 286.

rality,⁷⁰ religious worship,⁷¹ a theory,⁷² and (more specifically), a scientific theory,⁷³ a mathematical discovery,⁷⁴ and a symphony.⁷⁵ Such examples suggest not so much a category—even a broad category—but a family of related categories. It is necessary to see that Polanyi is not attempting to establish similarities between these "systems" per se, but that our participation in them can be only partially represented in terms of explicit knowledge. Polanyi explains: "The universe of every great articulate system is constructed by elaborating and transmuting one particular aspect of anterior experience."⁷⁶ An articulate system cannot be represented as a collection of facts that are explicitly known. They are the "happy dwelling places of the human mind."⁷⁷

The concept of "indwelling" reinforces the personal nature of knowing. A collocation of facts is not knowledge. A collocation of experiences is not knowledge. Facts and experiences represent knowledge only when we come to interpret them—when we make sense of them. Facts are not self-interpreting; they are interpreted by persons, and interpretation is made possible through the indwelling of articulate systems. In other words, to interpret facts and experiences requires an uncritical acceptance, at least for the time being, of a framework. In some circumstances, a personal evaluation may be made as to whether a framework is one to be trusted and indwelt; in others we may be largely unaware of our indwelling except in terms of the way in which we are able to make sense of things by means of it.

To participate in an articulate system, as an indwelling, is not to attain a fixed position but to actively engage in a heuristic vision. Not all scientific work reflects such participation: science has its quotient of routine work.⁷⁸ But the scientist's desire to press beyond the present frontiers of knowledge will be fulfilled through a vision that is facilitated by indwelling. By way of illustration, Polanyi explains: "Astronomic observations are made by dwelling in astronomic theory, and it is this internal enjoyment of astronomy that makes the astronomer interested in the stars. This is how scientific value is contemplated from within."⁷⁹ However, this joy is qualified when astronomic formulae are used in a routine way: "It is only

---

70. Ibid.
71. Ibid.
72. Ibid., 195.
73. Ibid., 286.
74. Ibid., 195.
75. Ibid.
76. Ibid., 283.
77. Ibid., 280.

78. It must be acknowledged that even routine scientific work requires frameworks, although such frameworks are relatively explicit and regulated in comparison with those which provide the potential for "heuristic vision."

79. Polanyi, *Personal Knowledge*, 195.

when he reflects on its theoretic vision, or consciously experiences its intellectual powers, that the astronomer may be said to contemplate astronomy."[80]

Competence in an articulate system is gained through the acquisition of the skills already attained by those who are active participants—indwellers of the system—whether this is theoretical knowledge, proficiency with the tools of experimentation, or some other pertinent expertise. But such knowledge and skills are acquired not as an end in themselves but in order that they can be used to contemplate further the realities from which the articulate framework is distilled. This process is certainly not limited to the sciences: "The task of inducing an intelligent contemplation of music and dramatic art aims likewise at enabling a person to surrender himself to works of art. This is neither to observe nor to handle them, *but to live in them*. Thus the satisfaction of gaining intellectual control over the external world is linked to a satisfaction of gaining control over ourselves."[81]

The impulse of science is to move beyond what is already known. An articulate framework, when indwelt in a creative and imaginative way, facilitates the contemplative experience of an entity or a phenomenon. It is within such contemplation that the potential for new discovery resides, and new discoveries must lead to a revision of the articulate framework. An important and highly significant discovery may lead to the formulation of a radically different articulate framework. "Scientific discovery, which leads from one such framework to its successor, bursts the bounds of disciplined thought in an intense if transient moment of heuristic vision. And while it is thus breaking out, the mind is for the moment directly experiencing its content rather than controlling it by the use of any pre-established modes of interpretation: it is overwhelmed by its own passionate activity."[82]

For Polanyi the desire of the scientist to ponder new problems is just a particular case of a more general urge present in human and, in some degree, higher animal life.[83] Humans are interested in puzzles and problems that challenge the body and the mind. It is, Polanyi's suggests, a "craving for mental dissatisfaction." He comments:

> The most radical manifestation of this urge to break through all fixed conceptual frameworks is the act of ecstatic vision. When we abandon ourselves to the contemplation of the stars we attend to them in a way which is not an astronomical observation. We look at them with great interest but without thinking about them. For if we did, our awareness of the stars would pale into that of mere instances of apposite conceptions; the focus of our interest being shifted beyond them, our awareness of them

---

80. Ibid.

81. Ibid., Polanyi, 196; my emphasis.

82. Ibid. This is essentially Polanyi's treatment of the phenomenon that Thomas Kuhn later takes up in his influential book on the history of science. See Kuhn, *The Structure of Scientific Revolutions*.

83. For example, a rat will attempt to devise a strategy to escape from a maze.

would become subsidiary to this focus and their vivid impact on the eye and the mind would be lost.[84]

For Polanyi contemplation is a unique form of experience. It "dissolves the screen, stops our movement through experience and pours us straight into experience; we cease to handle things and become immersed in them."[85] Contemplative experience represents the total participation of the person in that which is being contemplated.

As we have observed, articulate systems comprise a vastly diverse phenomena. What Polanyi calls "the facts of experience" bear in differing ways upon a system. In the natural sciences, for example, the bearing is much more specific than would be the case in religion or the arts. In the light of this, Polanyi speaks of the "verification" of science by experience while describing the process by which other articulate systems are tested and accepted as one of "validation." "Our personal participation is in general greater in a validation than in a verification. The emotional coefficient of assertion is intensified as we pass from the sciences to the neighbouring domains of thought. But both *verification* and *validation* are everywhere an acknowledgement of a commitment: they claim the presence of something real and external to the speaker."[86]

This discussion of the indwelling within articulate systems brings Polanyi to one of his key and radical propositions that the practice of science is dependent upon beliefs to which the members of the scientific community are, and must be, committed. Because this commitment is necessary to the working scientist, the work of science cannot be represented in non-committal terms. The logical rules and maxims of science point beyond themselves to a formulation of science that Polanyi calls "fiduciary."

Faith and Doubt

Faith

Polanyi's desire to explore the fiduciary nature of science was a radical departure from the consensus of opinion. As he noted in the introduction to an essay published in 1947, "People who believe in science do not usually regard this as a personal act of faith. They consider themselves as submitting to evidence which by its nature compels their assent and which has the power to compel a measure of assent from any rational human being."[87] This view of science emerged within an intellectual ethos significantly shaped by its rejection of authority, and a rejection

---

84. Polanyi, *Personal Knowledge*, 196–97.
85. Ibid., 197.
86. Ibid., 202; Polanyi's emphasis.
87. Polanyi, "Science: Observation and Belief," 10.

of the authority of the church in particular, as it had been exercised in medieval Europe. But Polanyi suggests that this freedom from authority left a vacuum. This was filled "as man tried to avoid the emptiness of mere self-assertion by establishing over himself the authority of experience and reason."[88] But it was precisely this that set us on the path to our present malaise. "[M]odern scientism fetters thought as cruelly as ever the churches had done. It offers no scope for our most vital beliefs and it forces us to disguise them in farcically inadequate terms."[89]

Polanyi's reasons for conceiving the situation in this way have already been noted in some detail, but I must now consider his response. In view of his criticisms of a scientism (which denied the role of authority) what, according to Polanyi, is the way out of the malaise? Here what Patrick Grant has called "the Augustinian component" of Polanyi's work comes to the fore.[90] The way forward, according to Polanyi, requires a glance backwards: "[W]e must now go back to St Augustine to restore the balance of our cognitive powers. In the fourth century AD, St Augustine brought the history of Greek philosophy to a close by inaugurating for the first time a post-critical philosophy. He taught that all knowledge was a gift of grace, for which we must strive under the guidance of antecedent belief: *nisi credideritis, non intelligitis.*"[91] This was the doctrine that directed the minds of Christian thinkers for a period of a thousand years until the decline of faith and the rise of the modern scientific worldview. In the growth of this worldview a radical revision of the meaning of "belief" was realized. "Belief" was no longer associated with a higher power conveying to us that which is beyond the range of observation and reason but, minimally, a personal acceptance that falls short of empirical and rational justification. The scheme of Augustine is thereby inverted and belief reduced to "an imperfection by which knowledge fell short of universality."[92]

But Polanyi believes we must go back to Augustine and openly assert, once more, that belief is the source of all knowledge. He writes: "Tacit assent and intellectual passions, the sharing of an idiom and of a cultural heritage, affiliation to a like-minded community: such are the impulses which shape our vision of the nature of things on which we rely for our mastery of things. No intelligence, however critical or original, can operate outside such a fiduciary framework."[93]

---

88. Polanyi, *Personal Knowledge*, 265.

89. Ibid., 265. Polanyi saw this "scientistic" view of the world as responsible for the destructive tyrannies of twentieth-century Europe. It was a philosophy that denied the place of the person in human knowledge. Polanyi claims that "homeless passions" were commandeered by totalitarian ideologies that sought to justify themselves as "scientific" and "necessary." His argumentation for this assertion is well developed. See, for example, *Personal Knowledge*, 224–45; and *The Tacit Dimension*, 56–63.

90. See Grant, "Michael Polanyi: The Augustinian Component," 438–63.

91. Polanyi, *Personal Knowledge*, 266.

92. Ibid.

93. Ibid.

Only in going back to this way can we escape from the problems inherent within the Enlightenment project. Polanyi explains:

> This ... is our liberation from objectivism: to realize that we can voice our ultimate convictions only from within our convictions—from within the whole system of acceptances that are logically prior to any particular assertion of our own, prior to the holding of any particular piece of knowledge. If an ultimate logical level is to be attained and made explicit, this must be a declaration of my personal beliefs. I believe that the function of philosophic reflection consists in bringing to light, and affirming as my own, the beliefs implied in such of my thoughts and practices as I believe to be valid; that I must aim at discovering what I truly believe in and at formulating the convictions which I find myself holding; that I must conquer my self-doubt, so as to retain a firm hold on this programme of self-identification.[94]

Not surprisingly, Polanyi regards Augustine—especially as he expresses himself in the *Confessions*—as a fine example of one who has offered a consistent and systematic expression based upon beliefs. Although Augustine gives an extensive autobiographical account of his pre-conversion experience, this is done from the perspective of the beliefs that he established through his conversion to Christianity. Polanyi makes the point: "He seems to acknowledge that you cannot expose an error by interpreting it from the premisses which lead to it, but only from premisses which are believed to be true."[95]

Polanyi, who spent the first half of his working life in pursuit of scientific discoveries, conceives of the holding of beliefs as a necessary precondition for such an endeavor. The exploration of the new and the unknown is the ongoing exposition of our beliefs: "Our fundamental beliefs are continuously reconsidered in the course of such a process, but only within the scope of their own basic premisses."[96] Polanyi describes his position, somewhat provocatively, as "an invitation to dogmatism."[97] This may be misleading if it is taken to be a denial of the heuristic function of beliefs, but this is not his intention. Polanyi uses the biblical imagery of the Garden of Eden to describe the present predicament of Enlightenment theories of knowledge:

> Humanity has been deprived a second time of its innocence, and driven out of another garden which was, at any rate, a Fool's Paradise. Innocently, we had trusted that we could be relieved of all personal responsibility for our beliefs by objective criteria of validity—and our own critical powers

---

94. Ibid., 267.
95. Ibid.
96. Ibid.
97. See ibid., 268. It is noteworthy that Thomas Kuhn spoke of "dogma" in science up until just before the publication of *The Structure of Scientific Revolutions*. See his essay, "The Function of Dogma in Scientific Research," in Crombie, *Scientific Change*, 347–69.

have shattered this hope. Struck by our sudden nakedness, we may try to brazen it out by flaunting it in a profession of nihilism. But modern man's immorality is unstable. Presently his moral passions reassert themselves in objectivistic disguise and the scientistic Minotaur is born.[98]

At the close of the chapter "The Logic of Affirmation," the key section on faith in *Personal Knowledge*, Polanyi gives a summary of his proposal that "[T]o restore to us once more the power for the deliberate holding of unproven beliefs. We should be able to profess now knowingly and openly those beliefs which could be tacitly taken for granted in the days before modern philosophic criticism reached its present incisiveness. Such powers may appear dangerous. But a dogmatic orthodoxy can be kept in check both internally and externally, while a creed inverted into a science is both blind and deceptive."[99]

Both his central assertion—about the holding of unproven beliefs—and his secondary comments about the possibility of keeping in check a dogmatic orthodoxy will be of importance to us as we consider the significance of Polanyi for theological work.

Doubt

Polanyi suggests that philosophical doubt is the "logical corollary" of objectivism.[100] Objectivism "trusts that the uprooting of all voluntary components of belief will leave behind unassailed a residue of knowledge that is completely determined by the objective evidence. Critical thought trusted this method unconditionally for avoiding error and establishing truth."[101] But it is necessary to expand upon this point by noting the crucial role of philosophical doubt. "Doubt has been acclaimed [in Enlightenment thought] not only as the touchstone of truth, but also as the safeguard of tolerance. The belief that philosophic doubt would appease religious fanaticism and bring about universal tolerance goes back to Locke, and this belief is still vigorously alive in our own day."[102]

Polanyi claims that, notwithstanding the reverence in which it has been held since Descartes, the method of critical doubt has not—indeed *cannot*—be rigorously followed in practice. Polanyi cites Hume as an example of a philosopher who was frank in this respect. He was prepared to set aside the conclusions of his own skepticism when he felt unable to follow them in an honest way. But

---

98. Polanyi, *Personal Knowledge*, 268. This is an allusion to Polanyi's theory of "moral inversion," which he believed to be the dynamic that, in the twentieth century, generated both communistic and Fascist ideologies.

99. Ibid. In the reference to "dogmatic orthodoxy" it may be possible to discern something of a polemical flourish. Any such "orthodoxy" would have to be a "post-critical" orthodoxy!

100. See ibid., 269.

101. Ibid.

102. Ibid., 271.

Polanyi also criticizes him because "he failed to acknowledge that by so doing he was expressing his own personal beliefs; nor did he claim his right and accept his duty to declare such beliefs, when this amounted to the silencing of doubt and the abandonment of strict objectivity. His dissent from scepticism was strictly unofficial, forming no explicit part of his philosophy."[103]

Polanyi's analysis proceeds by attempting to show the equivalence of doubt and belief. Polanyi comments: "The first point in my critique of doubt will be to show that the doubting of any explicit statement merely implies an attempt to deny the belief expressed by the statement, in favour of other beliefs which are not doubted for the time being."[104] Polanyi asserts that the difference between a positive statement and its denial is merely a matter of how the statements are worded and the acceptance or rejection of either must be evaluated according to the same criteria. The fiduciary component is present, equally, in both the acceptance and the denial. By way of illustration, Polanyi comments, "During the seventeenth and eighteenth centuries scientific beliefs have . . . opposed and discredited a whole system of supernatural beliefs and the authorities which taught these beliefs. We may regard this sceptical movement as altogether reasonable and be unaware of its fiduciary character until we are confronted with its blunders."[105] Science has its own history of error, and Polanyi recounts numerous stories in which evidence was ignored or overlooked because it pointed to something that was incompatible with the scientific worldview of the time.[106] It may be that a subsequent revision of a worldview may admit to a more favorable re-evaluation of the evidence, but it is only from a perspective gained from within a worldview that one may sustain a doubt about the reasonableness of a theory or a proposition. The perspective, and the worldview that supports it, are warranted only by the beliefs of scientists.

If a scientist does not engage with the claim of another scientist, it will likely be because he or she regards it as invalid. If he or she does engage with it, the level and degree of that engagement will reflect his or her evaluation of its significance. The scientist can sustain an agnostic position only if he or she is not concerned with the field of investigation, and generally one can only sustain an agnosticism if one lacks an interest in the subject. Polanyi concludes:

> There exists . . . no valid heuristic maxim in natural science which would recommend either belief or doubt as a path to discovery. Some discoveries are prompted by the conviction that something is fundamentally lacking in the existing framework of science, others by the opposite feeling that there is far more implied in it than has yet been realized. The first conviction

---

103. Ibid., 270.
104. Ibid., 272.
105. Ibid., 274.
106. See, for example, Polanyi's accounts of F. A. Mesmer's work in ibid., 51–52, 107–8, and Polanyi and Prosch, *Meaning*, 146.

may be regarded as more sceptical than the second, but it is precisely the first which is more likely to be hampered by doubt—owing to the excessive adherence to the existing orthodoxy of science.[107]

Commitment, Calling, and Universal Intent

Rooted within its Enlightenment heritage the traditional role of epistemology has been to define both truth and falsity in impersonal terms. The exclusion of personal commitments is required to justify claims to universal validity. Polanyi points out the profound disparity between this view and his vision of fiduciary knowing. He writes, "The framework of commitment leaves no scope for such an endeavour; for its acceptance necessarily invalidates any impersonal justification of knowledge."[108] Polanyi suggests the following dilemma for those who propose a standard of impersonal knowing: "The reflecting person is . . . caught in an insoluble conflict between a demand for an impersonality which would discredit all commitment and an urge to make up his mind which drives him to recommit himself."[109] Bertrand Russell attempted to resolve this dilemma by defining truth as the coincidence of subjective belief and the actual facts, but it is impossible, within the terms allowable in Russell's schema, to know if or when this has occurred. Polanyi, with his fiduciary program, shows that the dilemma can be resolved.

> The answer is this. The 'actual facts' are accredited facts, as seen within the commitment situation, while subjective beliefs are the convictions accrediting these facts as seen non-committally, by someone not sharing them. But if we regard the beliefs in question non-committally, as a mere state of mind, we cannot speak confidently, without self-contradiction, of the facts to which these beliefs refer. *For it is self-contradictory to secede from the commitment situation as regards the beliefs held within it, but to remain committed to the same beliefs in acknowledging their factual content as true.*[110]

A scientist will pursue a discovery that remains elusive, sustained by the conviction that the solution to the problem is hidden only because the approach adopted is somehow misguided. There may also be a tension between the conviction that something is known and the thought that the conviction might possibly be mistaken. In both cases there can be no Archimedean point from which the approach to the truth can be compared with the *actual* truth. It is only possible to compare different approaches—the articulate systems that we indwell. Polanyi

---

107. Polanyi, *Personal Knowledge*, 277.
108. Ibid., 303.
109. Ibid., 304.
110. Ibid.; Polanyi's emphasis.

states, "According to the logic of commitment, *truth is something that can be thought of only by believing it.*"[111]

For Polanyi this affirmation is not solipsistic, but it does recognize the profound relationship that exists between the commitments that we hold and the social and cultural contexts in which we are nurtured. Polanyi rejects the Cartesian *cogito* by asserting the communal co-efficient in human knowing. He writes:

> Articulate systems which foster and satisfy an intellectual passion can survive only with the support of a society which respects the values affirmed by these passions, and a society has a cultural life only to the extent to which it acknowledges and fulfils the obligation to lend its support to the cultivation of these passions. Since the advancement and dissemination of knowledge by the pursuit of science, or technology and mathematics forms part of cultural life, the tacit coefficients by which these articulate systems are understood and accredited, and which uphold quite generally our shaping and affirmation of factual truth, are also coefficients of a cultural life shared by a community.[112]

Recognition of the communal coefficient of our intellectual passions alerts us, again, to the fact that when we assert the truth, and do so with universal intent, our convictions arise out of a particular context. In this we appear to be confronted by a dilemma that if we hold convictions on the basis of a received authority, they do not appear to be *our* convictions. On the other hand, if we actively affirm them, it appears that our affirmation is *arbitrary*: why alight upon *these* convictions rather than others? Further, as Polanyi notes: "The exercise of authority will tend to appear as bigoted or as hypocritical, if it asserts as universal what is only parochial."[113] Does this imply that every affirmation is made in bad faith? It will do so only if it is made on the basis of an ill-founded received authority or if, as the objectivist has done, we propose a standard of impersonal knowledge. Polanyi, by illuminating the fiduciary and tacit elements of knowing, has sought to show that such a standard is illusory and meaningless. Polanyi accepts that any particular cultural context will be limited but does not conclude that such a limitation implies either invalidity or relativism. He writes "I accept these accidents of personal existence as the concrete opportunities for exercising our personal responsibilities. *This acceptance is the sense of my calling.*"[114]

Once the epistemic significance of personal participation is established, the question of the formation of calling (culturally, intellectually, emotionally, etc.) will appear not only a valid concern but a necessary and urgent one. What is the

---

111. Ibid., 305; Polanyi's emphasis.
112. Ibid., 203.
113. Ibid., 204.
114. Ibid., 322; Polanyi's emphasis.

mechanism by which human beings come to participate in a calling, and how is a cultural heritage communicated? Polanyi suggests:

> The affiliation begins with the fact that a child submits to education within a community, and it is confirmed throughout life to the extent to which the adult continues to place exceptional confidence in the intellectual leaders of the same community. Just as children learn to speak by assuming that the words used in their presence mean something, so throughout the whole range of cultural apprenticeship the intellectual junior's craving to understand the doings and the sayings of his intellectual superiors assumes that what they are doing and saying has a hidden meaning which, when discovered, will be found satisfying to some extent.[115]

The student must believe that the teacher possesses something that is meaningful, communicable, and true. The possibility of the transfer is contingent upon this belief. "The learner, like the discoverer, must believe before he can know."[116] The submission of the student to the teacher is "like an act of heuristic conjecture."[117] However, the dynamic of submission is not one of absolute submission. "Every acceptance of authority is qualified by some measure of reaction to it or even against it. Submission to a consensus is always accompanied to some extent by the imposition of one's views on the consensus to which we submit."[118] Conversely, even the most radical dissent from a recognized authority or norm must be asserted in terms that will be meaningful to those who affirm it. Revolutionaries or radical reformers must provide a bridge from that which they condemn to that which they affirm, because "dissent does not seek to abolish public authority, but to claim it for itself."[119]

Human nurture and formation occur in particular contexts, and it is only through such nurture and formation that we are able to participate and function effectively as human beings. These contexts provide ways[120] by which we endeavor to make sense of our lives and the world in which we live. They are, to recall an image used earlier in this chapter, our "spectacles": they provide us with a way of seeing. But our knowledge of them is primarily subsidiary, not focal.[121] We may render our knowledge of some aspects of them focal in certain circumstances (and may thereby consider some revision of them necessary) but this is exceptional rather than typical. The "spectacles" used in various contexts and communities differ and, consequently, the meanings established through the

---

115. Ibid., 207–8.
116. Ibid., 208.
117. Ibid.
118. Ibid.
119. Ibid., 209.
120. These "ways" are Polanyi's articulate systems.
121. Ordinarily we look *through* rather *at* the lenses of our spectacles.

use of them will be marked by a concomitant diversity. The distinctions between differing cultural spectacles are not easily understood, precisely because we are accustomed to evaluating their meaning by what we are able to see *through* them, and not by looking *at* them.

Polanyi's position here is no thoroughgoing relativism but an acknowledgement of the cultural particularity of a person's calling. Within that calling a person must bear his or her responsibility in the search for truth.[122] Polanyi illustrates this point by reference to the role of the judge in the law courts.

> By seeking the right decision the judge must *find* the law, supposed to be existing—though as yet unknown. This is why eventually his decision becomes binding as law. The judge's discretion is thus narrowed down to zero by the stranglehold of his universal intent—by the power of his responsibility over himself. This is his independence. It consists in keeping himself wholly responsible to the interests of justice, excluding any subjectivity, whether of fear or favour. Judicial independence has been secured, where it exists, by centuries of passionate resistance to intimidation and corruption; for justice is an intellectual passion seeking satisfaction of itself, by inspiring and ruling men's lives.[123]

There are parallels between the work of the judge in making a decision and the course of scientific discovery:[124]

> In both cases the innovator has a wide discretion of choice, because he has no fixed rules to rely on, and the range of his discretion determines the measure of his personal responsibility. In both cases a passionate search for a solution that is regarded as potentially pre-existing, narrows down discretion to zero and issues at the same time an innovation claiming universal acceptance. In both cases the original mind takes a decision on grounds which are insufficient to minds lacking similar powers of creative judgment. The active scientific investigator stakes bit by bit his whole professional life on a series of such decisions and this day-to-day gamble represents his most responsible activity. The same is true of the judge, with the difference, of course, that the risk is born here mainly by the parties to the case and by the society which has entrusted itself to the interpretation of its laws by the courts.[125]

The scientist engaged in the pursuit of a discovery gropes towards that which is hidden, but that he or she believes *may* be accessible. The choices made in this

---

122. This is the responsibility of which objectivism sought to relieve us in its claims to impersonal objective knowledge.

123. Polanyi, *Personal Knowledge*, 308–9; Polanyi's emphasis.

124. Polanyi is concerned here with scientific discoveries and momentous legal decisions. Such phenomena should be distinguished from routine scientific work and general legal administration.

125. Polanyi, *Personal Knowledge*, 309–10.

process are the scientist's own, but the scientist is constrained by the problem by which he or she is confronted.

> In so far as they are acting responsibly, their personal participation in drawing their own conclusions is completely compensated for by the fact that they are submitting to the universal status of the hidden reality which they are trying to approach. Accidents may sometimes bring about—or prevent—discovery, but research does not rely on accident: the continuously renewed risks of failure normally incurred at every heuristic step are taken without ever acting at random. Responsible action excludes randomness, even as it suppresses egocentric arbitrariness.[126]

Any significant scientific inquiry is bound up with uncertainty and the implications of new knowledge cannot be known from the beginning. What is referred to is believed to be real and, to use an idea to which Polanyi frequently returns, "to attribute reality to something is to express the belief that its presence will yet show up in an indefinite number of unpredictable ways."[127]

Polanyi's realism is to the fore in this part of his analysis. He writes, "An empirical statement is true to the extent to which it reveals an aspect of reality, a reality largely hidden to us, and *existing therefore independently of our knowing it*. By trying to say something that is true about a reality believed to be existing independently of our knowing it, all assertions of fact necessarily carry *universal intent. Our claim to speak of reality serves thus as the external anchoring of our commitment in making a factual statement.*"[128]

The scientist's intimations about the hidden reality are his or her own; they are personal and the product of the scientist's originality. But, as Polanyi wishes to emphasize, "they are not a subjective state of mind, but convictions held with universal intent, and heavy with arduous projects."[129] For the scientific discoverer, as with the judge, personal judgments—that are intrinsic to the heuristic striving—are balanced by the rigorous responsibility that must be exercised with regard to the reality that both scientist and judge endeavor to comprehend. But the personal component cannot be circumvented and every effort to present scientific discovery, or legal judgment, in impersonal terms can only serve to distort an understanding of the process. Polanyi explains:

> Desisting henceforth from the vain pursuit of a formalized scientific method, commitment accepts in its place the person of the scientist as the agent responsible for conducting and accrediting scientific discoveries. The scientist's procedure is of course methodical. But his methods are but the maxims of an art which he applies in his own original way to the prob-

---

126. Ibid., 310.
127. Ibid., 311. This is one of Polanyi's definitions of "reality."
128. Ibid.; Polanyi's emphasis.
129. Ibid.

lem of his own choice. Discovery forms part of the art of knowing; it can be studied by precept and example, but its higher performances require particular native gifts appropriate to particular subjects.[130]

Commitment provides a framework in which assent is delivered from randomness or egocentricity. A framework of commitment is the context from which affirmations can be made. Inherent within this framework is the existence of subsidiary affirmations that are relied upon, and if objections to these subsidiary affirmations were made, they could not *necessarily* be refuted. Thus such a framework "allows us to commit ourselves on evidence which, but for the weight of our own personal judgment, would admit of other conclusions. We may firmly believe what we might conceivably doubt; and may hold to be true what might conceivably be false."[131] Polanyi believes this to be a decisive issue in epistemology. Every act of knowing entails a tacit contribution on the part of the knower and, crucially for Polanyi, "this coefficient is no mere imperfection, but a necessary component of all knowledge."[132]

In visual perception it is possible to be confronted with a phenomenon which admits to two or more contradictory interpretations. One might think of the drawing used by Wittgenstein that can be seen as the head of either a duck or a rabbit, depending on how one looks at it.[133] One is able to switch from one perception to the other, but it is not possible to sustain both perceptions at the same time. Polanyi explains: "The only way to avoid being committed . . . is to close one's eyes. This corresponds to the conclusion reached before in my critique of doubt: to avoid believing one must stop thinking."[134] This demonstrates that even in a "primitive tacit act" such as perception, there is an active search for the truth in which a conclusion may be drawn in the face of alternative possibilities.[135] And Polanyi asserts: "There is . . . complete continuity between a perceptive judgment and the process by which we establish responsible convictions in the course of scientific research."[136]

---

130. Ibid., 311–12. The function of the scientific community—though not emphasized at this point—must not be lost to view. The scientist is no Cartesian soloist!

131. Ibid., 312.

132. Ibid.

133. Wittgenstein, *Philosophical Investigations (Second Edition)*, 194.

134. Polanyi, *Personal Knowledge*, 314.

135. In many acts of perception the kind of ambiguity which we find in the case of the duck-rabbit is absent. Nevertheless, perception is what Polanyi calls an "integrative" act and although it may be both unproblematic and almost instantaneous it does not exist apart from the *action* of the knower. I will return to Polanyi's treatment of this theme in later section on tacit knowledge in the present chapter and also in the final chapter—in the context of a discussion about imagination.

136. Polanyi, *Personal Knowledge*, 314. Note Polanyi's tendency to move freely back and forth between discussion of perception and discovery. This is no oversight or inconsistency but part of the strategy of his epistemological formulations. Polanyi writes, "I have tried to pursue systematically the kinship between perception and scientific discovery." Polanyi and Prosch, *Meaning*, 56.

Of course, the perception that we form in the face of ambiguous phenomena may be mistaken. We can only do the best we can as we seek to make sense of what we are looking at; but to withhold making a decision resolves nothing: "To postpone mental decisions on account of their conceivable fallibility would necessarily block all decisions for ever, and pile up the hazards of hesitation to infinity. It would amount to voluntary mental stupor. Stupor alone can eliminate both belief and error."[137] In many circumstances the integration that forms a perception is so fast that to speak of a postponement of a decision is inappropriate. We may, on the basis of a subliminal doubt about the veracity of a perception, take another look—as we might if we think we recognize someone while entertaining the doubt that we might be mistaken. But in so many cases our perception is correct—we recognize the pen, the paper, the book, the computer, the desk and chair etc., and we are able to get on with our business without difficulty.

Commitment is necessary, and yet any commitment held can neither defend itself against all objections nor make claims to incorrigibility on any other grounds: "To accept commitment as the framework within which we may believe something to be true, is to circumscribe the hazards of belief. It is to establish the conception of competence that authorizes a fiduciary choice made and timed, to the best of the acting person's ability, as a deliberate and yet necessary choice. The paradox of the self-set standards is eliminated, for in a competent mental act the agent does not do as he pleases, but compels himself forcibly to act as he believes he must."[138]

Despite the hazard of error, risks must be taken. "[T]o withhold belief on the grounds of such a hazard is to break off all contact with reality."[139] Again we may reject the charge that Polanyi's position is solipsistic. He affirms the existence of an external reality that may be approached and investigated by others. Polanyi resists strongly the suggestion that his position is relativistic on the basis that the external pole of human knowing is an external reality that makes a decisive claim upon all who approach it.

Polanyi insists that we must distinguish between different types of error. On the one hand, there may be a competent line of inquiry that happens to be erroneous; on the other, there are mental processes that are "illusory and incompetent." The latter may represent conclusions drawn on the basis of an inadequate depth of participation within a discipline. Implicit in this distinction is the recognition that knowing is a skillful achievement. One might think, for example, of knowledge

---

137. Polanyi, *Personal Knowledge*, 314–15.

138. Ibid., 315. Polanyi can sometimes speak in insufficiently differentiated terms about cognitive acts. In *Personal Knowledge*, in particular, he has a tendency to speak of conscious mental acts—the outcome of a period of deliberation—without noting the many circumstances in which the act is not deliberate. Indeed, most of our visual perceptions are more or less instantaneous, and although they may comprise tacit integrations that are intrinsically personal, they can scarcely be called "decisions" or, indeed, "passionate."

139. Ibid.

gained through complex scientific experimentation. This is the achievement of highly developed skills. An untrained person would not only be in danger of damaging experimental equipment but could not expect to draw competent conclusions from experimental data. Polanyi calls conclusions drawn on the basis of an inadequate participation in a framework or discipline "subjective."[140] Of course, an experienced scientist may make an experimental error or may draw an incorrect inference on the basis of correct experimental data, but such errors are, in Polanyi's view, to be distinguished from the errors of "subjectivity."

We have already seen that the grounds on which we hold to a framework of commitment can be neither fully articulated nor defended from all doubt. Polanyi comments: "We must commit each moment of our lives irrevocably on grounds that, if time could be suspended, would invariably prove inadequate; but our total responsibility for disposing of ourselves makes these objectively inadequate grounds compelling."[141]

A calling is not a rigid delimitation,[142] but its pervasive influence must be acknowledged. It is meaningless to ask what someone would think or say had they been brought up in a different society or in a different age, had their "calling" been otherwise. Just as we must live and die in the bodies that have been given to us—with all their possibilities and limitations—so it is with the social and cultural context into which we are born. Polanyi believes that our calling is to be embraced positively because: "Within its commitments the mind is warranted to exercise much ampler powers than those by which it is supposed to operate under objectivism; but by the very fact of assuming this new freedom it submits to a higher power to which it had hitherto refused recognition."[143]

Polanyi's rejection of an objectivism that divested people of the responsibility of holding beliefs explicitly reintroduces a recognition of the epistemic function of beliefs in knowing. Consequently we must say that what commitment offers, to those who will embrace it, is the legitimate grounds for affirming personal belief held with universal intent. On these grounds one can assert that one's participation is personal without being subjective (to adduce Polanyi's pejorative use of the term). "While it . . . lies beyond our responsibility, it is yet transformed by our sense of responsibility into part of our calling."[144] Our calling is prescribed by our historical particularity and from it we draw the resources to aspire to affirmations that we will make with universal intent. Polanyi believes we must make a radical and decisive move. We must leave the distortions of objectivism behind and take hold of the responsibilities that are rightly ours.

140. Note Polanyi's distinctive use of the term.
141. Polanyi, *Personal Knowledge*, 320.
142. Bear in mind that it is possible for us to transcend the frameworks which we inhabit.
143. Polanyi, *Personal Knowledge*, 323.
144. Ibid., 324.

Tacit Knowledge

Stefania Jha suggests Polanyi has often been misread. "In his epistemology he was mistaken to be a scientist mystifying scientific discovery rather than one attempting to explain its nonexplicit aspects."[145] In turning to consider Polanyi's theory of tacit knowledge, it will become apparent that such a negative evaluation is scarcely sustainable.

Polanyi's understanding of the tacit dimension of knowledge is clearly evident in *Personal Knowledge*, published in 1958. At that point he was already able to say that "Subsidiary or instrumental knowledge, as I have defined it, is not known in itself but is known in terms of something focally known, to the quality of which it contributes; and to this extent it is unspecifiable."[146] In *The Study of Man*, published in 1959, Polanyi goes as far as to say that "tacit knowing is . . . the dominant principle of all knowledge."[147] The tacit dimension is in evidence in many ways (and not least in his analysis of language) in his earlier publications, but this crucial element of his thought is worked out with greater precision in his article "The Logic of Tacit Inference"[148] and his book *The Tacit Dimension*, both of which were first published in 1966. The ideas in these publications are reinforced and, to some degree expanded, in *Meaning*, published in 1975. I will concern myself primarily with these works as we consider the theme of tacit knowledge.

Polanyi's starting point in *The Tacit Dimension* is a position that has already been established in his treatment of language in *Personal Knowledge*. In this later work the insight becomes pivotal, and Polanyi announces, "I shall [now] reconsider human knowledge by starting from the fact that *we know more than we can tell.*"[149]

That we know more than we can tell may be illustrated in various ways. We can be confident of recognizing the face of someone known to us among a million and yet our capacity to describe the person is severely limited. We can recognize a person's mood from their face without being able to say—except in a very vague way—how. This phenomenon, far from being unusual, is a feature of a vast number of human actions in which we achieve things without being able to articulate how we do it.

Polanyi acknowledges his debt to Gestalt psychology, which has shown how a whole is recognized by seeing its constituent parts *in a particular way*. In perceiving the whole, the parts are not seen as they would if they were attended to individually because, as the parts of a whole, they assume a particular *function*.

---

145. Jha, *Reconsidering Michael Polanyi's Philosophy*, 4.

146. Polanyi, *Personal Knowledge*, 88.

147. Polanyi, *Study of Man*, 13.

148. Polanyi, "The Logic of Tacit Inference." This article was also published in Grene, *Knowing and Being*, 138–58.

149. Polanyi, *Tacit Dimension*, 4; Polanyi's emphasis.

The parts cannot fulfill this function if they are being attended to directly; they can do this only as they are seen as part of a pattern. Gestalt shows that there are two distinct ways of "seeing." This insight is a clue to Polanyi's theory of tacit knowledge, but he takes issue with Gestalt insofar as it assumes that the process of integration, by which the parts are seen *as* a whole, is the result of a *spontaneous* equilibration as the particulars make their impression on the retina. Polanyi contends that this is not a *passive* but an *active* process.[150] He writes, "I am looking at Gestalt . . . as the outcome of an active shaping of experience performed in the pursuit of knowledge. This shaping or integrating I hold to be the great and indispensable tacit power by which all knowledge is discovered and, once discovered, is held to be true."[151]

In introducing his account of the structure of tacit knowing, Polanyi explains that it always involves two types of knowledge that he calls "the two terms of tacit knowing." We rely on our knowledge of the first term in order to attend to the second. This may be related to the second example by saying that the particular features of the face—the many physical phenomena manifested in it—comprise the first term of tacit knowledge, and it is in our reliance upon these clues that we are able to establish the second term, which is the mood of the face indicated by them. "[I]n an act of tacit knowing we *attend from* something for attending *to* something else."[152] Polanyi suggests, additionally, the adoption of anatomical language in which the first term becomes the "proximal" and the second the "distal." "It is the proximal term . . . of which we have a knowledge that we may not be able to tell."[153]

Polanyi's reason for wishing to emphasize the intentional nature of an integration is that the achievement is always *personal*. Subsidiary elements are not integrated into a focal whole apart from the participation of the knower. "[T]his pair is not linked together of its own accord. The relation of a subsidiary to a focus is formed *by the act of a person* who integrates one to the other. The from-to relation lasts only as long as a person, the knower, sustains this integration."[154] Polanyi writes: "knowing is action."[155] Purposive action cannot be conceived in impersonal terms.

In "The Logic of Tacit Inference," Polanyi identifies two distinguishable instances of the integrative process. In the first he identifies the case in which an object is perceived as a coherent entity. A ball moving in the direction of the viewer will appear to become larger (and may change in appearance in other ways,

---

150. Typically one in which it is possible to develop skills.
151. Polanyi, *Tacit Dimension*, 6.
152. Ibid., 10; Polanyi's emphasis.
153. Ibid.
154. Polanyi and Prosch, *Meaning*, 38. Polanyi and Prosch's emphasis.
155. Ibid., 42.

too), but the viewer will likely be able to determine, because of many subsidiary clues, that there is one object, and that it is not increasing in size but moving closer to the observing eyes. In this case the subsidiary clues are largely distinct from the focal object. But the situation is different when the distal term is located in the same place as the proximal clues, as in the case of a physiognomy. This is the second instance. The features of the face upon which we rely for recognition are, as it were, in the same spot as the focal term. We are aware of them only insofar as they bear upon that on which we are focused: the face. Although it is by the features that we recognize the face, we cannot, except in a vague way, say how we do this. Something akin to the dynamic of this latter situation occurs when the discovery of a new theory integrates various observations into a new theoretical appearance. Despite the distinctions that must be made between these two forms of integration, it must be noted that "tacit knowing does exercise in both cases its characteristic powers of integration, merging the subsidiary into the focal, the proximal into the distal."[156]

Polanyi analyses the relationship between the two terms of tacit knowing in some depth by identifying the different structures implied in it.[157] First is the "functional structure." This is the way in which the proximal or subsidiary term of tacit knowing is subordinated to the distal or focal term. Polanyi explains that "Since this functional relation is set up between two kinds of awareness, its directedness is necessarily conscious."[158] I am uncertain whether Polanyi's emphasis on consciousness is well placed here. The great majority of integrations by which we perceive things are performed, as I have noted already, almost instantaneously. I concur with Polanyi that one of the reasons we are able to make them is that we possess perceptual skills that have developed over time, but far more often than not, our perception is a performance in which the conscious effort required to make the integration is negligible. The critical point is not the degree to which the integration is conscious, but that subsidiary clues can become the means by which focal knowledge is established through the application of such internalized skills.

A second structure is the "phenomenal." This refers to that which *appears* in the act of tacit knowing. "A perceived object acquires constant size, colour and shape; observations incorporated into a theory are reduced to mere instances of it; the parts of a whole merge their isolated appearance into the appearance of the whole."[159] It is in the appearance of the distal term (perceived as a comprehensive entity) that we become aware of the proximal term of the integrative act.

---

156. Polanyi, "The Logic of Tacit Inference," 3. Although Polanyi describes just two instances there are, presumably, many others.

157. See ibid., 3–4, Polanyi, *Tacit Dimension*, 10–13 and Polanyi and Prosch, *Meaning*, 35–36.

158. Polanyi, "The Logic of Tacit Inference," 3–4.

159. Ibid., 4.

A third aspect of the relationship between the two terms of tacit knowing is its "semantic structure." It is by way of the elements of the proximal term of tacit knowing that the distal term appears, and we say, in recognition of this appearance, that the distal term is the *meaning* of the elements of the proximal term. A frowning countenance is composed of a multitude of largely unspecifiable facial features: the *meaning* of these features is the frown as it is recognized as the distal term. Or, as Polanyi puts it elsewhere, "The subsidiaries of from-to knowing bear on a focal target, and whatever a thing bears on may be called its meaning."[160] Polanyi cannot speak of the *meaning* of a thing without acknowledging its *reality*.[161]

From these structures of tacit knowing emerges the final one—the "ontological structure." Here Polanyi's realism is explicit. "The act of tacit knowing . . . implies the claim that its result is an aspect of reality, which, as such, may yet reveal its truth in an inexhaustible range of unknown and perhaps still unthinkable ways."[162] For Polanyi an act of knowing, if it is valid, is contingent upon the existence of a reality that exists independently of the knower. This is what he calls the "external pole"[163] or "external anchoring"[164] of tacit knowing.

Polanyi believes that the processes of human perception may be extended to include the use of tools, probes, and the like. Polanyi observes that our body is the "ultimate instrument" by which we attain our practical and intellectual knowledge. He comments: "Our own body is the only thing in the world which we normally never experience as an object, but experience always in terms of the world to which we are attending from our body. It is by making this intelligent use of our body that we feel it to be our body, and not a thing outside."[165] However, in the use of a probe, for example, the skilled surgeon does not handle the probe as an external object but uses it as an extension of his or her own body. The probe is held in the hand, and the sensations that the surgeon picks up from the wall of the cavity being explored are mediated through the hand. But the surgeon does not attend *to* the sensations in his or her hand but *from* them. In Polanyi's terms, the probe is made to function as the proximal term of tacit knowing. I have already offered an account of Polanyi's concept of indwelling, but some repetition is justified at this point since it plays such a crucial role in his epistemology. He explains:

> Whenever we use certain things for attending *from* them to other things, in the way in which we always use our body, these things change their appearance. They appear to us now in terms of the entities to which we are

---

160. Polanyi and Prosch, *Meaning*, 35.

161. In an article dealing with Polanyi's realism Phil Mullins has noted the close proximity of his usage of "real" and "meaningful." See Mullins, "The Real As Meaningful," 42–50.

162. Polanyi, "The Logic of Tacit Inference," 4.

163. See Polanyi, *Personal Knowledge*, 404.

164. See ibid., 311.

165. Polanyi, *Tacit Dimension*, 16.

attending *from* them, just as we feel our own body in terms of the things outside to which we are attending *from* our body. In this sense we can say that when we make a thing function as the proximal term of tacit knowing, we incorporate it in our body—or extend our body to include it—so that we come to dwell in it.[166]

The functional relationship between the surgeon's probe and the exploration of a cavity may readily be extended to include any number of practical tools, but may be extended further to include the use of "intellectual tools"—theories, concepts, moral codes and so forth. Here we meet once more with Polanyi's important (if unfortunately named) concept of articulate systems. As I noted earlier, the articulate system is for Polanyi an extremely broad category (or family of related categories). The diversity contained within it makes generalization difficult, but in the context of the present discussion, the significance of an articulate system is that it functions as the proximal term of tacit knowing. We do not look *at* the articulate system, we look *with* it. When we attend from an articulate system (we might think, for example, of a theory) in order to attend to something else, we interiorize it. It becomes, in effect, an extension of our own body and we indwell it.[167] We might, for example, think of the heliocentric view of the universe. It was through his indwelling of this view of the universe that Newton was able to discover the laws of gravitation. In making his discovery, Newton was not looking *at* the Copernican view but looking *with* it. Had he indwelt a Ptolemaic view he would not have made his discovery because what he was able to uncover was not implied in a geocentric view of the universe.

In addition to showing how an articulate system can be made to function as the proximal term in discovery, this analysis also illuminates at least three other important aspects of tacit knowing. The first is that to indwell an articulate system one must have developed an understanding of those aspects of the system that are explicit and that have been articulated,[168] as well as an awareness of what is or may be implied by this knowledge. Again, it is difficult to generalize, but the indwelling of an articulate system will often be possible only after a period of apprenticeship, nurture, or training. The second is that discovery is the *imaginative* indwelling of an articulate system. In addition to this indwelling, there is the factor of creative genius by which a gifted person may see more of what is implied in a particular articulate system.[169] The final point is that the potential for error is ever present. The ideas and theories that we must indwell in the pursuit of new horizons of

---

166. Ibid., 16; Polanyi's emphasis.

167. "Body" ought to be understood as shorthand for "mind-body," as when we indwell something the indwelling is one of body *and* mind.

168. The formalized aspect of science, for example.

169. Indwelling functions at many different levels: Newton's indwelling of the Copernican view of the universe, for example, was one in which the highest level of imaginative engagement was present.

discovery are not and cannot be known to be infallible even if they are known to be effective. The theories and concepts that we may come to understand and subsequently, through the indwelling of them, rely upon for pursuing new discoveries, we trust as representations of what is real. But this is a fiduciary component in our heuristic endeavors. We can offer no final proof, as we have no "direct" access to that reality. As I noted before, a theory, insofar as it is indwelt, functions somewhat like a pair of spectacles and, as Polanyi points out, "You cannot use your spectacles to scrutinize your spectacles."[170] By wearing spectacles, we are enabled to see things that would otherwise be unclear to us. We evaluate the function of the spectacles we wear on the basis of the perception that they facilitate. We accredit our perception on the basis of our faith in the spectacles.

Our inability to fully specify the proximal term of tacit knowing will, inevitably, appear to the objectivist as a limitation of knowledge. Polanyi disagrees. The critical point is not that there is a shortfall in our explicit knowledge of the proximal term, although there is clearly a sense in which this is so. (As we have seen, it might be possible for the elements of the proximal term to become part of our focal knowledge. But, insofar as this can be done, by looking *at* these features we exclude the possibility of looking *from* them.) Polanyi's analysis demonstrates the *positive* character of tacit integration. "It brings home to us that it is not by looking at things, but by dwelling in them, that we understand their joint meaning."[171] This point will be reinforced by reflecting upon the consequences of seeking focal knowledge of a proximal term by way of a few examples. If we stare intently at a particular minute feature of a face, we are no longer aware—or are only hazily aware—of the face's expression (to which the detail we observe makes some contribution). The surgeon can attend to the sensations of the probe in his or her hand but will thereby lose the facility to use the probe to attend to the cavity. In playing the piano, to introduce a further example, we may attend to the placement of our fingers on the keyboard, but this will interrupt our ability to play fluently. In these and any number of other circumstances a satisfactory performance or achievement can be re-established by interiorizing the particulars once more. But Polanyi observes:

> [T]his recovery never brings back the original meaning. It may improve on it. Motion studies, which tend to paralyze a skill, will improve it when followed by practice. The meticulous dismembering of a text, which can kill its appreciation, can also supply material for a much deeper understanding of it. In these cases, the detailing of particulars, which by itself would destroy meaning, serves as a guide to their subsequent integration and this establishes a more secure and more accurate meaning of them.[172]

---

170. Polanyi and Prosch, *Meaning*, 37.
171. Polanyi, *Tacit Dimension*, 18.
172. Ibid., 19.

The outcome of such a procedure is not always a happy one. Polanyi suggests that in some circumstances "the damage done by the specification of particulars may be irredeemable. Meticulous detailing may obscure beyond recall a subject like history, literature and philosophy."[173] What Polanyi opposes is the view that the particulars offer a truer conception of things. In focusing upon the particulars we do not clarify but obfuscate their joint meaning.[174]

At this point in Polanyi's analysis, his opposition to the dominant views of the philosophy of science resurfaces once more. Modern science aims at establishing strictly detached, fully articulated, objective knowledge. But Polanyi has shown that "tacit thought forms [are] an indispensable part of all knowledge."[175] Consequently he believes that the declared and explicit aims of science "turn out to be fundamentally misleading and possibly a source of devastating fallacies."[176]

The Ubiquity of the Tacit

In the preface to *Personal Knowledge*, Polanyi writes: "This is primarily an enquiry into the nature and justification of scientific knowledge. But my reconsideration of scientific knowledge leads on to a wide range of questions outside science."[177] Evidence of Polanyi's background in science is never far from view in his writings, but in his book, *Meaning*, which he co-authored with Harry Prosch, his engagement with the implications of his epistemology for subjects outside science becomes more sustained. In *Meaning* Polanyi explores an extension of his theory of tacit integration in specific areas including metaphor, art, myth, and religion. I will consider his comments about religion in the brief excursus that follows this chapter, but it will not be possible to give any consideration to the other themes that appear in his last book. All I will do in this brief section is note Polanyi's belief that his theory of tacit integration applies to all areas of knowing, and that there is a much greater degree of continuity in the ways of knowing across a variety of disciplines than has generally been recognized.

In *Meaning* Polanyi argues against the rigid distinctions that, it is supposed, separate the arts and the sciences. In the first place he insists that even in the empirical aspects of science, the imagination of the "artist" is at work: "We may conclude quite generally that no science can predict observed facts except by relying with confidence upon an art: the art of establishing by the trained delicacy of eye, ear and touch a correspondence between explicit predictions of science and

---

173. Ibid.
174. An insight with parallels in Gestalt theory.
175. Polanyi, *Tacit Dimension*, 20.
176. Ibid.
177. Polanyi, *Personal Knowledge*, vii.

the actual experience of our senses to which these predictions shall apply."[178] He goes on to insist: "We must . . . amend our ideal of science by accrediting skills and connoisseurship as valid, indispensable, and definitive forms of knowledge. This amendment . . . will open the way to a far-reaching relaxation of the tension between science and the nonscientific concerns of man."[179]

In one essay Polanyi suggests that his theory of tacit knowledge brings into question the sharp distinction supposed to exist between faith and reason:

> The traditional division between faith and reason, or faith and science . . . reflects the assumption that reason and science proceed by explicit rules of logical deduction or inductive generalization. But I have shown that these operations are impotent by themselves. To know is to understand, and explicit logical processes are effective only as tools in search of the solution to a problem, commitment [sic] by which we expand our understanding and continue to hold the result. They have no meaning except within this informal dynamic context. Once this is recognized, the contrast between faith and reason dissolves, and the close similarity of this structure emerges in its place.[180]

It is because of the essentially unspecifiable way in which our multifarious indwellings facilitate the integrations by which our focal knowledge is achieved that Polanyi is able to say that "All knowledge is . . . either tacit or rooted in tacit knowing."[181] If we see all of our knowledge in terms of such dynamic structures, we cannot uphold the rigid distinctions that have been drawn between science and the humanities.

Language

An important aspect of our cultural life, and one to which a considerable amount of space was devoted in the last chapter, is our use of language. Polanyi gives considerable attention to this topic in *Personal Knowledge*. Expanding his justification of the personal nature of knowledge, Polanyi wishes to indicate the indeterminate and existential nature of language.

Words used in a sentence are confidently relied upon and used directly. A word used with quotation marks is being used in a skeptical or oblique way, unless a quotation is intended. Polanyi comments: "Since a word remains the same whether used directly or obliquely, the difference between uttering it confidently or sceptically must lie wholly in the tacit coefficient of its utterance. This difference

---

178. Polanyi and Prosch, *Meaning*, 31.
179. Ibid., 32–33.
180. Schwartz, *Scientific Thought and Social Reality*, 126.
181. Polanyi and Prosch, *Meaning*, 61.

identifies formally the unspecifiable personal coefficient attached to the confident use of a descriptive term."[182]

In forming a definition of a word, we must attend to the way in which we use it. We must have a sense of when the word is used authentically and when it is not. "The formalization of meanings relies therefore *from the start* on the practise of unformalized meaning. It necessarily does so also *in the end*, when we are using the undefined words of the definitions."[183] Herein is the inherent risk of what Polanyi calls the tacit co-efficient of meaning. To use a word in an oblique way is to draw attention to the fact that the meaning of the word is in question, but this can only be done in the context of a sentence in which the rest of the words are used with confidence. Without such confidence (which could conceivably be misplaced), we would be led into infinite regress.

When we use a word confidently and feel that it is appropriate for its purpose, we make a personal choice. Polanyi suggests that "When we say that a word is precise (or apt, or fitting, or clear, or expressive), we approve of an act of our own which we have found satisfying while carrying it out. We are satisfied by something we *do* in the same way as when we make sense of blurred sights or faint noises; or when we find our way or recover our balance."[184]

Polanyi identifies the use of language[185] as the primary reason for humanity's superiority over other animals. This observation may sound out of place from a philosopher who has drawn particular attention to the importance of inarticulate knowledge, but this apparent incompatibility can be easily resolved: "The two conflicting aspects of formalized intelligence may be reconciled by assuming that the articulation always remains incomplete; that our articulate utterances can never altogether supersede but must continue to rely on such mute acts of intelligence as we once had in common with chimpanzees."[186] Polanyi goes on to suggest that "If, as it would seem, the meaning of all our utterances is determined to an important extent by a skillful act of our own—the act of knowing—then the acceptance of any of our own utterances as true involves our approval of our own skill. To affirm anything implies, then, to this extent an appraisal of our own art of knowing, and the establishment of truth becomes decisively dependent on a set of personal criteria of our own which cannot be formally defined."[187]

---

182. Polanyi, *Personal Knowledge*, 250.

183. Ibid.; Polanyi's emphasis.

184. Ibid., 252; Polanyi's emphasis.

185. Polanyi describes language as "formal instruments of thought" and he includes within this category writing, mathematics, graphs and maps, diagrams and pictures. It would, doubtless, be possible to think of others.

186. Polanyi, *Personal Knowledge*, 70.

187. Ibid., 70–71. This personal act cannot, of course, be understood apart from the communal context or "calling" in which it occurs.

Polanyi wishes to demonstrate the significance of pre-linguistic experience; the kind of experience that parallels other animals that do not have language. An anatomist exploring by dissection a complex topography may be using intelligence much like a rat in a maze. Like the rat that is unable to explain how it has found its way out of the maze, the expert will be unable to offer a fully articulate account of what he or she has come to know. It is a knowledge that is ineffable. Polanyi observes: "We may say in general that by acquiring a skill, whether muscular or intellectual, we achieve an understanding which we cannot put into words and which is continuous with the inarticulate faculties of animals."[188] What is understood here has a meaning for the skilled anatomist, and it has a meaning in itself, but this is not the meaning of a sign in denoting an object. Its meaning is what Polanyi calls "existential." As animals lack language, all animal knowledge is of this existential nature.

However, to say that we have knowledge that is ineffable is not to say that we are unable to speak of it at all. Rather, it is to say that we can only articulate part of what we know. Polanyi identifies a further aspect of the tacit co-efficient of language: not only does tacit knowledge go beyond what we are able to articulate, in the reception of what *is* articulated, the receiver is directed not to what is contained in the symbolic forms of the articulation but, rather, to that to which they point. "Even *while* listening to speech or reading a text our focal attention is directed towards the meaning of the words, and not towards the words as sounds or as marks on paper."[189] Polanyi draws attention to the possibilities and the dangers inherent in the use of language: "The mind which entrusts itself to the operation of symbols acquires an intellectual tool of boundless power; but its use makes the mind liable to perils the range of which seems also unlimited. The gap between the tacit and the articulate tends to produce everywhere a cleavage between sound common sense and dubious sophistication, from which the animal is quite free."[190]

It is thus clear that in their use of language humans commit themselves to a double indeterminacy. In the first place, there is the gap between our knowledge and our articulation of it; and in the second place, there is a gap between what we have said and our subsequent reflection upon it. "For just as, owing to the ultimately tacit character of all our knowledge, we remain ever unable to say all that we know, so also, in view of the tacit character of meaning, we can never quite know what is implied in what we say."[191]

It is also necessary to attend to the relationship between words and sensory perception. Polanyi talks of the way in which the meaning of denotative words is shaped in the process of applying them in particular situations over time. Polanyi

---

188. Ibid., 90; Polanyi's emphasis.
189. Ibid., 92; Polanyi's emphasis.
190. Ibid., 94.
191. Ibid., 95.

comments: "These linguistic identifications are in fact based primarily on the sensory identification of objects at varying distances, under varying angles and varying illumination, and merely extend the theory of the universe implied in our sensory interpretations to the wider theory, implied in the vocabulary by which we talk about things."[192] This is the significance of sensory perception for the tacit components of articulate knowledge. In a limited way each new situation may be regarded as unprecedented. Not only do we see familiar things in new circumstances, but we are confronted by new things. How do we make sense of such things? Polanyi explains that

> The adaptation of our conceptions and of the corresponding use of language to new things that we identify as new variants of known kinds of things is achieved subsidiarily, while our attention is focussed on making sense of the situation in front of us. Thus we do this in the same way in which we keep modifying, subsidiarily, our interpretation of sensory clues by striving for clear and coherent perceptions, or enlarging our skill without focally knowing how by practising them in ever new situations. The meaning of speech thus keeps changing in the act of groping for words without our being focally aware of the change, and our gropings invest words in this manner with a fund of unspecifiable connotations.[193]

Polanyi points out that different languages represent different conclusions reached by different peoples at different points in history. As such they are distinct conceptual frameworks. "The confident use of nouns, verbs, adjectives and adverbs, invented and endowed with meaning by a particular sequence of groping generations, expresses their particular theory of the nature of things."[194]

At this juncture it is important to note the relationship between what has been said about language here and what was said in the previous chapter. In chapter 2 the influence of Wittgenstein's language philosophy was evident. It is surprising to find that in his explicit observations on Wittgenstein, Polanyi adopts a very negative tone. This is exemplified in a comment on Wittgenstein in *Personal Knowledge*: "The understatement that language is a set of convenient symbols used according to the conventional rules of a 'language game' originates in the tradition of nominalism, which teaches that general terms are merely names designating certain collections of objects—a doctrine which, in spite of the difficulties admittedly attached to it, is accepted today by most writers in England and America, in abhorrence of its metaphysical alternatives."[195] Polanyi also criticizes Wittgenstein for overstating the significance of grammar. All this suggests that Polanyi seriously misunderstood Wittgenstein, if he had read him at all. Not only does he

---

192. Ibid., 97.
193. Ibid., 112.
194. Ibid.
195. Ibid., 113.

misrepresent Wittgenstein's later thought; he also fails to so see the close affinities that exist between Wittgenstein's work and his own. C. B. Daly is surprised that Polanyi did not recognize in Wittgenstein an ally.[196]

As we have seen, like Polanyi, Wittgenstein was aware of the complex relationship between life and language. He saw that words are not always used in the same way, and that in the differing usages we see "family resemblances" but also distinctions. These arise because they are being used in different life contexts, or communities of practice. Wittgenstein's method is *a posteriori*—"don't think, but look."[197] This is remarkably similar to Polanyi's approach. Using "justice" as his paradigm case, Polanyi writes: "we must *use* the word 'justice,' and use it as correctly and thoughtfully as we can, while watching ourselves doing it, if we want to analyse the conditions under which the word properly applies. We must look, intently and discriminatingly, *through* the term 'justice' at justice itself, this being the proper use of the term 'justice,' the use which we want to define."[198] Polanyi goes on to explain that simply looking *at* the word "justice" can only destroy rather than establish its meaning. So for Polanyi, like Wittgenstein, it is in the *use* of the word that its meaning is to be discerned. Daly makes the comment that "the most striking similarity between Polanyi and Wittgenstein in their philosophy of language is that both see language as meaningful only within the wider context of culture, tradition, and ways of human living."[199] Wittgenstein is innocent of the conventionalism of which Polanyi accuses him. His purpose, like Polanyi's, is to confront positivistic theories of language by showing their inadequacy in describing language as it is used.

Polanyi's negative evaluation of Wittgenstein appears to rest upon a misunderstanding of his work. The philosophies of language of Polanyi and Wittgenstein are far more complementary than the former was able—for whatever reasons—to acknowledge.

Concluding Remarks

As we noted at the beginning of the chapter, Polanyi does not, in any of his published works, present a systematically developed theory of knowledge by means of systematic argumentation. I want to suggest that, rather than a limitation—or even a failing, this might be regarded, at least in some limited way, as an attempt to embody, methodologically, the content of his theory.

---

196. This case is argued at length in an essay entitled "Polanyi and Wittgenstein" by C. B. Daly. See Langford and Poteat, *Intellect and Hope*, 136–68.

197. Wittgenstein, *Philosophical Investigations (Second Edition)*, 31.

198. Polanyi, *Personal Knowledge*, 116. Polanyi's emphasis. It must be emphasized that it is something akin to Wittgenstein's "don't think, but look" which is in view here, and not the Platonic "Forms."

199. Langford and Poteat, *Intellect and Hope*, 146.

Polanyi's theory of tacit knowledge demonstrates that the standard of comprehensive lucidity, so reverenced in objectivist philosophies, is fallacious. Crucially it ignores the "from-to" aspect of our knowing and the forms of indwelt knowledge implied in this. A focal knowledge of things is achieved through the integration of subsidiary elements, and in the integrative process our knowledge of the subsidiary elements will be more than we can tell. We are not looking *at* this knowledge, we are looking *from* it.

Polanyi adopts a variety of strategies for articulating his theory of knowledge. These strategies appear, perhaps inevitably, as the elements of his theory. As will be apparent from the exposition above, these elements of his thought frequently spill over into each other and any rigorous separation of them is inappropriate. I have grouped my reflections under ten sub-headings, but there is nothing of critical importance about this number, nor is there any particular significance to be attached to the sequence in which they appear. The exposition of the theme "problems and discoveries" precedes, for example, that of "passions" and it appears to me that there is a significant logical link here. But the themes of "indwelling" and "tacit knowledge," among others, also exhibit important logical links with that of "problems and discoveries." If there are elements of development to be discerned in the sequential appearance of the themes, and often this does seem to be the case, these are of minor significance in comparison with their collective function *as the subsidiaries whose meaning is understood in terms of our achievement of tacit knowledge.*

Polanyi adopts a rigorously *a posteriori* approach in his philosophy. His theory of knowledge is an attempt to make explicit the subsidiary elements that comprise our actual experience of coming to know things. A theory of knowledge is not a prescription for "how to know things" but an attempt to articulate "how things are known." As such we must acknowledge that Polanyi's theory of knowledge—in consistency with its own doctrine—cannot be complete. It is an attempt to articulate the way in which we come to know things while acknowledging that this achievement is ineffable and that the theory is and can only be an "attenuated summary."[200]

Our ability to come to know things is not contingent upon our theory of knowledge. Nevertheless, as Polanyi's theory would suggest, there are circumstances in which by gaining focal awareness of the subsidiary elements in which we participate, some failings may be discerned. Our subsequent performance can then be improved, once the elements are allowed to resume their subsidiary function. Polanyi's passionate engagement in developing a new theory reflects his belief that the objectivist theories of knowledge that he opposed were not only

---

200. See Polanyi, *Personal Knowledge*, 171.

mistaken but pathological.[201] A theory of knowledge may be, in Polanyi's own terminology, "an attenuated summary" of how we come to know things, but such a term should not blind us to their destructive potential. For Polanyi the study of the theory of knowledge is not a philosophical pastime but a matter that has a significant bearing on the integrity of a culture and the various components of which it is comprised—not least theological expression.

It is difficult to overstate the philosophical ambition and scope of Polanyi's work. He seeks to achieve nothing less than the radical reform of our understanding of knowledge as it has developed from the philosophy of Descartes, through the Enlightenment, and culminated in what was, for Polanyi, the contemporary thought of the logical positivists. This ambition is implied in the subtitle of his *magnum opus*, "towards a postcritical philosophy." Polanyi's work represents one of the first reactions to critical, objectivizing thought and might appropriately be regarded as an early postmodern philosophy. I noted, in the last chapter, Colin Gunton's assessment of the achievement of Barth as "something of a *tour de force*, plucked from the intellectual air by an act of intuitive genius."[202] It would not be out of place to attribute to Polanyi a similar accomplishment. It is doubtless *because* of the scope of Polanyi's work that it can, on occasions, lack certain nuances, and runs risks of overgeneralization. I have noted, for example, the daunting breadth of the term "articulate system," and yet Polanyi will often talk of our participation in such systems without differentiation. There may be important parallels between the ways in which we indwell a symphony and a scientific theory, but there are also differences! I am not, of course, attempting a detailed critique of Polanyi here but merely pointing to an example of his tendency to generalize.

It is clear that in his theory of knowledge, Polanyi's paradigm case is *scientific* knowledge and, as an accomplished practitioner of scientific research, he makes acute observations in respect of scientific knowledge. It is here that Polanyi's philosophical method is most consistently *a posteriori*. In dealing with themes and subjects in which his own personal participation is less full and sure, his approach can be less finely attuned to the phenomena with which he is dealing. Here Polanyi's impulse towards an *a posteriori* method can be compromised by his desire to discern general patterns of epistemic processes. In these circumstances his insights can be considerably less acute as we shall see in the excursus that follows.

---

201. As I have already hinted, Polanyi believed the destructive totalitarianisms of the twentieth century were, to a significant degree, a product of objectivizing and depersonalizing epistemologies.

202. Gunton, *Theology through the Theologians*, 53.

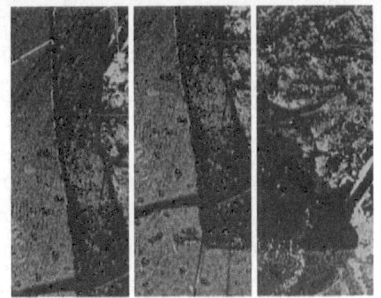

Excursus: Polanyi and Religion

Introduction

THE TASK WHICH Polanyi set himself in *Personal Knowledge*, as noted in the previous chapter, was to inquire into "the nature and justification of scientific knowledge."[1] Although, in his inquiry, he is led to consider a "wide range of questions outside science,"[2] his approach in the latter task is significantly influenced by the way in which he formulated the former. *Personal Knowledge*, Polanyi's *magnum opus*, typifies his work as a whole. He starts with science, and epistemological questions in science, and then moves on to consider other matters. One of the questions outside science to which Polanyi is led is that of religion. How does Polanyi pose this question? I now turn to an exposition of the theme of religion in his work.

Polanyi's breadth of scholarship is often breathtaking. He has the ability to weave together diverse and complex themes within relatively small compass. In the present context it may be difficult to offer an exhaustive account of Polanyi's writings on the subject of religion but it is possible to point to the works which exhibit a concentration upon the theme.

Exposition

Personal Knowledge

ARTICULATE SYSTEMS

In *Personal Knowledge* there are two substantial passages in which we find exposition of religious themes. They are found between pages 195–202 and 279–86 under the headings, "Dwelling In and Breaking Out" and "Religious Doubt,"

---

1. Polanyi, *Personal Knowledge*, vii.
2. Ibid.

respectively. Here the theme of religion is conceived in terms of Polanyi's articulate systems—the "happy dwelling places of the human mind."[3]

Polanyi describes religious engagement in a typically elusive statement: "Religion, considered as an act of worship, is an indwelling rather than an affirmation. God cannot be observed, any more than truth or beauty can be observed. He exists in the sense that He is to be worshipped and obeyed, but not otherwise; not as a fact—any more than truth, beauty or justice exist as facts. All these, like God, are things which can be apprehended only in serving them."[4]

The choice to indwell an articulate system[5] is a matter of faith: one cannot demonstrate the truth or falsity of an articulate system. This is so for any articulate system, and it is true for religion. As we saw in the previous chapter, an articulate system is the elaboration of an aspect of anterior experience. In the case of religion, according to Polanyi, this is the "supernatural."[6] Polanyi suggests, "The convert enters into the articulate framework of worship and doctrine by surrendering to the religious ecstasy which their system evokes and accredits thereby its validity."[7]

Polanyi describes the Christian religious service[8] as "a framework of clues which are apt to induce a passionate search for God."[9] The Christian search is a heuristic impulse that to some degree parallels the experience of scientific discovery. This appears to imply that in religion, as in science, there is something to be found—it is a valid inquiry: "A heuristic impulse can live only in the pursuit of its proper enquiry. The Christian enquiry is worship. The words of prayer and confession, the actions of the ritual, the lesson, the sermon, the church itself, are the clues of the worshipper's striving towards God. They guide his feelings of contrition and gratitude and his craving for the divine presence, while keeping him safe from distracting thoughts."[10]

As may be the case with other articulate systems by which we apprehend the world there is, in addition to our indwelling of it, an impulse to "break out." As we noted in the previous chapter, in contemplation our participation is, at least for a moment, changed, and instead of "handling" the things we experience we become

---

3. Ibid., 280. Although this is the dominant theme in *Personal Knowledge*, another theme, the theme of tacit integration, is also strongly implied.

4. Ibid., 279. Note the way in which Polanyi links religion and worship.

5. It may be that in some cases our indwelling of an articulate system is less a choice and more to do with accidents of birth—the age, location, and family into which we are born.

6. This comment does not appear to be in harmony with his comments in *Meaning*, and various other places, unless one takes worship, and the kinds of integrations achieved in worship, to be "supernatural" in the sense that they contain supernatural aspects and/or relate to supernatural realities. And, interestingly, this does appear to be implied in *some* of Polanyi's discussion of religion.

7. Polanyi, *Personal Knowledge*, 283–84.

8. I take it that Polanyi is referring to congregational worship at this point.

9. Polanyi, *Personal Knowledge*, 282.

10. Ibid., 281. It is arguable whether all the elements of a church service are always effective in keeping the worshipper safe from distracting thoughts!

"immersed" in them. "Contemplation dissolves the screen, stops our movement through experience and pours us straight into experience; we cease to handle things and become immersed in them."[11] This is the moment in which we may come to see things differently and may find our conceptual grasp of that which we comprehend deepened or transformed in a more radical way. In this context, Polanyi speaks of the experience of the religious mystic. The path to God is found in the sustained effort at detachment from *all* frames of knowledge:

> The whole framework of intelligent understanding... sinks into abeyance and uncovers a world of experience uncomprehendingly as divine miracle. The process is known in Christian mysticism as the *via negativa* and the tradition which prescribes it as the only perfect path to God stems from the *Mystic Theology* of Pseudo-Dionysius. It invites us, through a succession of 'detachments', to seek in absolute ignorance union with Him who is beyond all being and all knowledge. We see things not focally, but as part of a cosmos, as features of God.[12]

Polanyi conceives of this form of mystic contemplation in salvific terms: "The Christian mystic's communion with the world seeks a reconciliation which is part of the technique of redemption. It is man's surrender to the love of God, in the hope of gaining his forgiveness and admission into His presence."[13] For Polanyi the experience of the Christian is unique. He writes, "the dwelling of the Christian worshipper within the ritual of divine service differs from any other dwelling within a framework of inherent excellence, by the fact that this dwelling is not enjoyed."[14] Additionally, he claims that it is "By these ritual acts the worshipper accepts the obligation to achieve what he knows to be beyond his own unaided powers and strives towards it in the hope of a merciful visitation from above."[15]

In the previous chapter, we made reference to the importance for human beings of puzzles and problems that draw us into an imaginative engagement with reality. It seems that for Polanyi, Christian worship, in which we seek after God, is, in a sense, the most pure form of this phenomenon in that it inspires a passion that is never resolved. The mystic's detached contemplation is his surrender to the love of God made in the hope of receiving forgiveness and being received into God's presence. But there is no resolution; "The ritual of worship is expressly designed to induce and sustain this state of anguish, surrender and hope. The moment a man were to claim that he had arrived and could now happily contemplate his own perfection, he would be thrown back into spiritual emptiness."[16] This is a striking

11. Ibid., 197.
12. Ibid., 197–98.
13. Ibid., 198.
14. Ibid.
15. Ibid.
16. Ibid.

feature of Polanyi's understanding of religion, and one which receives considerable emphasis in *Personal Knowledge*.[17] The believer's indwelling is perpetually uncomfortable and unresolved. Unlike the problems of the scientist, for whom a discovery resolves the tension, "Christian worship sustains, as it were, an eternal, never to be consummated hunch: a heuristic vision which is accepted for the sake of its unresolved tension."[18] Polanyi suggests that the Christian worshipper may only be comforted by the image (though *only* the image) of "a crucified God."[19]

DOUBT

As we participate or dwell within an articulate system, we do not look *at it* but *from it*. It was suggested in the previous chapter that, for this reason, the system functions somewhat like a pair of spectacles. By indwelling an articulate system, we entrust ourselves to it and the vision it offers to us. It is with this in mind that we must read Polanyi's comments on faith and doubt in relation to religion:

> As a framework expressing its acceptance of itself as a dwelling place of the passionate search for God, religious worship can say nothing that is true or false. Words of prayer are addressed to God, and while other parts of the service *speak of* God, they are mostly declarations of interpersonal relations—such as the praise of God. Some parts of worship, like the credo, admittedly make theological assertions, and the lessons from the Bible are couched in plainly narrative language. But the accent of the credo lies on the words: 'I believe' which emotionally endorse worship, while the extracts from the Bible are not quoted in the course of a Christian religious service in order to convey information, but as starting points for teachings that sustain the faith. All such statements function as subsidiaries to worship.[20]

Polanyi does not believe that the statement "God exists" can be the subject of explicit doubt because it is an a-critical statement made, by a person who makes it, with a greater or lesser degree of confidence. Here we recall Polanyi's differentiation between acceptances in natural science—where he speaks of *verification*—and in "mathematics, religion or the various arts"[21]—where he speaks of *validation*. Polanyi says that religious worship is a heuristic vision and stands alongside the great intellectual systems such as mathematics, fiction, and the fine arts. We do not say that they are "true," but we entrust ourselves to them (or withhold our trust) with a greater or lesser degree of confidence.

The aspect of anterior experience upon which the Christian articulate system is constructed is, for Polanyi, the supernatural. The biblical miracles are certainly

17. See ibid., 324.
18. Ibid., 199.
19. Ibid.
20. Ibid., 281; Polanyi's emphasis.
21. Ibid., 202.

in view here. In a discussion on the subject of miracles, Polanyi criticizes Hume and others who rejected miracles on the basis of a lack of factual evidence. He suggests to the contrary: "[I]f the conversion of water into wine or the resuscitation of the dead could be experimentally verified, this would strictly disprove their miraculous nature. Indeed, to the extent to which any event can be established in terms of natural science, it belongs to the natural order of things. However monstrous and surprising it may be, once it has been fully established as an observable fact, the event ceases to be regarded as supernatural."[22]

A miracle must have happened if it is to be of any significance: "Of course, an event which has in fact never taken place can have no supernatural significance; and whether it has taken place or not must be established by factual evidence. Hence the religious force of biblical criticism, shaking or, alternatively, corroborating certain facts which formed the main themes of Christianity."[23]

Polanyi suggests that there are two important ways in which religious faith may be assailed by doubt. Firstly, its internal evidence might be questioned in the way the meaningfulness of an innovative work of art might be questioned. Polanyi suggests that we may refuse or hesitate to indwell such articulate systems for fear that we may thereby lose or weaken our grip on reality.[24] There is, of course, no test that can be applied when we are faced with such a dilemma: "This kind of doubt is the hesitancy of an acceptance. Our reluctance to accept the habitation offered to our minds may be craven or wise, and so we may prove eventually to have been dull or rash."[25] Secondly, doubt may attack Christian faith in that it is striving for that which cannot be attained. There is something of a paradox here. The lack of consummation, which Polanyi regards as intrinsic to the Christian faith, may increase to the degree where faith is destroyed altogether.

In the Western world, over a period of 300 years, the effect of advancing historical and scientific knowledge has had the effect of substantially weakening religious belief. But, while reducing the religious meaning of things, such advances have offered no alternative meaning. Polanyi comments: "If the universe were in fact meaningless, the destruction of religious beliefs would have been fully justified. Since I do not believe that the universe is meaningless, I can admit only that the rejection of religion was reasonable in view of the grounds on which religious doctrines were asserted at the time."[26]

---

22. Ibid., 284.

23. Ibid. Polanyi's meaning here is not clear to me. If a miracle happened, would it not be "observable" even if it couldn't be "experimentally verified"?

24. A fear that the "spectacles" will distort rather than facilitate our seeing.

25. Polanyi, *Personal Knowledge*, 285.

26. Ibid., 286. Polanyi's belief in the meaningfulness of the universe is closely related to his theory of hierarchy. This is an important aspect of Polanyi's work but, given its limited bearing on the subject matter of the present work, it has been necessary to forgo a treatment of it. For a succinct summary of this theory in the context of the rest of his work see, Polanyi, "Transcendence and Self-Transcendence."

Meaning

In Polanyi's last published book, *Meaning*, which he co-authored with Harry Prosch, the subject of religion is revisited. The scope of Polanyi's concerns expressed in *Meaning* is very broad. Its approach may be distinguished from that of *Personal Knowledge* in that the emphasis shifts from the fiduciary component of knowledge and the indwelling of articulate systems to that of tacit integration. At the heart of this work is Polanyi's identification and description of the integrating processes involved in all knowing. Polanyi writes, "*all* meaningful integrations (including those achieved in science) exhibit a triadic structure consisting of the subsidiary, the focal, and the person."[27] In *Meaning* it is in the imaginative process of integration that the *personal* nature of knowledge (always central to Polanyi's project) emerges. Polanyi explores the nature of this integrating process in relation to metaphor, art and myth, and, indeed, religion.

As noted in the previous chapter, Polanyi is concerned to show that the triadic structure of tacit knowing is present in all knowing, and in this regard no distinction may be made between the sciences, the arts, morality, and religion. The role of imagination must be acknowledged for the sciences as it is for the arts, the humanities, morality, and religion.[28] Whatever other appropriate distinctions may be made, it cannot be claimed that science stands in a more sure or authentic relation to reality on the basis of the absence of personal participation and human imagination.

Polanyi suggests that for the contemporary mind an acceptance of these commonalities is problematic. It finds it difficult to conceive of intangibles, such as religion and morality, as having any existence independently of humanity. He explains:

> In order to hold these meanings securely in the reverence they seem to him to demand, contemporary man . . . needs a theory of these meanings that explains how their coherence is no less real than the perceptual and scientific coherences he so readily accepts. He needs to see how his obvious personal involvement with these meanings is necessarily and legitimately part and parcel of the reality they actually have, that his personal involvement is not at all a reason to regard them as mere subjective fantasies.[29]

Polanyi deals at some length with the subject of myth, focusing primarily on creation myths.[30] He wishes to make a distinction between the integrations

---

27. Polanyi and Prosch, *Meaning*, 64; Polanyi's emphasis.

28. I shall have more to say on this matter in the final chapter.

29. Polanyi and Prosch, *Meaning*, 68. In this passage it appears that Polanyi is preparing a case for the independent reality of such entities. As his argument unfolds, he does indeed claim that they are "realities," but what precisely he means by this is less than clear, as we shall see.

30. See ibid., 120–48.

achieved in myth and those achieved in science. The integrations required in making a scientific discovery may be very considerable, but once they have been established, we become accustomed to working with them and they become quite "natural" to us.[31] It seems that the difficulty of making the integrations fades with familiarity. But the integrations of myth[32] do not enter into our ordinary world and our ordinary lives. They do not work in such a sphere. They must be detached from our daily lives. The incompatible elements that we integrate in myth remain incompatible. They must be joined together in every new instance by an act of our imagination as we contemplate them. They do not, in Polanyi's view, become "natural." Such integrations Polanyi calls "transnatural."

Polanyi suggests that the myths of the "primitive mind"[33] "bristle with absurdities."[34] It sustains views which, to the modern mind, seem extraordinary. But Polanyi believes that the cognitive processes involved in both archaic and modern minds are the same. The outcomes differ because the range of acceptable tacit integrations is far greater for the archaic mind than for the modern mind.[35] It is only the *range* which is at issue since the integrative process is integral to all forms of human knowledge.[36] We must not disregard the fact that all our empirical knowledge is rooted in subsidiaries that are, to a greater or lesser extent, unspecifiable. Are such myths true? For Polanyi the creation myths are certainly more true to our experience than the picture of "barren atomic topography" offered to us by those who follow the ideal of detached observations.[37] Nevertheless, he acknowledges that such a view may not be acceptable to a modern generation.

I turn now to the explicit treatment of the theme of religion in *Meaning*. There is evidence to suggest that in chapter ten of *Meaning*, entitled "Acceptance of Religion," Harry Prosch has substantially fleshed-out rather than edited the material of Polanyi's with which he was working.[38] Consequently we ought to be

31. For example, and even as non-scientists, we have little difficulty with conceiving the apparent rising and setting of the sun as the movement of the earth around its axis. The difficulty associated with the discovery of this was considerably greater!

32. Polanyi claims that the same is true of poetry and art, although the integrations of these are not as far-reaching or all-encompassing as the integrations in myth.

33. Polanyi does not expand on what is intended in this vague and undifferentiated term.

34. Polanyi and Prosch, *Meaning*, 132.

35. Polanyi also suggests that the archaic mind has a greater disposition to see significance in events and is less likely to treat them as coincidental. This is the point of distinction in which *we believe* the modern mind to be more correct in its evaluations.

36. Polanyi explains that when the process of tacit integration in human knowledge is denied by the modern mind it commits itself to an essentially nonsensical way of conceiving things.

37. Here Polanyi has the reductionistic Laplacean view of the universe in mind. For a succinct exposition and comment on this view see Polanyi, *Personal Knowledge*, 139–41.

38. Much of the material in chapter 10 of *Meaning* is not to be found in the lecture manuscript (Texas and Chicago series, 1969) also entitled "Acceptance of Religion" on which the chapter was based. (See "Polanyi Collection: Regenstein Library, University of Chicago." Box 40, Folder 1.) I am unaware of any similar material in any of Polanyi's published or unpublished work. It is striking that

cautious in attributing to Polanyi the material on Holy Communion, ritual, praise, and prayer to be found in the book. Nevertheless, it is apparent that it is only some illustrative material that might not be attributable to Polanyi; the general structure of the argument certainly is.

Polanyi writes: "Religion ... is a sprawling work of the imagination involving rites, ceremonies, doctrines, myths, and something called "worship." It is a form of "acceptance" much more complex, therefore, than any of the other forms we have been attending to."[39] He continues, "religion involves sacred myths that inform rites and ceremonies, imbuing their intrinsically metaphoric meaning with something more than the kind of poetic or artistic meaning they would possess simply as metaphorical works of art."[40] The sacrament of Holy Communion is identified as an important ceremony in Christian worship. The ceremony embodies several things:

> We embody our own temporal, inchoate experiences, stretching over a long period of time, in the unification of one moment—which also embodies our unification *with* one another in the same moment. If this happens to be a traditional ceremony, hallowed by time, engaged at regular intervals—perhaps by generations of the same people and their descendants—the ceremony will border upon the sacred or religious. Let us say rather that it could move easily into the obviously sacred or religious with the addition, in time, of a myth describing how the ceremony was "once upon a time" ordained by a god.[41]

In this way the Holy Communion is detached from the prosaic act of eating and drinking and from all temporal meanings. Through the myth, we enter into the Great Time[42] in which we are united not only with our forefathers but with the whole creation, and we participate in the ultimate meaning of things.[43] In Holy Communion there is a mutual embodiment of rite and myth. But it is detached from everyday life and, claims Polanyi, is made sacred in this detachment. Polanyi believes that the timing of such ceremonies is important. However, the action of the ritual has a meaning not in ordinary time but in the Great Time—the time before all-time which has and needs no date. It is the myth which gives a rite its larger meaning, and the rite is embodied in the myth. In a curious sense, a myth

---

Polanyi's lecture manuscript contains only six paragraphs at the end of the piece which deal directly with religious matters. In *Meaning*, however, there is a large amount of material about the Holy Communion, praise, prayer, ritual and worship.

39. Polanyi and Prosch, *Meaning*, 152.
40. Ibid.
41. Ibid., 152–53; Polanyi's emphasis.
42. A term that Polanyi borrows from Mircea Eliade.
43. See Polanyi and Prosch, *Meaning*, 153.

itself has no body except the rites that it creates. Expanding his comments on the Holy Communion, Polanyi writes:

> In general, bodily nourishment is thought to interfere to some extent with nourishment of the soul. This apparent fact is what lies behind the universally acknowledged efficacy of fasting for purposes of spiritual edification and progress. Yet the two supposed incompatibles (nourishment of the body and of the soul) are combined in the rite of Holy Communion. There are also obvious incompatibilities involved in considering the same physical objects to be both flesh and bread, both blood and wine—to say nothing of the impossibility of deriving an infinite supply of food from one finite human body. The whole ritual, combined with the myth, bristles with irresolvable incompatibilities. But it is the fusion of these incompatibles, accomplished by our imagination, that gives a meaning to the whole transaction and moves our religious feeling so powerfully—if we are Christian.[44]

Polanyi goes on to look at other incompatibles in Christian worship. He asks questions such as "How could God be pleased with our worship?" "How can intercessory prayer be in anyway meaningful?"[45] He compares such acts of worship and prayer with a murder on stage in a theatrical production: in the latter what appears to be happening is actually *not* happening, while in the former case what appears not to be going on (because it makes no logical sense) "*is* actually going on."[46]

Polanyi conceives of worship as a very particular kind of indwelling through which he claims, we "see God."[47] And we can *only* come to see God in this way. God's existence cannot be established on any other grounds. God is known in the worship of God. "Through our integrative, imaginative efforts we see him as the focal point that fuses into meaning all the incompatibles involved in the practice of religion. But, as in art—only in a more whole and complete way—God also becomes the integration of all the incompatibles of our own lives."[48] Polanyi envisages here the manifold aspects of our lives: pleasures and pains, hopes and fears, loves and hates, loose ends and blind alleys.

> In a practical sense these fundamental incompatibles are often resolved by throwing away one or the other. The megalomaniac rejects his frailties, the opportunist rejects his obligations, and the suicide rejects his hope. The sane man, we say, holds all these incompatible factors together in a sort of

---

44. Ibid., 154.

45. See ibid., 155.

46. Ibid.; Polanyi's emphasis. Polanyi does not expand upon or attempt to elucidate what he means by this statement.

47. Ibid., 156. This remarkably blunt, realist language sits uneasily with other things he says of God.

48. Ibid.

permanent tension, hoping that somehow he may be given the power to do what he knows he must, but living in the meantime humbly within the limits of his capacities—within his "calling" in the broadest sense of this word. As a matter of fact, this is the sort of faith and hope that a *scientist* has when he faces a problem he does not know how to resolve but which he tackles anyway.[49]

Polanyi believes that such a faith is necessarily blind and difficult to maintain, especially under pressure. He suggests that such imaginative fusions are given short shrift where it is thought pure reason is the arbiter. "[I]t is easy for such faith and hope to be supplanted by the supreme arrogance of a Marxism, which forgets or denies human limitations, or by the freedom of a Sartre, which forgets the obligations we find in our position, or by the despair of a Camus, which abandons all hope as objectively groundless."[50] Here Polanyi recognizes what he elsewhere calls the "Pauline scheme," in which we must dwell in the hope of meeting with the grace of God:

> Our myths tell us of the Fall and of how and why we are excluded from the Paradise we long for as our natural state. But they also tell us of the Redemption and of the power and grace of God that is to be dispensed to us as needed. So we are freed from our worry about our (to us) insurmountable limitations. But we are not freed from obligation to "the Law," and therefore we cannot become complacent. Rather, we are humbled before God in the recognition of our dependence upon him for the ultimate victory through Christ.[51]

But to this he adds (in my view disappointingly) that "None of these beliefs makes any literal sense. They can be destroyed as easily as the actuality of Polonius' death upon the stage, should anyone attempt to defend its reality in the world of facts. Both are works of the imagination, accepted by us as meaningful integrations of quite incompatible clues that move us deeply and help us to pull the scattered droplets of our lives together into a single sea of sublime meaning."[52] The content of the myths may appear entirely implausible, and yet in the stories of creation, miraculous birth, crucifixion, and resurrection there is "a meaning that is born and remains at the level of feeling but which is nonetheless a genuinely universal personal meaning and not merely a subjective personal meaning."[53] Polanyi continues:

---

49. Ibid.; Polanyi's emphasis.
50. Ibid., 156–57.
51. Ibid., 157.
52. Ibid.
53. Ibid., 159.

> [E]ven when all the representational details in the myths are clearly and frankly regarded as impossible . . . the *import* of these details must still be thought to be *plausible*. For . . . the contents of a religion will have as their import the story of a fundamentally *meaningful* world . . . Therefore, if we can regard religious myth as plausible, the sort of world that religious myth represents—a meaningful world—must be thought by us to be plausible . . . In other words, it must be plausible to us to suppose that the universe is, in the end, meaningful.[54]

The meaningfulness so strongly implied in religious myth will not be acceptable so long as it is believed that the world is fundamentally meaningless. The meaning implied in the narrative myths of religion clashes with the meaninglessness implied in the reductionistic, atomistic philosophy embraced by modern culture. In Polanyi's view, this clash is the source of popular disenchantment with religion.

In the chapter that follows, entitled "Order," Polanyi argues for the meaningfulness of things on the basis of purposeful evolutionary achievement.[55] By this argument, he suggests, "We might justifiably claim . . . that everything we know is *full* of meaning, is not absurd at all, although we can sometimes fail to grasp these meanings and fall into absurdities."[56] Polanyi concludes: "The religious hypothesis, if it does indeed hold the world to be meaningful rather than absurd, *is* therefore a viable hypothesis for us. There is no scientific reason why we cannot believe it."[57] However, finding no scientific reason why not to believe in the "religious hypothesis" is not necessarily to believe it. We cannot be religious without having a religion any more than we can speak without having a language. Religious meaning can only be sought in the concrete form of a religious tradition.

This is a significant problem as many in Polanyi's time—as in the present day—do not "inherit" a religion. Such people can become believers only through conversion. Polanyi is not trying to effect religious conversion through what he writes, but he does consider that his work might function as a prelude to it. He hopes that he might contribute to the "unstopping of ears," so that some may hear should a "liturgical summons" come their way.[58] But he agrees with St. Augustine that it is not our part to initiate such a summons: "It is a gift of God and may remain inexplicably denied to some of us."[59]

---

54. Ibid., 159–60; Polanyi's emphasis.

55. The function of this chapter parallels Polanyi's purposes in the fourth part of *Personal Knowledge*, 327–405.

56. Polanyi and Prosch, *Meaning*, 179; Polanyi's emphasis.

57. Ibid., 179; Polanyi's emphasis.

58. See ibid., 180.

59. Ibid.

Other Significant Articles

I would like to make brief mention of three articles penned by Polanyi: "Faith and Reason,"[60] "Science and Religion,"[61] and an unpublished paper, "About Religious Faith."[62] These articles are significant for understanding Polanyi's views on religion, but not in the way that one might expect. Despite their titles, none of the three pieces deals with religious or theological themes except insofar as they illuminate an epistemological theme—which is their main concern.

"Faith and Reason" contains an exposition of Polanyi's distinction between focal and subsidiary knowledge. He looks at medical diagnostics and scientific discovery and goes on to challenge the traditional division that is made between faith and reason (scientific knowledge being associated with the latter). In this it is supposed that reason proceeds by logical deduction or inductive generalization. Polanyi insists that our reasoning powers are void of meaning without a context of informal or tacit assumptions that we cannot fully articulate. Polanyi comments, "Once this is recognized, the contrast between faith and reason dissolves, and the close similarity of this structure emerges in its place."[63] Polanyi's task in this article is to draw attention to the harmony between faith and reason and to illuminate the continuities between scientific and religious knowing.

The scope of "Science and Religion" is somewhat broader. Here Polanyi rehearses the familiar themes of tacit and focal knowledge, indwelling, and the insights of Gestalt. However, he goes on to reiterate the themes of hierarchy and dual control, found in the latter part of *Personal Knowledge* and elsewhere, suggesting that "an adequate theory of knowledge must involve a true conception of man and the universe and be supported by it."[64] Polanyi's hierarchical ontology leads on, he believes, to a cosmic vision that may resonate with some of the basic teachings of Christianity. Polanyi suggests: "If this project succeeds, it would achieve a more satisfactory reconciliation of human convictions than would the acknowledgement of strictly separate dimensions for science and religion."[65] Here, as in "Faith and Reason," Polanyi wishes to demonstrate "the close neighbourhood of science and religion to which a [i.e., Polanyi's] revised theory of knowledge leads us."[66]

---

60. First published in Polanyi, "Faith and Reason," subsequently published in Schwartz, *Scientific Thought and Social Reality*, 116–30.

61. "Polanyi, "Science and Religion.""

62. "Polanyi Collection: Regenstein Library, University of Chicago," Box 42, Folder 11, dated July 1972.

63. Schwartz, *Scientific Thought and Social Reality*, 126.

64. Polanyi, "Science and Religion," 8. It must be acknowledged that it has not been possible to do justice to this aspect of Polanyi's philosophy in the present work.

65. Ibid., 11.

66. Ibid., 14.

The final piece is an essay entitled "About Religious Faith."[67] This was written at a time when Polanyi's mental powers were waning. Nevertheless, many familiar themes are present. In this paper he reflects on the disasters of European history, the phenomenon of moral inversion, the dangers of reductionism and the processes of tacit integration. However, in spite of the title, Polanyi barely touches on the matter of religion. It is only in the final paragraph of the paper that Polanyi tells us: "This is briefly what I wanted to say; namely that the progress of science is less significant for our fates and ways, as we are immersed in a system of emotional powers by which—or against and beyond which—lies all that we can do for the sake of men and their religious existence."[68] I must admit that I am not entirely clear what Polanyi means here, but he is clearly suggesting that religion has a weightier bearing than science on the meaning of human existence.

Evaluation

Working from Science to Religion

Polanyi, as philosopher, is tireless in developing epistemological themes and seeking to establish their significance across a broad range of concern. An important element in Polanyi's work is his desire to generalize.[69] This can be seen in the articulate systems of *Personal Knowledge* and the integration of incompatibles of *Meaning*. In the first passage of *Personal Knowledge* in which Polanyi deals with religious themes,[70] he considers mystical contemplation as a particular case of the general phenomenon of "breaking out" of an articulate system. He has considered the significance of this scheme for scientific discovery, now he is looking to apply it in other spheres. In the second passage[71] he considers the nature of doubt and indwelling in relation to Christian worship, having reflected on the theme of belief and doubt and upon its significance in scientific progress. In *Meaning* the theme of integration of incompatibles, as a particular form of tacit integration, is applied to religious practice, having been expounded in relation to art, metaphor, and myth.[72] I have also offered a very brief exposition of three articles which, while purporting to address the theme of faith and religion, do not in fact deal with it in any substantial way.

---

67. "Polanyi Collection: Regenstein Library, University of Chicago," Box 42, Folder 11. This is an unpublished paper.

68. Ibid., 8.

69. Polanyi's tendency is to generalize beyond the realm of natural scientific work on the basis of insights that he has established within it.

70. See Polanyi, *Personal Knowledge*, 195–202.

71. Ibid., 279–86.

72. See Polanyi and Prosch, *Meaning*, 149–60.

Polanyi, as a systematizer, comes to religion with a generalizing scheme in hand—a scheme that is, more often than not, derived from his work in science.[73] He never starts with religion, religious belief, or Christianity as phenomena, nor does he appear to derive his generalizing schemes (or interpretive frameworks) from an indwelling of the religious life. Polanyi typically starts with the nature of scientific knowledge and it is here, primarily, that his ideas emerge.

One must not forget that for the first half of his working life, Polanyi was a physical chemist, a scientific researcher and, indeed, a researcher of international repute. Polanyi knows about science from his deep engagement with it and when he raises epistemological questions in relation to science it must be said, emphatically, that he knows what he is talking about (c.f. the biographical comment on Polanyi made by Marjorie Grene and quoted in the previous chapter). This is undoubtedly one of the reasons why his philosophizing, insofar as it relates to science, is strongly *a posteriori*. But when he deals with religion, he is far less grounded in his subject matter, and the systems and schemes that he has developed, largely in the context of the sciences, can become overly prescriptive.[74]

Polanyi's Failure to Do Justice to the Phenomenon of Religion

Polanyi gives the appearance of being wary of dealing with the phenomena of religious faith, practice, and tradition in a direct way.[75] When Polanyi refers to religious themes, he is often following up a theme that has already been established in another context,[76] or demonstrating the degrees of continuity in the way that we come to know across religion and science, faith and reason. In both endeavors, the phenomenon of religious belief and practice is typically truncated or completely ignored.

In *Personal Knowledge*, Polanyi describes the search for God in terms of his theory of heuristic passion. But the desire to "discover" God must be distinguished from others because it is a desire which cannot be fulfilled. It is the

---

73. In his later writing, especially in *Meaning*, certain forms of schematization are drawn from his comparatively brief (though by no means insignificant) engagement with the study of metaphor, art, and myth.

74. An example of Polanyi's prescriptive method is to be found in his treatment of the sacrament of Holy Communion in *Meaning*. Quite apart from his bizarre description of how the rite developed, in which he makes no attempt to engage with ecclesiological accounts, his suggestion that Holy Communion integrates various incompatible meanings of food (including a positive nutritional one for our bodies and a negative spiritual one for our souls) owes everything to his *a priori* scheme and very little indeed to any meaning that has been attributed to it by the church or theology.

75. When Polanyi speaks of religion, he seems, more often than not, to be referring to the Christian religion. This is typically implicit—particularly in his later writings—but there are occasions when he makes explicit reference to Christianity. He does, very occasionally, refer to Zen Buddhism, but it may be assumed that a reference to religion is a reference to Christianity unless he states otherwise.

76. An example of this would be "breaking out" in *Personal Knowledge*. See Polanyi, *Personal Knowledge*, 195–99.

discovery that can never be made. I do not deny that what he says may have some resonances with the kinds of things that might be said from within the religious traditions, but, nevertheless, it is woefully inadequate. For example, from within the Christian tradition, the theme of ongoing pilgrimage must be balanced by those of God's acceptance, of knowledge of God, and of the comfort of the Holy Spirit. There is insufficient space (and, in all honesty, I do not think it is appropriate or worthwhile) to make detailed criticisms of what Polanyi does say about religion. In place of this I will make some summary remarks.

A central and surprising weakness in Polanyi's treatment of religion is his failure to recognize the corporate nature of its life and dissemination. This is a surprising failing because Polanyi's understanding of the communal aspects of science is acute. Indeed, his appreciation of the dynamics of the inculcation of skills, connoisseurship, and the importance of the social coefficient of knowledge as these function in science cries out for consideration in his treatment of religion, but Polanyi fails to make the connections.[77]

If we are to take Polanyi's comments on religion to refer primarily to the Christian faith, a further set of issues come into focus. Where, in Polanyi's exposition, do we hear of incarnation? Where do we find an acknowledgement of the God of revelation or the work of the Holy Spirit? Where does Polanyi explore the authority of Holy Scripture, the creeds, and confessions of the church? He may touch on such matters in passing, but they play no formative part in his analysis of religion. It seems that Polanyi tends to subsume Christianity under a generic "religion."

It has been debated at some length whether, for Polanyi, God exists independently of our thought about him.[78] I doubt whether Polanyi sustained a consistent position on the question. But, to the extent to which a positive response can be given, Polanyi's God is one who may allow us to search for him but is hardly a God who takes the initiative—a God who searches for us: a God of prevenient grace.

An Emerging Theme

Despite the serious inadequacies of Polanyi's treatment of religion, one is often left with a sense that Polanyi has a positive disposition towards religion and to Christianity in particular. For periods of his life he attended Christian worship and he was part of J. H. Oldham's group, the *Moot*—which was largely comprised of Christian intellectuals. He had many Christian friends and acquaintances—

---

77. To the general observation that Polanyi pays little heed to the Christian traditions when speaking about the phenomena of Christian faith I would add that his failure to perceive the importance of community and the traditions of the community at this point is likely the result of the great emphasis which he places on the mystical tradition. (Polanyi has a highly individualistic interpretation of *this* tradition.)

78. See, for example, the articles in *Zygon* 17 (1982) 3–87.

Oldham among them—and in later life he developed a friendship with T. F. Torrance, who became his literary executor. As we have seen, Polanyi had associations with Paul Tillich and worked closely with theologian Richard Gelwick towards the end of his life.

I think that Polanyi's positive disposition towards religion and Christianity is discernable both in the general trajectory of some of his arguments and in certain specific comments. As we have already noted, the thrust of both "Faith and Reason" and "Science and Religion" is to challenge the belief of modernity that the ways of knowing in faith and reason, and science and religion, are fundamentally distinct. Polanyi's epistemology illuminates the role of belief in scientific knowledge and offers a radical critique of science conceived as an impersonal, value-free, and objective endeavor. Polanyi shows that there is a greater degree of continuity between religious and scientific knowledge than has generally been acknowledged.

As I have already suggested, Polanyi is concerned with ontology as well as epistemology. His hierarchical ontology affirms an essentially meaningful universe. Although I have not been able to expound this aspect of Polanyi's work, it is implicated in his treatment of religion. For Polanyi, perhaps *the* key to religion, as he sees it, is its affirmation, in its narrative myths, of a meaningful universe. He sees this affirmation running contrary to a dominant reductionistic and materialistic modern view that denies such meaning. It is precisely because of its affirmation of meaning that religion is rendered unpopular in the modern situation.

Polanyi sees religion as disempowered, but entertains the thought that if the distortions of modernity are corrected, it may emerge, once more, as a force. This view is underlined in the last paragraph of *The Tacit Dimension*. Polanyi, reflecting upon humanity's need for a purpose bearing on eternity, writes: "Perhaps this problem cannot be resolved on secular grounds alone. But its religious solution should become more feasible once religious faith is released from pressure by an absurd vision of the universe, and so there will open up instead a meaningful world which could resound to religion."[79] This theme of paving the way for religion finds a strong echo in *Meaning*. In his last book, Polanyi concludes his consideration of the theme of religion by commenting that it "is not directed toward effecting conversions to any religion. At the most, it is directed toward unstopping our ears so that we may hear the liturgical summons should one ever come our way."[80]

Polanyi's affirmation of religion is an affirmation of religion's claim that the universe is meaningful. In the light of this, it is not difficult to see why he believes that (in an indeterminate and indirect way) he is working in the service of the emancipation of religion. As such it is, perhaps, unsurprising that Polanyi is happy to speak about religion without distinguishing between different religions

---

79. Polanyi, *Tacit Dimension*, 92.
80. Polanyi and Prosch, *Meaning*, 180.

and speaks specifically of the Christian faith while paying scant attention to its traditions of practice and doctrine. R. L. Hall makes the concomitant complaint that Polanyi's writing on religion is insufficiently grounded in history. "If we are thinking of religion in the historical sense, that is, of the Western experience, especially the Judaeo-Christian tradition, then Polanyi's account of religion simply will not do."[81]

Polanyi's interest in religion may have a particular kind of validity, but it must be acknowledged to be highly idiosyncratic. More particularly, it cannot be said to be an approach which is born out of an indwelling of any particular religious tradition, which one would expect to be the *sine qua non* of a "Polanyian" contribution to religious or theological understanding.

Polanyi and Theology

Having offered an exposition and evaluation of Polanyi's comments on religion, it is necessary to proceed to assess the possibilities of Polanyi's work for theology in anticipation of the more specific task of considering how his theory of knowledge might contribute to a doctrine of revelation.

It is clear why Polanyi has had a significant influence among theologians.[82] In both his employment of certain terms (such as "faith," "belief," "commitment," etc.), and his attack on various dualisms ("faith and reason," "science and religion," etc.) his contribution is a congenial one. However, because of his failure to deal in any adequate way with the phenomena of religious life and thought, and his tendency to approach religious themes in the light of *a priori* conceptualities forged in the crucible of his engagement with scientific thought,[83] he can disappoint the theological reader of his work.

It is not surprising that there has been a contentious debate about what Polanyi believed about religion.[84] As we have noted above, there have been disagreements about whether or not Polanyi held a realist understanding of the existence of God. Even close collaborators came to quite different conclusions about Polanyi's personal Christian convictions, and this is illustrated by the comments of T. F. Torrance and Harry Prosch.[85] On the one hand, Torrance writes of Polanyi's "deep Christian commitment influenced particularly by St Paul's teaching about

---

81. Hall, "Michael Polanyi on Art and Religion," 17.

82. One list of theologians influenced by the work of Polanyi is found in Dulles, "Faith, Church, and God: Insights from Michael Polanyi." See the first two footnotes of this article.

83. And to this we must add, with respect to *Meaning*, more perfunctory engagements in the study of art, myth, and metaphor.

84. See, in particular, the extended discussion in *Zygon* 17 (1982) 3–87.

85. Both were writing of their personal engagement with and experience of Polanyi when he was living in Oxford in the 1970s.

redemption and Augustine's stress upon faith as the door to understanding."[86] On the other hand, Prosch comments: "At one point Polanyi did seem to think of himself as a fully practicing Christian. When I knew him he obviously was not one."[87]

Martin Moleski is surely correct when he writes: "Because of Polanyi's lack of formal training in theology and because of his independence from any particular Christian tradition, it may be somewhat unfair to expect precision and clarity from him in his reflection on religious issues."[88] My opinion is that any kind of inquiry that seeks to get to the consistent heart of Polanyi's position, or to establish Polanyi's position in relation to one strand or other of the Christian faith is fundamentally flawed. While Polanyi sees the significance of religion for his work and, conversely, sees significance in his work for religion, these are not explored in relation to any explicit understanding of religion or (and more significantly) from any deep commitment to—or indwelling of—any particular religious tradition.

The great strength of Polanyi as a philosopher derives from his profound knowledge of science from the perspective of an accomplished practitioner. This rich engagement in science must be contrasted with Polanyi's comparatively sparse involvement in the Christian church and its theological traditions. He did have some knowledge of Christian worship and was aware of the work of a small number of theologians—notably Paul Tillich—but Polanyi's participation in and knowledge of these was very limited.

Polanyi's explicit engagement with religion and theology does not have a great deal to offer the theologian, but this should not yield the conclusion that his work, as a whole, is to be disregarded by the theologian. Moleski makes the point that "one may have an epistemology like Polanyi's but not share his theology."[89] This is because "The theological implications of epistemology derive from additional *assumptions* about the nature of divine reality and the possibility and content of divine revelation."[90] Additionally, and significantly, a "Polanyian theology"[91] ought also to draw upon the forms of life and practice *as they are* found in the Christian church.

Polanyi's work has much to offer the theologian. However, the *way* in which Polanyi is taken up in theology must, in my estimation, be subjected to careful methodological scrutiny. Any discipline must allow its methods to be formed and

---

86. Torrance, "Michael Polanyi and the Christian Faith—A Personal Report," 28.

87. Prosch, "Polanyi's View of Religion in *Personal Knowledge*: A Response to Richard Gelwick," 46–47.

88. Moleski, *Personal Catholicism*, 142.

89. Ibid. Although Polanyi deals with certain theological issues, we would question whether Polanyi has a "theology." Nevertheless, Moleski's point on epistemology is well made.

90. Ibid., 143; Moleski's emphasis. I would be cautious about using the term "assumptions" in this context since it might imply an *a priori* conceptuality.

91. By which I mean something like "the kind of theology that Polanyi ought to have written"!

to develop in response to the object of its concern.[92] Theology, too, must adopt a methodology wherein it is faithful to its object, and to the extent to which theology does this, it might be regarded as a science. Indeed, according to Karl Barth, "The only way which theology has of proving its scientific character is to devote itself to the task of knowledge as determined by its actual theme and thus to show what it means by true science."[93] As such theology does not forsake its theme by subjugating or correlating it to the concerns of the natural sciences but ascribes the epithet of "science" to theology precisely because it is faithful to its object and is so in a rigorous and *a posteriori* way.

Much more could be said about the "object" of theology. I would certainly want to point to the importance of the church as the community of believers and the significance of participation in that community with its biblical, creedal, and doxological heritage and its various forms of life. Christian theology is reflection upon, and a humble attempt to purify and clarify, the church's language and practice, which it ventures in response to the ways in which God has made himself known.

Polanyi's religious and theological views, even if they can be understood as a coherent whole, certainly cannot be received uncritically. Indeed, if my evaluation of his contribution in this sphere is correct, it might be better if they were set aside. But Polanyi's epistemological insights are of a different order. It may be that many of them were established in relation to the concerns of the scientific community, but they illuminate philosophical distortions deeply rooted in the contours of Western thought. Such distortions do not cease at the doors of the church or the desk of the theologian. Polanyi may not have done a good job in establishing the significance of his epistemological insights in theology and religion but this does not mean that the job *cannot* be done.

The task of theology is a human one, although it must contend with God's self-revelation, and it cannot hold God in its hand as capital. It must deal with revelation—recollecting the ways in which God has made himself known and thereby transformed and shaped the life, thought, and language of a community. It must utilize language, concepts, and philosophies that are ready to hand and it must develop practices that facilitate participation in what God has made known. Of course there is nothing absolute about any of these things: they will always be imperfect and inadequate for the task, and they must be adapted, transformed in responsiveness to their source. Theology's task is, inevitably, an ongoing one. If Polanyi has identified errors into which Western patterns of thought have fallen, his corrective will be of importance for theology to the degree to which it has itself fallen into the same errors.

---

92. This is perspicuously absent in Polanyi's approach to religion.
93. Barth, *Church Dogmatics I/1*, 10.

Polanyi believes that in taking up Augustine's motto *nisi credideritis, non intelligitis*, he is returning to something that has been lost. He also realizes that he is drawing from the wisdom of the Christian tradition even if he knows relatively little about its context. Trevor Hart makes the point that in drawing on Polanyi's thought, "we are reclaiming insights and emphases once borrowed from Christian theology, but which in the climate of modernity, theologians themselves have too often been afraid to own."[94]

Polanyi, drawing on his profound experience in science, provides profound insights into the epistemic processes involved in scientific life and work at a time when the scientific community's self-understanding had been significantly distorted by the contributions of the philosophy of science. He recognized that in his endeavor to establish and justify the nature of scientific knowledge, he must consider many fields outside of science. One may wish that when Polanyi came to consider theology, he might have brought the same depth of insight. However, it must be frankly acknowledged that Polanyi was not sufficiently equipped for such a task. Nevertheless, Polanyi's project—if it is conceived primarily as one of epistemological correction—*can* be fruitfully employed in theological studies, as I will now seek to demonstrate.

---

94. Hart, *Faith Thinking*, 49.

CHAPTER 4

Barth and Polanyi
in Conversation

Introduction

IN CHAPTER TWO I suggested that in Karl Barth's exposition of revelation in the early volumes of *Church Dogmatics* the themes of "response" and "participation," though present, are understated. It is important, for the purposes of this work, to demonstrate the importance of such human involvement if Barth's theology and the epistemology of Michael Polanyi are to be brought into conversation. Since this proposal, upon which I depend, has been contested by some scholars it is appropriate to pause before proceeding to consider the kinds of criticism of Barth in which the validity of such an approach may be called into question.

In his description of revelation, Barth will typically speak of the freedom and sovereignty of God on the one hand, and human impotence (indeed, opposition) on the other. Such a view is evident in a comment made by Barth noted in the first chapter: "When revelation takes place, it never does so by our insight and skill, but in the freedom of God to be free for us and to free us from ourselves, that is to say, to let His light shine in our darkness, which as such does not comprehend His light. In this miracle, which we can only acknowledge as having occurred, which we can only receive from the hand of God as it takes place by His hand, His kingdom comes for us, and this world passes for us."[1] Is there a place for human response or participation in revelation conceived in this way? On the basis of such a statement alone, it might seem that human response may be affirmed but limited to one of "acknowledgement." It is not immediately clear how a place for human participation can be established since, according to Barth, there "is something God Himself must constantly tell us afresh . . . [T]here is no human knowing that

---

1. Barth, *Church Dogmatics* I/2, 65.

corresponds to this divine telling."² Ronald Thiemann, in many ways a sympathetic interpreter of Barth, writes:

> Barth is so insistent that God's revelation takes place only when and where the sovereign God chooses that he sunders every connection between human speech and divine revelation other than that which God creates in the very act of revelation. Consequently there can be no grounds for Christian truth-claiming other than God's gracious electing will. From Barth's point of view theological justification of God's prevenience demands not an intellectual *inquiry* but simply a faithful *acknowledgement* of God's gracious revelation when and where it occurs.³

Thiemann shares one of Barth's concerns that theology must distinguish clearly between the Word of God and innate "fallen" human capacities, and that it must resist any temptation to correlate them. But Thiemann "cannot follow . . . [Barth's] radical disjunction between human speech and divine reality."⁴ Thiemann believes that the price Barth's approach has paid is too high: "[it] 'solves' the problem of revelation, viz., the relation of God to human concepts and categories, by severing all relations between the two and taking refuge in the miracle of grace to bring them together."⁵ Thiemann's counter-suggestion is that while no innate connection between human concepts and divine revelation should be sought, "Christian faith demands that once God has claimed a piece of creaturely reality as his own and bound himself to it, then we are warranted in accepting the God-forged link between the human and divine."⁶

There are two lines of response to Thiemann that I would like to take up. The first is a counter-contention: if Barth paid the high price of severing the connection between God and human conceptions of him, it was in response to the high price the liberal tradition had paid for asserting "God-forged links between the human and divine." It was on the basis of such claims that many of Barth's theological teachers sought to justify German engagement in the First World War, and it was the acceptance (on the part of the German church and, in particular, its theologians) of German nationalism (which would emerge as a devastating force again in the 1930s) that precipitated Barth's departure from the theological tradition in which he had been nurtured.⁷ The association of the will of God

---

2. Barth, *Church Dogmatics* I/1, 132.

3. Thiemann, *Revelation and Theology*, 95. Thiemann's emphasis. Against Thiemann it might be said that Barth's *Church Dogmatics* (which is surely to be understood as a response to God's grace at some level) is more aptly described as an "inquiry" than an "acknowledgement"!

4. Ibid.

5. Ibid.

6. Ibid.

7. For a biographical account and theological comment on these events see McCormack, *Karl Barth's Critically Realistic Dialectical Theology*, esp. 111–17.

and a national identity is possible without recourse to the concept of "an innate human capacity," but the key question is not whether the capacity is innate, but whether revelation is considered to be at the disposal of human conceptuality. Once such a claim is made, God's "revelation" becomes a human possession, and God is no longer free in it. This is undoubtedly the kind of counter-criticism that Barth would make to Thiemann.

A second line of response is to ask whether Thiemann's criticism is adequate given other emphases that we find in Barth. Thiemann claims that Barth "sunders every connection between human speech and divine revelation other than that which God creates in the very act of revelation," and that, as a consequence there are no enduring God-forged links between the human and the divine. In response to this, several things may be said. Firstly we must say that because revelation is an event in which God establishes a relationship—and not a datum that is passed from God to humanity—Thiemann is correct in claiming that Barth denies that in revelation God is "bound to a piece of creaturely reality," if by that we imply that God's revelation can become a possession. For Barth the life of faith is one in which the relation between God and creature must be constantly renewed. The believer lives in recollection of God's past revelation and in expectation of his future revelation. But does this, of necessity, imply that the only possible human response to revelation is one of acknowledgement? While acknowledgement may be the first response, it is apparent that Barth believes that much more can be said.

Contrary to Thiemann's claim, there is a clear sense in which Barth *does* uphold a connection between human speech and divine revelation. As we noted in chapter 2, he insists that there is a positive relationship between revelation and human concepts. While we cannot claim parity between the two, Barth explicitly rejects any view which would assert total disparity. What *can* be said of God in the event of his revelation in Barth's view is something positive, but partial. Furthermore, it is not possible to say *how* our words and concepts relate to God. God may reveal himself—and we may participate in the event in which this happens—but we cannot, as it were, observe our participation as if we were outside it. And yet it would be precisely this kind of perspective that would be necessary in order to determine the relationship between it and our words and concepts. T. F. Torrance illuminates the nature of the problem when he writes: "[E]ven in revelation what is revealed remains mystery for it is not the kind of reality that can be brought under our human controlling or dividing and compounding—it transcends us and remains exalted far above us even in being revealed and apprehended."[8]

Thiemann's criticism reflects a reading of Barth that firmly rules out the kinds of human participation which, at various places in the first three part volumes of *Church Dogmatics*, Barth explicitly rules in. It may be noted here (as it

---

8. Torrance, *Theology in Reconstruction*, 30.

was earlier) that Barth is, in large part, responsible for such misreadings. In the early volumes of the *Church Dogmatics* in particular, Barth's discussion of revelation is far more concerned to emphasize the sovereignty of God than to explore responsive human participation in his revelation. Nevertheless, the latter element is certainly not always absent.

It is appropriate to acknowledge that there may well be a tension within Barth's theology in that some of the statements that he makes about the sovereignty of God in his revelation do not easily mesh with other strands of his thought in which, for example, he explores the significance of the Word of God becoming a human word. It is not necessary to regard such tensions as inconsistencies although it is not difficult to see why others have done so.[9]

Thiemann's critique does highlight this tension in Barth's doctrine of the Word of God, but the solution he proffers will lead back to exactly the kinds of difficulties from which Barth fought to extricate theology. I would contend that a more satisfactory development of the doctrine is to be found in an essentially sympathetic reading of Barth in which the kinds of human participation in the revelation of God of which he does speak are both extended and more fully stated.

We have considered at some length criticisms of Barth that imply that his description of revelation precludes the possibility of a responsive human participation in it. In response, an attempt has been made to show that Barth's description of revelation is not inconsistent with such a possibility. It is apparent that Barth's primary task in describing revelation in the early sections of *Church Dogmatics* is polemical to a significant degree, and by it he wishes to differentiate his own position from the liberal position against which he had reacted. He wants to emphasize that revelation is God's self-presentation to humankind and that, as such, it cannot become a human possession: it cannot be captured or controlled. However, this does not in fact preclude the possibility of our participation in it.

The situation is clarified to a considerable degree when we turn from Barth's theological—we might say "theoretical"—treatment of revelation to a consideration of his own employment of it elsewhere in his dogmatics. When we consider a work of the scope of *Church Dogmatics*, it is certain that we are dealing with more than an *acknowledgement* of revelation. But are we to conceive of Barth's

---

9. In reading Barth's *Church Dogmatics* it is appropriate, and indeed necessary, to bear in mind that his project is one which is carried out in conscious contradistinction to the theologies of liberalism in which he had been nurtured. Barth's doctrine of revelation is, as well as being a constituent part of his dogmatics, the principal locus within which he is able to explicate the distinctiveness of his line of approach *in the context of the theological and ecclesial ethos in which it was written*. I would contend that to read *any* theological dogmatics as timeless and context-less truths can only hinder the reader's ability to understand an author's intention. In a situation in which a substantial and radical challenge is being offered to the dominant contours of theological discourse—as was the case during the writing of the early volumes of *Church Dogmatics*—one might expect these issues to be of greater significance. In my opinion, Thiemann has been insufficiently sensitive to this issue in his interpretation of Barth's doctrine of revelation and has, consequently, failed to grasp the coherence of Barth's position.

dogmatic work as something other than a participation in revelation? To the contrary: Barth seeks to produce a dogmatic work in response to what God has made known in his revelation. *As such, it is entirely appropriate to conceive of his writing as a participation in revelation.*

Bringing Barth and Polanyi into Conversation

One point that I have emphasized in my discussion of Polanyi's epistemology is that his description of the way in which knowledge comes about is deeply rooted in his own experience of scientific research. Polanyi believes that the account that we offer of how we come to know things ought to derive from a reflection upon the way in which those things have come to be known. In other words, his method is *a posteriori*. It is noteworthy that Polanyi's insights are typically less secure when he ventures to speak of areas away from science in which his personal participation is less sure footed. In the excursus that precedes this chapter, it was noted that this is the case when he deals with theology and religion.

It has been my contention that Polanyi's restricted participation in the life of the church and theology inevitably placed a severe limitation upon his contribution in this sphere. Although I am convinced that his epistemological insights have the potential to sharpen theology's self-understanding, "One cannot deduce theology from epistemology any more than one can deduce omelettes from eggs."[10] And so I have sought to discern the significance of Polanyi's insights in the context of a more adequately articulated theology. In attempting this, I have delimited the task by focusing upon the doctrine of revelation, and I have taken Barth's doctrine of the Word of God as my point of departure.

Two significant reasons for choosing Barth as my primary representative theologian are his considerable emphasis upon the doctrine of revelation and his commitment to develop an *a posteriori* dogmatics. In this latter emphasis, it is possible to discern a methodology that reflects some significant affinities to that of Polanyi, *in that* Barth wishes to speak of God *a posteriori* out of the knowledge of God.

Having noted this affinity, it is also important to acknowledge that the desire to claim the insights of Polanyi's philosophy (which is so deeply rooted in his concern for the physical sciences) for theology in general and for Barth's doctrine of revelation in particular is not without its problems. Indeed, the very basis upon which this is taken up has been confronted with challenges and warnings from within and without—which is to say from both Barth and his critics.

From within we are confronted by Barth's desire to establish a clear differentiation between theology and the sciences. At the outset of his *Church Dogmatics*

10. Moleski, *Personal Catholicism*, 139.

Barth issues an impassioned warning against the inclusion of theology among the sciences. He writes:

> Since the days of Schleiermacher, many encyclopaedic attempts have been made to include theology in the sciences. But the common objection may be made against all of them that they overlook the abnormality of the special existence of theology and therefore essay that which is radically impossible. The actual result of all such attempts has always been the disturbing or destructive surrender of theology to a general concept of science and the mild unconcern with which non-theological science, perhaps with a better sense of realities than theologians with their desire for synthesis, can usually reply to this mode of justifying theology.[11]

In responding to this anxiety of Barth, I want to make the point that my purpose in engaging with what may be described as a philosophy of science is not the *justification* of theology. I am not making an attempt to include theology under the same head as the other sciences (although I do not question that this has been done on many occasions and, no doubt, to bad effect, as Barth suggests). My purpose is to *consider* (i.e., not to *prescribe*) the ways in which we come to know things across the disciplines. There is no suggestion here of a commonality of approach. I freely acknowledge the distinctive themes of the various disciplines, and that the ways in which those themes are taken up ought properly to be determined by the nature of those themes. What I am attempting is to identify some quite fundamental distortions in the theory of knowledge that have been bequeathed to us by Enlightenment philosophy and which themselves serve to distort a properly differentiated approach in the various disciplines. This I believe to be Polanyi's contribution to a general epistemology. Consequently I can heartily agree with Barth in his assessment that "The only way which theology has of proving its scientific character is to devote itself to the task of knowledge as determined by its actual theme."[12] It is only as we compare the methods of theology and the natural sciences *as they are determined by their theme* that I wish to comment upon any similarities or dissimilarities that might be discerned. In adopting an *a posteriori* method, I necessarily rule out any *a priori* judgment about the presence or absence of similarities between the way in which we come to know things in theology and the natural sciences.

With regard to the challenges from without, I have already noted at several points that critics of Barth have suggested that his doctrine of revelation is so formulated that it represents an eclipse of all human forms of knowing, implying that, beyond the response of acknowledgement, there is nothing more to be said of an active and creative process by which we may engage in establishing a place

---

11. Barth, *Church Dogmatics I/1*, 10.
12. Ibid.

for human participation in revelation. I have rejected such a line of criticism and have offered my reasons. I will not repeat them now.

It is worth acknowledging, however, that in my discussion of Barth's doctrine of revelation, the emphasis has been placed upon methodological questions of how it might be possible to speak of participation in revelation in broadly "Barthian" terms. As such, I have not paid much attention to how Barth conceived the formation of human knowledge *as* participation in the revelation of God. It is to an illustration of such work in Barth's corpus that I now turn. Here I will present Barth operating as a theologian in pursuit of the truth and, in some very significant ways, as parallel to the scientist that Polanyi has in mind as he pursues the truth in his own discipline.

The work upon which I shall focus is Barth's treatment of church confessions.[13] This choice is of particular significance as Barth was very much involved in the drafting of the Barmen Declaration, which addressed vital issues for the church in the wake of the Nazi regime's rise to power in Germany in 1933. Although the Barmen Declaration has not generally been regarded as a confession of the church, it is clear that its intentions are not radically distinct from those of the theological confession. And, more to the point, it dealt with a matter of gravity that might mean life or death for members of the church to which it was addressed. In this section of *Church Dogmatics*, we see Barth reflecting upon confession as a particular and acute form of theological expression, with its venerable history in the church, and doing so as a practitioner.[14] This is an example of Barth's "responsive participation" in revelation, and one in which epistemological issues are to the fore.

My method, in this section, will be to represent Barth's description of church confession, and bring it into conversation with the insights of Polanyi's epistemology. I will attempt to show several things: a) parallel insights shared by Barth and Polanyi, b) points at which Barth's exposition might be helpfully developed in the light of Polanyi's work, and c) the distinctions to be made between theology and the natural sciences that derive from their distinct themes.

Reiteration of Barth's Method: Scripture and Revelation

For Barth, Holy Scripture is of paramount importance, not because it is revelation in and of itself, but because it witnesses to it. The authors do not speak of their spiritual wisdom (although they may have this); they speak of what has been revealed to them: "That which we have seen and heard." "Not every man can speak God's Word. For not every man has heard it. But those who have heard it can and

---

13. We will focus upon Barth, *Church Dogmatics* I/2, 620-60.

14. Barth had participated in the drafting of the Barmen Declaration less than four years before penning this passage of the *Church Dogmatics*.

must repeat it."[15] For Barth, Scripture, as this witness, "is like the unity of God and man in Jesus Christ."[16] It is creaturely, and yet it speaks with high authority because it speaks of the God who comes to it from beyond its own sphere. As the Bible witnesses to past revelation, so it promises future revelation and as we read and hear it, we may be drawn into participation in it. Barth insists that,

> [O]f itself the mere presence of the Bible and our own presence with our capacities for knowing an object does not mean and never will mean the reality or even the possibility of the proof that the Bible is the Word of God. On the contrary, we have to recognise that this situation as such, i.e., apart from faith, only means the impossibility of this proof. We have to recognise that faith as an irruption into this reality and possibility means the removing of a barrier in which we can only see and again and again see a miracle.[17]

Later, Barth expands: "the miracle which has to take place if the Bible is to rise up and speak to us as the Word of God, has always to consist in an awakening and strengthening of our faith."[18]

The eternal presence of Christ is concealed from us in our earthly existence. He is revealed in a sign expressed in the witness of apostle and prophet. But they are signs and human-temporal. They cannot stand by themselves for what they signify. Barth writes:

> [T]he act of their institution as signs requires repetition and confirmation. Their being as the Word of God requires promise and faith—just because they are signs of the eternal presence of Christ. For if they are to act as signs, if the eternal presence of Christ is to be revealed to us in time, there is a constant need of that continuing work of the Holy Spirit in the Church and to its members which is always taking place in new acts. If the Church lives by the Bible because it is the Word of God, that means that it lives by the fact that Christ is revealed in the Bible by the work of the Holy Spirit. That means that it has no power or control over this work. It can grasp the Bible. It can honour it. It can accept its promise. It can be ready and open to read and understand and expound it. All these things it can and should do. The human side of the life of the Church with the Bible rightly consists in all these things. But apart from these things, the human side of its life with the Bible can consist only in the fact that it prays that the Bible may be the Word of God here and now, that there may take place that work of the Holy Spirit, and therefore a free applying of the free grace of God.[19]

---

15. Barth, *Church Dogmatics I/2*, 491.
16. Ibid., 501.
17. Ibid., 506.
18. Ibid., 512.
19. Ibid., 513–14.

For Barth, "The door of the Bible texts can be opened only from within."[20] It is another matter whether we wait and knock at *this* door or whether we seek others. The very presence of the texts urges the former response: "The existence of the biblical texts summons us to persistence in waiting and knocking. Their concrete form is a challenge to concrete effort. We can sum up all that must be said on this point in the statement that faith in the inspiration of the Bible stands or falls by whether the concrete life of the Church and of the members of the Church is a life really dominated by the exegesis of the Bible."[21]

Barth is aware that in presenting the Word of God in this way, there is a danger that the Bible is asserted as the Word of God on the basis of *our* faith, and that allows insufficient emphasis upon the objectivity of the Bible as the Word of God. This is a danger and must be acknowledged as such, but it is unavoidable. There is no external criterion that can be appealed to. Barth suggests we must trust "that the action of God in the founding and maintaining of His Church, with which we have to do in the inspiration of the Bible, is objective enough to emerge victorious from all the inbreaks and outbreaks of man's subjectivity."[22]

In this we see a parallel with Polanyi's epistemology, which insists that *in the general case* our knowledge is based upon commitments (or "faith") that cannot be defended. This is why *in the general case*, Polanyi says, "Any enquiry into our ultimate beliefs can be consistent only if it presupposes its own conclusions. It must be intentionally circular."[23] And, consequently, "the whole of my argument is but an elaboration of this circle; it is a systematic course in teaching myself to hold my own beliefs."[24] Barth makes a strikingly similar comment when he writes of "the circle of our freedom which as such is also the circle of our captivity."[25]

Barth claims, "Certainly it is not our faith which makes the Bible the Word of God. But we cannot safeguard the objectivity of the truth that it is the Word of God better than by insisting that it does demand our faith, and underlie our faith, that it is the substance and life of our faith."[26] Barth goes on to say,

> we have to understand the inspiration of the Bible as a divine decision continually made in the life of the Church and in the life of its members. That it took place once for all in the resurrection of Jesus Christ and in the outpouring of the Holy Spirit, as the establishment of the Church, is not disputed. But this is known and acknowledged in its objectivity by the fact that we recollect and expect the same divine decision in the

---

20. Ibid., 533.
21. Ibid.
22. Ibid., 534.
23. Polanyi, *Personal Knowledge*, 299.
24. Ibid.
25. Barth, *Church Dogmatics I/2*, 535.
26. Ibid., 534.

preservation of the Church, and our own fellowship with Jesus Christ and in the Holy Spirit.[27]

At this point we must note an important distinction between theology and the natural sciences. For theology there is, and there always will be, a returning to the biblical witness with the expectation that in it God's Word will be spoken—God will make himself known in the church. It is not so with the natural sciences. In these sciences we do not always return to the same textual source. The works of Ptolemy, Copernicus, Kepler, Newton, Clark Maxwell, and Einstein reflect a greater or lesser degree of continuity with respect to each other and the lives, as well as the works, of such great thinkers remain inspirational for future generations of scientists. However, within the bodies of knowledge that evolve in the natural sciences, there is no fixed textual point to which the scientist must return, time and again, in the way that the theologian must return to Holy Scripture.

Although Holy Scripture is not in and of itself the revelation of God, Barth's clear intention is to suggest that we can have every expectation that the Word of God will be spoken to the church and to its members through it. Barth believes that it is precisely this for which the church and its members must pray, wait, and listen. We can also say that our participation in revelation is linked to Scripture in this way.

Barth's discussion of the confessions of the church presupposes that the Word of God *will* be spoken through the Scriptures. As we consider Barth's discussion of the confessions of the church, all that has been said in these introductory comments is presupposed. Here we find a theological practitioner reflecting upon the way in which the truth is established—as a human endeavor—in his own discipline. In this regard we find Barth engaged in his discipline in a way that parallels Polanyi in significant respects: the skilled practitioner describing what it is like to do the job.

Barth on Church Confession: A Polanyian Reading

It is Barth's belief that, notwithstanding time and place, the church confesses the same God who makes himself known in the Bible. This is the basis upon which the church can make a united confession and upon which it may seek to express a common faith. But what does Barth mean by "confession"? In venturing a definition, he writes: "A Church confession is a formulation and proclamation of the insight which the Church has been given in certain directions into the revelation attested by Scripture, reached on the basis of common deliberation and decision."[28]

The point of departure for Barth is the fact that God reveals himself. The first thing to be noted about Polanyi's epistemology is that it claims that this is how we

27. Ibid., 534–35.
28. Ibid., 620.

come to know *anything*.[29] It is necessary to pay careful attention to the nuances of Polanyi's critical realism. He distinguishes clearly between "real" and "tangible." What is tangible is real, but not all that is real is tangible. He speaks of the "profundity" of a reality. In comparing the profundity of a tangible cobblestone and a less tangible person he writes "Persons . . . are felt to be more profound, because we expect them yet to reveal themselves in unexpected ways in the future, while cobblestones evoke no such expectation."[30] Polanyi relates this to epistemic processes as he continues: "This capacity of a thing to reveal itself in unexpected ways in the future I attribute to the fact that the thing observed is an aspect of reality, possessing a significance that is not exhausted by our conception of any single aspect of it. To trust that a thing we know is real is, in this sense, to feel that it has the independence and power for manifesting itself in yet unthought of ways in the future."[31] This is the way in which Polanyi expresses the transcendence of "the real" in respect of any concept of it. Notwithstanding the veiling that is concomitant with the unveiling in God's self-revelation, it is the similarities, rather than the dissimilarities, that stand out in this comparison of the knowledge of God and the knowledge of other things.

Barth proceeds by expanding upon the characteristics of a confession explaining that "[It] involves the expression of an insight given to the Church. Holy Scripture has been given to the Church as the source of its knowledge of divine revelation. It is not individuals, or any group of individuals, but the Church itself, represented by those who can and must speak in its name, which has to give an account of its faith to itself and the world in the confession of the Church."[32]

Scripture, as the creaturely resource through which the Word of God is made known, has been given to the church. There are not many churches but one church, because the church proclaims the Word of God, and it must do so on the basis of the Scripture that has been given as a witness to this Word. Barth is conscious of the fallibility of what must be attempted. He writes: "There is no confession without . . . risk and danger. And obviously for those who venture to come before the Church with a confession, there is also the danger that they will have the witness of Holy Scripture in their favour, but that in the rest of the Church they will speak to deaf ears and therefore, isolated with the Word of God, they will necessarily be in their Church heretics and oddities, unauthorised innovators or even invincible reactionaries."[33] Barth suggests that "The courage to accept the

---

29. In the excursus, I remarked upon the irony that Polanyi adopted religious imagery to depict a self-revealing universe while denying the same kind of power to a self-revealing God.

30. Polanyi, *Tacit Dimension*, 32. While Polanyi is right in claiming that persons are more profound than cobblestones, he is wrong to imply (as he does here) that our knowledge of cobblestones is exhaustive, and that we can have no expectation to learn more of them.

31. Ibid. Polanyi's use of "observation" ought to be extended to include other forms of perception.

32. Barth, *Church Dogmatics I/2*, 622.

33. Ibid., 622–23.

risk involved is at least one test of the genuineness of their enterprise."[34] He says, in addition, "However limited and oppressed the authors of a confession may be in the church, if they really have to confess, i.e., to confess the Word of God, they cannot possibly dare to speak of themselves and from their own small corner, or in order to secure recognition for themselves and this corner."[35]

I shall consider the matter of fallibility later. Here I note the close parallels between these comments of Barth and Polanyi's conviction that the consummation of a scientific discovery is to be found in the embracing of that discovery by the scientific community. The claim of the scientist, who believes that he has made a discovery, is made with "universal intent." There can be no suggestion that the scientist has attained a private insight that will merely satisfy his or her own curiosity. The intellectual passions which gave rise to the new vision seek a response, and in the absence of such a response there is strife. "[W]e suffer when a vision of reality to which we have committed ourselves is contemptuously ignored by others."[36] Scientific discoveries are made, as Polanyi has shown, not through following an explicit, mechanistic procedure but through a passionate personal grappling with a problem. Furthermore, they are not made apart from the scientific community but through a profound participation or indwelling within it—in all its forms of life: theoretical, practical and social. For a discovery (which could only have been conceived of in the context of participation in such a community) to be rejected by fellow participants within the community can only be the source of much discomfort.

Barth writes, "The confession of the Church involves an insight which is given or gifted to the Church. This is bound up with the fact that it has not invented its content, but discovered it in Holy Scripture and as a gift of the Holy Spirit."[37] There is something of "the moment" in a confession. It is not a theological summary or synopsis but something of urgent concern to the whole church. "We can confess only if we must confess. Theological work of a theoretical or practical kind is not the instrument of this compulsion. Theological work as such is quite unable to produce a Church confession, although it is indispensable to its formation when a confession arises, and if it is serious its final goal must always be the Church's confession."[38] The situation that demands confession is not so much one in which the church discerns a truth but one in which the truth finds the church.

> If the Church's confession involves an insight given to the Church, then the confession cannot understand itself or rightly let itself be understood as an exposition of favourite ideas, or convictions, or the so-called reflections of

---

34. Ibid., 623.
35. Ibid.
36. Polanyi, *Personal Knowledge*, 150.
37. Barth, *Church Dogmatics I/2*, 624.
38. Ibid.

faith. It certainly rests on exegesis, but it is more than biblical inquiry. It certainly arises only with a dogmatic consciousness, but it will proclaim more than a theologoumena. It is certainly proclamation, but its power will not be only that of edification. The faith of its authors will be heard in it, but it will not be because of this subjective faith that it has a right to be heard.[39]

Here it seems that we find a contrast between the task of the church confessor and that of the natural scientist (although I think there is a parallel in respect of general dogmatic work). Nevertheless the participation of the confessor, like the scientist, involves the taking up of particular skills. A grounding in general theological work is, to adopt Barth's word, "indispensable." As a result, Polanyi's understanding of skills comes into view. In acknowledging that error is always possible, he distinguishes between two types of error. There is the error made by the one who participates deeply in the tradition in its practical and theoretical forms; and there is the error of one who does not so participate. The first kind of error is inherent in the human condition and in the ways in which we come to know, but those of the latter are "illusory and incompetent"—not as a result of a lack of intellectual ability (although this *might* be so), but because the one who makes them does not participate (by way of the skills that are implied in such a participation) in the relevant form of life.[40]

There is no sense in which the confession is sourced by human skills, but skills are necessary for its expression. One cannot make a church confession unless one is committed to the form of life that is to be found in the church, and unless one participates in the discipline of theology that seeks to serve it. Anyone claiming to speak to and for the church from outside such "commitment situations" would be, on that basis, discredited. Their voice would not deserve to be heard. Barth writes:

> The confession of the Church always involves the statement and expression of the insight given to the Church in definite limits. This limitation does not contradict either the intended universality of the confession or the certainty proper to it as Church dogma. On the contrary, it is in this very limitation that it is universal and Church dogma, and therefore has ecclesiastical authority.[41]

What Barth expresses here implies at least some part of the critique of objectivism we find in Polanyi's writing. How do we come to know things? We come to know things *as persons* and as persons existing at a particular time, in a particular place, and within particular communities. If such particularities (or "limitations," as Barth calls them), invalidated our efforts to acquire knowledge, there would be no knowledge. (The objectivist's standard of indubitable knowledge, implying some-

---

39. Ibid., 624–25.
40. This is precisely the kind of criticism which we have made of Polanyi with respect to his writing on theology and religion.
41. Barth, *Church Dogmatics* I/2, 625.

thing like a "view from nowhere," is an unattainable one for human knowing, as Polanyi has shown.) No. This is the way in which we *do* come to know things. The limitations are genuine limitations, but they provide us, at the same time, with our possibilities, and without them we can know nothing.

The particularities take many forms. There is the general socio-cultural context in which we are nurtured in early childhood—what Polanyi describes as our "calling." Barth says, "It cannot be denied that the definite limits which can be seen in all confessions stand in a constantly shifting relationship to political, cultural and economic groupings and movements."[42] But of prime significance in this context is the life of the church. In its concrete form, the life of the church manifests not only many continuities but also considerable diversity. But the source of its life does not. It is the Word that is made known in the church in its diverse forms through Holy Scripture. The power of the confession to unify the church is found in the Word of God.

What Barth does not say, but that which finds full expression in Polanyi's work, is that these particularities or limitations are "indwelt." Our knowledge of them is not, for the greater part, explicit but tacit. Because they are forms of life that we indwell, we do not attend *to* them, but *with* them, or *from* them. They become, to adopt Polanyi's description, an extension of our own bodies. Or, as was suggested in chapter 3, they represent the spectacles through which we see the world. Therefore, although we are able to say things about the forms of life that we indwell, much of what we know is tacit. Indeed, according to Polanyi, "All knowledge is . . . either tacit or rooted in tacit knowing."[43]

Confession arises in the context of conflict. Barth writes, "A Church confession with Church authority has always arisen in a definite antithesis and conflict."[44] It always has a pre-history. "It consists . . . in controversies in which the existing confession of the common faith and therefore the existing exposition and application of Holy Scripture is called in question because the unity of the faith is differently conceived, and there is such different teaching on the basis of the existing unity that the unity is obscured and has to be rediscovered."[45] As such, the church must express itself more precisely if it wishes to preserve unity.

The example of the theological liberalism of the eighteenth and nineteenth centuries is an interesting case in point. It saw itself in dialectical relationship with the conservative counter-movement. However, in face of opposition, "liberal toleration has, of course, usually reverted very quickly to a fairly extreme intolerance."[46] Barth sees this as inevitable: "How can it be otherwise than that

---

42. Ibid., 626.
43. Polanyi and Prosch, *Meaning*, 61.
44. Barth, *Church Dogmatics I/2*, 628.
45. Ibid.
46. Ibid., 629.

heresy, if only in the attenuated form of a general doctrine of toleration, should want to be not merely one opinion, but the doctrine of truth, the expression of Church unity, and that therefore it is bound to be intolerant whether it will or no?"[47] Consequently "The battle of confession must be waged . . . as a battle for the very substance, a battle for the life and death of the Church."[48] There is no question that there are battles and conflicts within the natural sciences, but such battles must be distinguished from those with which the church confession engages. The conflicts that emerge within science do not challenge the identity of the scientific community at the same depth. The confession confronts a challenge to the well-being of the church in a way in which the discoveries of a Newton or an Einstein (and the conflicts associated with them) do not challenge the well-being of the scientific community. This is a function of the fact that the identity of the church is sustained by the Word of God, as it returns time and again to the witness of Holy Scripture in a way unparalleled in science. The identity of science may be significantly changed by a Newtonian or Einsteinian revolution, but such discoveries are not only integrated into an enlarged scientific worldview but come to be seen as significant stages in the progress of science. In Polanyian terms, a new discovery, once established and integrated, becomes part of the tacit knowledge that is indwelt by scientists who venture to new insights. While new insights may be gained in the church (and old insights lost!), the idea of progress must be distinguished from the progress that is known in the sciences. There is a dogmatic core in the thought of the church which, were it surrendered, would be tantamount to the surrender of the Christian faith.

In order to think of a parallel in science to the kind of challenge to which the church confession responds, one would have to envisage a challenge to what we think of as modern science, as it has developed over several centuries, by a credible alternative. It is interesting to note that Polanyi considers this to be a serious possibility. Modern scientific knowledge is largely unspecifiable. It is passed from one generation of scientists to the next, from master to apprentice, through the transference of largely tacit skills. If this transference of *skills* was to be seriously interrupted, the seemingly unassailable position of modern science could be challenged. It is worth noting that Polanyi discerned such a challenge in the Soviet Union's co-option of science into the service of the Five-Year Plan. It is instructive to note that in attacking the totalitarian position and defending the freedom of science, Polanyi adopted a style that strongly resembles that of the church confession. It was impassioned, highly focused, and addressed to the widest possible audience. I think that the similarities are far from accidental.

Barth writes: "In the form of a decision a new expression of the old unity of faith must now be sought and found: an expression which brings out the other

47. Ibid.
48. Ibid.

way and direction, in which (unlike the representatives of the counter-doctrine) we find ourselves bound by Holy Scripture, an expression which makes manifest the judgment of Holy Scripture in the current controversy as the confessors claim to have heard it."[49] But he warns, "It is not a matter of an academic or an individual decision but before and behind the confession stands the actual life of the Church. Preaching and instruction will correspond to the confession. It is, therefore, a part of the recurrent worship and congregational life of the Church which is voiced in the confession."[50]

To speak in general terms, the kinds of conflict that arise in the natural sciences make only a modest impact upon the general population, regardless of the turbulence that they may cause within the scientific community. The issues implied in the genesis of a church confession, by comparison, are *typically* the concern not only of the theologically trained but of the person in the pew also. It is instructive to reflect upon some of the disturbances that have emerged within the Church of England, for example, that have troubled the British churches since the Second World War: The "Honest to God" debate initiated by Bishop John Robinson; the discussion of the nature of the resurrection of Jesus, initiated by Bishop David Jenkins; the debate about the ordination of women and, more recently, issues relating to human sexuality. All these issues have been the concern not just of clergy and theologians but of a great many other church members. Although these concerns have not been met by church confession, they illustrate ways in which issues that *might* become the concern of church confession touch the lives of the many and not only those of an intellectual sub-culture.

Barth does not disguise the inherently conflictual nature of the church confession. The confession expresses both a "Yes" and a "No." The confession speaks with conviction in the uncertainty and confusion of a particular contemporary situation to call the church back to clarity and unity on the basis of what the Word of God says through the witness of Scripture. It comes as an unwelcome word to those who defend the ideas or doctrines that are condemned. However, the confession is not expressed in order to destroy unity. Rather, it makes clear where, or on what basis, unity can be found. The confession must speak with authority. Barth writes: "If we have not the confidence (or the explicit confidence) to say *damnamus*, then we might as well omit the *credimus*, *confitemur*, and *docemus* and return to the study of theology as before. The time is not ripe for confession."[51] This all serves to highlight both the weight of a confession and the consequences that attend it. Is the *damnamus* pronounced not on the basis of the Word of God but on the basis of "strife of opinions and emotions"? A condemnation or, indeed, a false affirmation that is the expression of ephemeral human opinion will bring

49. Ibid.
50. Ibid.
51. Ibid., 630.

further danger to the church. There is danger on both sides because on either side the unity of the Church is threatened.

Since the confession is always occasioned by what the confessors take to be an error it is, inevitably, a *reaction*. Barth asks, "[D]oes not that limit the insight expressed in it—not to speak of the fallibility of its authors, the temporal limitation of their exegetical and dialectical methods, their power of self-expression? When we consider all these points together, the spatial, temporal and material limitations of all confessions, we may well ask how in these circumstances there can ever be any authority at all in any confession."[52] Might it not be the case that what is said in confessions may *all* be reduced to such limiting factors? Does not the whole enterprise collapse into a kind of cultural-cum-ecclesial relativity? Is it not all a matter of subjectivity or cultural relativism? Barth suggests that if we see things in such a way, we have not seen the positive human aspect: "It means that we have not yet understood this limitation as a mark of the particular humanity of the confession, and it is important that it should be understood in that way. The particular humanity of the Church's confession consists in the freedom, the joy of responsibility, the certainty and the love, in which it has always taken place in spite of the limits of those who make it."[53]

Such a response is strongly supported by Polanyi's affirmation of the personal and communal coefficient of our knowing. Knowledge, according to Polanyi, has no meaning apart from persons. And persons are only able to make truth claims out of the social and intellectual contexts which they indwell. Apart from such indwellings (that are, admittedly, limited and fallible), nobody would be able to say anything. A search for the truth arises out of a particular context for which we can make no *absolute* claims; but, Polanyi asserts, "I accept these accidents of personal existence as the concrete opportunities for exercising our personal responsibilities. *This acceptance is my sense of calling.*"[54]

It is out of this "calling" that we seek the truth. But our explorations, although facilitated by the limited perspectives that we inhabit, are not *determined* by them. In our search for the truth, we are confronted with a reality that, if we are to grasp it, must be allowed to shape the way in which we conceive it. We cannot say anything we like. We must say what we find ourselves constrained to say as we submit to the pressure that the reality exerts upon us—as we respond responsibly to that pressure. Our calling represents the "internal pole" of our knowing;[55] but this, in a responsible personal act, is brought into relationship with an "external pole," which is the reality which we seek to know. Because of the transcendent nature of this reality—its existence is independent of our knowledge of it—what

---

52. Ibid., 633–34.
53. Ibid., 634.
54. Polanyi, *Personal Knowledge*, 322; Polanyi's emphasis.
55. Understood communally rather than individualistically.

we say of it is not "free" but delimited by that reality. As a result, we speak of it with "universal intent." The confession in the church acknowledges the Word of God, as it is mediated to us through Scripture, as a reality which exists independently of our knowledge of it. What is said in confession must be responsible in its acknowledgement of this.

Polanyi's recognizes a sense in which all things can be known only insofar as they give themselves to be known—although he is well aware that this language is metaphorical. Polanyi distinguishes between the way in which, for example, inanimate matter reveals itself and the way human persons reveal themselves. We deal with much greater depth of reality in relation to the latter. Our knowledge of a person is significantly determined by what that person wishes to reveal of themselves. The subjective disposition of the object is of considerable significance. The doctrine of revelation—as it has been developed in the first two chapters—conceives of God as enclosed in his subjectivity in such a way that we may know him *only* insofar as he gives himself to be object to us and even then in the paradoxical ways of veiling and unveiling.

Barth suggests that if God's Word and will are the real subject of what happens in church history, a different picture arises: "If we . . . agree on this, then we will certainly not deny the varied limitations of all Church confessions, but we will also reckon with the fact that they have a meaning not only from below, but also from above, in the fact that it is the Word and will of God and not creaturely powers and forces which have imposed upon these confessions their different limits."[56] In this respect, we ought appropriately to speak of the *will* of God as the external pole of our knowledge of the Word of God. According to Barth, it is Holy Scripture that speaks to the church in this time and this place, or in that time and that place; this is the way in which the will of God, which is established above, is communicated. If we may speak of God's Word and will as the subject of the history, it is not unreasonable to think of church confession carrying the authority of the church in doing so. As Barth points out, the apparent paradox that the authority of the church resides "in the very thing which seems to compromise it, i.e., in the limitation which betrays its humanity."[57] What is human and limited is confronted, challenged and transformed in its responsive participation in the Word of God.

The authority of a confession is, and must be established, *within* such constraints. It will be clear enough whether a confession is of the Western or Eastern tradition, old or new, and it may also be possible to discern what particular ephemeral concern provides the focus for its expression. But if it is tested by Scripture—and therefore the Word and will of God—and if it bears the character of obedience, the perception of truth breaks through the contextual constraints

---

56. Barth, *Church Dogmatics I/2*, 635; this "limitation" is, of course, the church's "possibility."
57. Barth, *Church Dogmatics I/2*, 635.

(or limits). It may be seen that "the confession arose under the compulsion of a necessity, which as such was also a permission, that the limit of its insight is that marked out by the Word of God and therefore does not merely humble the confessors but strengthens and encourages them in the human venture of their *credimus, confitemur, docemus,* and also their *damnamus.*"[58]

There are strong resonances with Polanyi's position in what Barth is saying here. Both recognize that the communal aspect of our knowing is both essential and fallible, and both recognize the potential for transcendent realities to transform the ways in which we understand and speak of them (although Polanyi clearly does not acknowledge the Word of God as a reality as Barth does).

Barth believes that it is required of a confession that the majority of the Church members are able to affirm it, and consequently the discussion and conclusion that relate to it should be on "the widest possible basis." "A confession has to speak in the name of the Church and to the Church. Therefore two or three must be gathered together—with some order and willingly and publicly—if what is said is to be a confession."[59] Barth writes, "If there is no *consensus ecclesiae* there is no *ecclesia*, and therefore no *confessio ecclesiastica.*"[60]

However, if in the processes that led to the establishment of a confession, there is little order—indeed, if there is disorder and violence! (famously the case at Nicaea)—however deplorable this may be, it does not *per se* invalidate its outcome. "What really decides its authority is simply its content as scriptural exposition, which is necessarily confirmed or judged by Scripture itself. This content can impart something of its own value and significance even to a confession which is open to question on formal grounds."[61] This is not to say that the church ought to be unconcerned about the origination of a confession. Indeed, every effort must be made to establish orderly procedure. However, the force of the confession comes not from the good order in which it was initiated nor is the lack of force attributable to bad order. In each case the matter will be decided by whether what is said is confirmed in the church by the Word of God.

By the nature of the confession it is necessary that it is published as broadly as possible. "A confession demands publicity."[62] Once again, the challenge that is implied in it will not go away. "But where the confession is obedience, the anxiety implied in this question is removed, for it is self evident that the confession should be made public."[63]

---

58. Ibid., 636–37.
59. Ibid., 637.
60. Ibid., 638. Historically it seems that such a consensus can be extremely difficult to establish.
61. Ibid.
62. Ibid., 639.
63. Ibid., 640.

For confession, there is a question of whether it speaks the right word at the right moment with the right weighting. Barth states, "What is to be proclaimed by a herald has to be not only right but important."[64] Here Barth appears to be referring to an idea that parallels in some ways Polanyi's discussion of the way in which scientists identify important problems and attribute significance to facts. For Polanyi, it is the selective passion of the scientist (the "wise neglect" of many observations) that ensures that science does not become lost in a mass of trivialities. As confession is concerned with the Word and will of God, the decision cannot be reduced to the theological skill of the confessor; but for Barth, the theological skill of the confessor is certainly in view since he affirms that "There can be no confession without the background of solid, theological work."[65]

The seriousness of the confession must always be before us: "it says Yes and No—not as God says Yes and No, but in the human sphere, and yet in that sphere with an appeal to God Himself, and therefore with a definite assertion and denial of the unity of the Church, and with a definite indication in what sense and within what limits there is or is not fellowship with God."[66] The counter-pressure against the confession always represents a temptation. The desire for a quiet life and an easy peace may distract the confessor. But even to limit the degree to which the confession is published is tantamount to affirming that which is condemned within it.

> [W]ith all the mutual strangeness and division in the Church, where there is a real Church there is also an unbroken continuity between the Church then and now and an unbroken connexion between the Church there and here. There is no Church where fellowship is completely lacking in even one of these two dimensions, where in what appears to be a Church there are no fathers behind us and no brethren beside us. But having both, in both directions we hear the voice of a Church confession, within definite limits and on a definite road we take part in the story of the exposition and application of Holy Scripture, and we have therefore a definite responsibility to definite decisions made earlier and elsewhere in the Church.[67]

Our responsibility to the "fathers" and to the "brethren" is our responsibility before God in recognition of the fact that the truth that we seek, within the limited context of our particular historical and geographical situation, is the truth which was sought by those of other times and other places. Again, we note that the particular dynamic of the confession is to be distinguished from that which is operative in the natural sciences because across history and geography the confessor returns to the witness of Scripture. It is important to note, however, that

---

64. Ibid., 641.
65. Ibid.
66. Ibid., 643.
67. Ibid., 647.

there is a strong parallel insofar as the task of confession and the task of natural scientific work are tasks that are conducted within community. Barth writes, "No one has ever read the Bible only with his own eyes and no one ever should."[68]

When we think of confession in the present, we can and we must remember the other confessions of the church. What they say has a weight that we do not ascribe to other voices. The confession is not something that stands between the Word of God and the word of man, "but a human word figuratively ranked before all other human words."[69] Barth makes the barbed comment that "It is a pure superstition that the systematising of a so-called historico-critical theology has as such a greater affinity to Holy Scripture itself and has therefore in some sense to be heard before the Apostles' Creed or the *Heidelberg Catechism* as a more convincing exposition of the biblical witness."[70]

Barth believes that, after Holy Scripture, the confessions should be given first place in the church. When we have heard them, *then* we must be ready to hear other voices or draw from our own insight. But we must remember that in listening to the witness of the church confessions, what we say (having heard what we must hear) is still *our* responsibility. As the confessors (of whom we hear) fulfilled their responsibility in giving their reading of Scripture, we fulfill our responsibility with our own reading of the Scriptures. We are not bound to the confessions as to a law, but that does not mean that we do not respect them. They become, as it were, our starting point: "For at this point it takes a third and genuinely spiritual form. It becomes a constant antithesis, the horizon of our own thinking and speaking. Naturally, within this horizon it is a question of our own free thinking and speaking, for which we must bear the responsibility, which is not bound by any law except that of its object, and therefore only by Holy Scripture."[71]

This is the way in which Barth sets forth and also delimits the freedom in which we may move. We are not free to say what we wish. We must listen for the Word of God in Scripture. We must also listen to the previous confessions of the church—not as a final authority but as a venerable guide. We cannot seek the truth *as if* these confessions had not been spoken. As Barth puts it, "in this sphere we are not sovereign in the sense that we are alone, with no antithesis, no horizon. We cannot think and speak as in the absence, but only as in the presence of the confession."[72]

It is of considerable interest to note that Barth does acknowledge that the force of previous confession comes to succeeding generations of the church not only through explicit articulation. In what reflects at least part of a Polanyian insight,

---

68. Ibid., 649.
69. Ibid.
70. Ibid., 649–50.
71. Ibid., 651.
72. Ibid.

Barth acknowledges ways in which the confessional insights come to inhabit the tradition in less explicit forms, and exert their authority in such ways.[73] Barth writes:

> We can make this plain by the external fact that the Christian worship in which our own exposition and application of Holy Scripture is most solemnly expressed usually takes place not freely or in a neutral place, but in a "church" which even by its architecture and furnishings more or less directly and faithfully reminds those who gather in it . . . of their "confessional position." Even if it is mainly a witness to the helplessness of the 19th century the "Church" confronts us with Church history. And what happens in it happens not only in the presence of God and His angels, not only in the presence of the departed spirits of the past, but also—with whatever freedom and responsibility—in the presence of the confession, by which in strength or weakness, in loyalty or apostasy, our "Church" is this particular "Church." In the same way the hymn book which, good or bad, is always used in worship, confronts us with Church history. Together with the text of the Bible our own exposition and application of the word of the Church's praise is a third trigonometrical point, and at a varying distance behind it there always stands the Church's confession. Finally, even the order of worship can more or less definitely play the same role.[74]

In this way Barth does acknowledge that the explicit statement of the church confession does not exhaust its influence upon the church. He does discern, if not in a particularly developed way, that there are ways in which the confession confronts us indirectly. The force of the confession can be pervasive in its indirect forms. Barth explains:

> We cannot avoid this fact of the—noted or unnoted—presence of the Church's confession in every present aspect of the Church's life. If we think that we are so free or so committed that after hearing the confession we must go our own way independently of it, the confession does not cease, directly or indirectly to speak, *tacitly* opposing its word to our word, not as any kind of voice, but as the voice which has been peculiar to our Church from its inception and still characterises its being to this day.[75]

Barth is explicitly acknowledging that the confession, in its influence upon the church, cannot be limited to its form as an explicit statement. As such, he points, in some significant ways, towards an understanding of knowledge as an indwelling.

An important aspect of the church's confession is its ability to speak across the ages and geography. Despite the limitations of context and the particularity of the concerns of a confession, it has the potential to speak in the present. Barth asks,

---

73. It would be incorrect to imply, however, that Barth's acknowledgement of the tacit dimension reflects anything approaching the depth of treatment it receives in Polanyi's writings.

74. Barth, *Church Dogmatics I/2*, 651.

75. Ibid., 651–52; my emphasis.

"What can explain . . . [this] except that it is a document of obedience to the Holy Spirit of the Word of God and therefore an instrument of His power and His ruling?"[76] Our reception of the Word of God is both made possible and limited by the particularity of our calling. But despite the diversity of contexts out of which the church has listened for the Word of God in Scripture, the God who makes himself known in this way is the same God. Notwithstanding the significance of contexts in which the response to God's revelation is made, God's being shows through. What was received and expressed in the form of a confession "there and then" has authority "here and now" in that it is the same God who speaks and makes himself known through the witness of Holy Scripture. Barth suggests, "To have and be authority in this sense and therefore to confirm its imperative and binding and normative character, it needs only—but very earnestly—to be seen and understood as the silent but present antithesis of the Church's daily life, as the horizon within which—under the lordship of the Word of God—it is conducted."[77]

Barth insists that there is a unity in faith. The confession speaks of this unity, to the end that the church will find itself in it. The confessions of the church point to particular times and places where the way has been shown towards unity in the face of that which disturbed it. Barth points out that even when we feel compelled to hold to something apparently or actually opposed to a confession, the statement of the confession remains before us, with all its weight and authority. In this way it cannot be forgotten even though we feel unable to affirm or repeat what it says. It does not cease to affect us, and even in our opposition to it (at whatever point), we continue to respect it.

In making a distinction that again hints at the tacit dimension, Barth writes: "It is not by agreeing with these statements and appropriating them, but by learning the *direction* from these statements that we respect the authority of the confession."[78] Although Barth leaves us in no doubt that, after Scripture, he attributes to the confession the highest of human authority, it is, nevertheless, a *human* authority and fallible as such. Revelation is not captured in the confession. In speaking of the "direction" of the confession, Barth implies a *tacit* understanding that transcends what is *explicitly* stated in the confession. He is not simply pointing to the gap between the event of revelation and human reflection upon it (although this is certainly in view). He is suggesting that there is something to be discerned in the confession that is not fully articulated in the words, concepts, and propositions that it adopts. This is what Polanyi would call our tacit understanding, and the way in which Barth expands upon this theme only lends support to such an interpretation. Barth proceeds to suggest that there are times when we

---

76. Ibid., 653.
77. Ibid.
78. Ibid., 655; my emphasis.

must depart from the confessions in some—or even many—of their statements out of a discernment of this "direction." He writes:

> A certain positive criticism of the confession cannot be avoided when we respect its authority, when therefore we go further in the direction indicated by it, and therefore in our own responsibility in relation to the Church in the here and now. Even if there is no cause to oppose them directly, its statements have at all points to be extensively interpreted. They have to be read with underlinings and emphases and accentuations which they never had then, which they do not have when considered "historically," but which they necessarily acquire when they are the antithesis and the horizon of the present-day Church. The necessity of this positive criticism of the confession may lead to the emergence of a new confession, i.e., a confession which repeats the old one according to the new knowledge of the present-day Church. This is not merely reconcilable with the authority of the confession, but may even be demanded in some way by the authority of the confession as rightly understood, in that it does not bind us to itself but to Holy Scripture, in that it does not challenge us primarily to agreement with its statements, but to persistence in the unity of faith and only for that reason and in that sense to agreement with its statements.[79]

In this statement it is the limitations of the confession that come to the fore. Everything that the church may say comes under the limit of a particular time and place. The problem is not that we can never ascribe to a confession the status of an infallible authority. Perfection is not reached within the limits of our temporal strivings. Barth writes: "in practice we have to recognise that every Church confession can be regarded only as a stage on a road which as such can be relativised and succeeded by a further stage in the form of an altered confession. Therefore respect for its authority has necessarily to be conjoined with a basic readiness to envisage a possible alteration of this kind."[80]

In view of what has been said of the confessions—and of the many ways in which what they imply has shaped the church's life—we may appropriately adopt Polanyi's language of indwelling. In listening for the Word of God in Scripture in the "here and now," we do not focus *on* the confessions;[81] we focus *with* or *through* them. This is the way in which, according to Polanyi, the scientist relates to the body of scientific theory upon which he draws in order to make a new discovery. He or she does not look *at* it, but *with* it. I contend that there is a parallel here with the church confessions. The confessions provide the "spectacles" that we wear in approaching Holy Scripture.

---

79. Ibid., 656.
80. Ibid., 658–59.
81. This is impossible not least because our understanding of them transcends what we are able to say about them.

But, as Polanyi points out, in addition to the need for a scientist to indwell a body of scientific theory, there is also a desire to "break out." The theories upon which we typically depend in order to come to new understandings are fallible and may be mistaken. Polanyi suggests that it is in contemplation (i.e., when we become absorbed in the realities that our theoretical understanding seeks to represent) that our theoretical grasp is relaxed. It is in *this* moment that we *may* gain a new insight into the reality with which we are engaged. This, for Polanyi, is part of the process of scientific discovery in which our understanding of the world is modified.

There is a parallel in the way in which we seek the truth in Scripture. As we listen to Scripture, our hearing is powerfully conditioned by the confessional perspective that we indwell. But this limit is not an *absolute* limit. The Word of God, as it speaks through Scripture, may call into question, in some way, the understandings that we indwell, and we might have to reconsider whether some element of our explicit confession is in need of revision. This, in Polanyi's terms, would be an example of "breaking out," and it appears that Barth has some such idea in mind in his discussion of confessions.

There are, then, parallels between the ways in which our knowledge develops in the natural sciences (as Polanyi describes it) and the confessions (as Barth describes them). But it is important to acknowledge that there are also distinctions. These are crucial, and derive from the radically distinct subject matter of the respective inquiries. The sciences deal with physical phenomena—and in many cases inanimate physical phenomena—that fall into the broad category of created being. The confessions deal with the creator God whose divine being is utterly distinct from all that he has made. We are comparing and contrasting human knowledge of dumb creaturely reality and that of the inscrutable God who exercises complete freedom over his own self-disclosure.

It may be pertinent at this point to return to one of Polanyi's more startling suggestions that even inanimate physical phenomena can "reveal" themselves in such a way that our conceptualization of them is called into question (this, in Polanyi's understanding, is the capacity of the real to manifest itself in unanticipated ways). But, as noted above, this kind of language is obviously metaphorical. An inanimate object is *de facto* passive in the "revelatory" process, and it would be scarcely appropriate to speak—even in metaphorical terms—about the *decision* of such an object to make itself known. But this kind of claim and language is entirely appropriate when employed in respect of our knowledge of God. If, following Barth, we acknowledge the Word of God as subject of the church's history as well object to us, it is not only appropriate but necessary to speak of God's *decision* to reveal himself and of our knowledge of him being dependent upon this. If it is appropriate to speak of inanimate phenomena revealing themselves in unanticipated ways and challenging the conceptualities we have of them (as I think it is), it is all the more certain that we must speak of God—and our knowledge of God in these terms.

Concluding Comment

In this chapter I have sought to explore the significance of the epistemological thought of Michael Polanyi for an understanding of participation in revelation in the form of a "Polanyian" commentary upon Barth's discussion of church confession in his *Church Dogmatics*. In doing so, I have attempted to demonstrate ways in which the insights of Polanyi, which have been articulated primarily in the context of the natural sciences, can illuminate the processes involved in the kind of theological task in which Barth is engaged. It is interesting to note that many of the themes that comprise Polanyi's post-critical philosophy are, to a degree, acknowledged in Barth's work. However, I contend that the Polanyian reading offered in this chapter extends the reflexive insights contained within Barth's own exposition and is suggestive of yet further developments.

One reason for engaging with Barth's treatment of church confessions is, as noted at the outset, to gain insight into the way in which he seeks to speak in response to the revelation of God—to consider one way in which he seeks to "participate in revelation." As I have shown, there are theologians who have argued that Barth's doctrine of revelation, as it is expressed in the early volumes of *Church Dogmatics*, leaves little room for human participation beyond "acknowledgement." In my expounding this excerpt from Barth's work, it is clear that this is not the conclusion that Barth has drawn, and it has also been possible to discern some of the contours of his constructive method. I contend that the methodology that Barth adopts at this point ought to inform any interpretation of his doctrine of the Word of God. Such a strategy would certainly preclude some of the conclusions drawn by a theologian such as Thiemann.

Having offered this Polanyian reading of Barth, I will proceed in the next chapter to consider a variety of other ways in which the insights of Polanyi might be adopted in attempting to articulate a fuller understanding of human participation in revelation. Given the lack of space, it will be necessary to adopt a high degree of selectivity. What can be done in building on the work of the present chapter is to offer a selection of examples of how Polanyian insights might be brought to bear, as well as to indicate how this might operate at different levels. Alan Torrance, as we have seen, has offered a careful and thorough account of the "semantic level" of our participation in revelation; I shall now seek to consider aspects that are not adequately articulated under this heading—not least the "bodily" and "epistemic."[82]

---

82. The meaning that I attach to these categories will emerge in the context of the next chapter, and I will defer any attempt to anticipate this at the present juncture.

CHAPTER 5

Revelation and Participation

Introduction

THE STRUCTURE OF chapter 4 was substantially derived from Barth's discussion of the confession of the church in volume I/2 of *Church Dogmatics*. It offered what I described as a "Polanyian exposition" of Barth's work. As such, the scope of its content was largely delimited by the structure of Barth's own writing on the theme. This line of approach was useful not only in demonstrating ways in which Polanyi's insights offer scope for extending and reformulating Barth's representation of the theme, but also for illuminating the degree to which Barth was already operating with ideas that parallel strands of Polanyi's post-critical thought. Although Barth would undoubtedly have had little time for Polanyi's theological and religious writings, it is not difficult to see how his epistemological work would have proved fruitful in the kind of project in which Barth was engaged.

Barth's discussions of church confession might be described as a study of the method by which the church participates in revelation. The confession arises as the church seeks to articulate theological truth in the context of doctrinal conflict, by looking to the witness of Scripture and seeking the illumination of the Spirit. This provides one example of what Barth believes we can and, indeed, ought to say on the basis of revelation. It has been noted at various points that Barth's explicit treatment of the doctrine of revelation in the early parts of *Church Dogmatics* might call into question the legitimacy of speaking of participation in revelation.[1] I have contended, however, that what Barth says explicitly of the doctrine of revelation ought to be interpreted in the light of what he is seeking to achieve in the rest of his theological writings. After all, it would be extraordinary to suggest

---

1. This is the view of Ronald Thiemann, for example.

that Barth did not conceive of his work as it is expressed *Church Dogmatics* and elsewhere as a response to, or participation in, revelation.[2]

This state of affairs offers good reason for revisiting and reconsidering Barth's doctrine of revelation. Thus after articulating Barth's position in chapter 1, I sought to critique and reformulate a broadly Barthian doctrine of revelation in chapter 2. In doing so, I drew substantially upon Alan Torrance's work, in which he seeks to move on from what he describes as Barth's "revelation model" to a "worship model." The latter model identifies ecclesial worship as the event in which the community of the church is drawn into participation in the trinitarian communion. An important emphasis here is *participation*.[3] Through this model, Torrance is able to expand upon Barth's description of revelation as "event." The worship model recasts Barth's somewhat undifferentiated revelation "event" in the form of an identifiable human activity in which persons are drawn by God into fellowship with himself. This participation, which God makes possible, is a transformative one, and Torrance's principal focus is upon the semantic aspects of this transformation (*metanoia*).

In completing chapter 2, I did not complete what I have to say about the revision or restatement of the doctrine of revelation. While affirming Torrance's work as a valuable extension of Barth's doctrine, I believe that his worship model is itself in need of further extension. The continuation of the development of the doctrine of revelation was interrupted by an exposition of the epistemology of Michael Polanyi in chapter 3.[4] It was here I sought to establish resources for extending this work. The resources assembled in chapter 3 have already been put to work in the exposition of Barth in chapter 4, but now I return to the explicit development of the doctrine of revelation in the light of insights gained from Michael Polanyi's theory of knowledge.

Critical Engagement with Alan Torrance

Torrance's description of semantic participation in revelation represents a significant development of Barth's doctrine of revelation. His comments on language as a communal phenomenon contain crucial insights for guiding us away from a distorting Cartesian individualism. At various points, Torrance speaks of the importance of the community of the church as the context in which semantic revision occurs in response to God's revelation. He suggests that, for example, "[T]he use of a theological term presupposes a community which provides the

---

2. Barth is, of theologians, one of the most vehemently opposed to theology conceived in terms of human religious insight *apart* from revelation.

3. It might be noted, in parentheses, that this *participation* is a participation in that which is offered by Christ as the incarnate One on our behalf.

4. And an exposition of Polanyi's theological and religious writings in the excursus.

context of its use, that is, the rules of the use of the term. Terms are used in the context of social participation with respect to which certain rules apply."[5] But, while Torrance deals with the transformation of human language—and the human *metanoia* associated with this dynamic—in the ecclesial context, he does not go on to consider the pre-linguistic, supra-linguistic, and non-linguistic aspects of ecclesial life. The importance of these forms of life for semantic participation are acknowledged by Torrance from time to time,[6] but, while his analysis of semantic participation is nuanced and highly developed, the significance of other forms of participation in the ecclesial community is not. I contend that it is necessary to develop the detailed explorations of these other forms of participation that we find in Torrance's treatment of the semantic.[7]

It is clear that there is conceptual space in Torrance's work for development along such lines. For example, he speaks of "the priority of participation over interpretation"[8] and, significantly, "The 'performative' logic of grace as held forth in infant baptism."[9] According to Torrance, baptism is "irreducibly bound up with its purpose of training a child (in and through its being brought up to understand what its baptism means) in the "skill" of interpreting the world from the perspective of the paradigm associated with the ontological and existential realities held forth in baptism."[10] Although this is not developed, it is implicit in such a comment that not only does Torrance wish to speak of semantic participation (which is, substantially, the burden of his book); he also acknowledges the development of particular cognitive skills as other forms of participation in revelation. Indeed, with regard to his discussion of infant baptism, it seems that he is concerned with what might be called "epistemic" participation and transformation. Torrance, in embracing the "priority of participation over interpretation" distances, himself from the individualistic Cartesian *cogito* and aligns himself with the view, embraced by Wittgenstein among others, that our interpretation, including our understanding of language, is always established in relation to our participation in particular life contexts.[11]

---

5. Torrance, *Persons in Communion*, 336.

6. As Torrance adopts a substantially Wittgensteinian position, it is not surprising that other aspects of participation enter the picture, although this appears to be largely tacit. It is more often implied than it is articulated.

7. In the context of this work it is possible to give little more than a suggestion of how such an approach might be developed. I will offer examples as I proceed, but what is offered can be no more than suggestive of a much larger project.

8. Torrance, *Persons in Communion*, 339.

9. Ibid.

10. Ibid.

11. This insight is also acknowledged in Gilbert Ryle's distinction between knowing *how* and knowing *that*. See Ryle, *Concept of Mind*, 26–60.

In chapter 3 some of the similarities between the thought of Wittgenstein and Polanyi were noted (of which the latter seemed to be unaware). Both men concurred that if we are to understand a word, we must look to the way it is used in a particular context or community. Polanyi and Wittgenstein both reject a nominalism that attaches fixed or general meanings to words in abstraction. They assert that words are (to borrow Torrance's technical term for a more general purpose) "commandeered" within a particular context, and that the meaning of a word cannot be separated from this context without loss of meaning.

For Torrance, Wittgenstein, and Polanyi, it is on the basis of our participation in a particular form of life that the possibility for reflection upon it arises. Explicit knowledge arises from within a life-context. The unique insight of Polanyi (which finds no direct parallel in the work of Wittgenstein) is to be found in his theory of tacit knowledge. As we saw in chapter 3, Polanyi identifies and differentiates two terms of tacit knowing: the focal and the subsidiary. We can know something *focally* only by way of *subsidiary* knowledge upon which we rely. When we consider language in the light of this general epistemological insight, we notice two distinct lines of application. Firstly, in our use of language we are only subsidiarily aware of the shape of the words on the page or the sound of the words as they are spoken. Such symbols and sounds point beyond themselves to the things that they denote and with which we are focally concerned. We must *indwell* the symbols and sounds of language in order to attend to their meaning. Secondly, when we use language, what is said explicitly must inevitably draw upon a reservoir of tacit knowledge. What we bring to explicit articulation is, in this respect, the focal term, but in doing so we rely upon our tacit knowledge (of which we are only subsidiarily aware) that has developed through our participation in a particular form of life.

In theology we are concerned with the church. The language that the church adopts is in view here, but we must be aware that this language is irreducibly bound up with various forms of ecclesial life. Many of these contain a linguistic component but, in participating in them, we participate in more than language.[12] Torrance, in following Wittgenstein, may be correct in asserting that we cannot think of language in terms of attaching words to things that are already known pre-linguistically, in what amounts to a one-step process; but I wish to follow Polanyi in his insistence that there is knowledge that cannot be articulated: "we know more than we can tell." It is to a consideration of the knowledge that cannot be articulated that I now turn.

Recall the example of the anatomist noted in the section "Language" in chapter 3.[13] The anatomist possesses knowledge that is ineffable: it is more than

---

12. Here I have in view the whole gamut of ecclesial practices: from the forms of worship with their liturgies, hymns, songs, prayers, Bible readings, physical postures, etc., to their engagement in the wider community in service, evangelism, and prophetic witness (and any number of other practices besides).

13. The illustration is drawn from Polanyi, *Personal Knowledge*, 90.

can be told. The anatomist is able to speak of what he or she knows but can express it only in part. To borrow Ryle's terminology, the anatomist may speak of his knowledge "that" but cannot speak in the same way of his knowledge "how." And it is this latter knowing that is, in many ways, the most interesting and important. The only way in which the anatomist can convey his or her knowledge "how" (his "know-how") is indirectly through nurturing another in the skills he or she possesses.[14] Language will have a part in this but it will be a limited part. When two skilled anatomists converse with one another, they communicate, of course, by using language, but the success of their communication depends upon a tacit co-efficient in which, on either side of the conversation, what is said is supplemented by a whole body of knowledge that is shared. Such knowledge cannot readily be made explicit, but it is nevertheless knowledge that is depended upon. We know more than we can tell.

I have sought to establish the need to extend Torrance's understanding of semantic participation in such a way that other forms of participation are explicitly acknowledged and brought into view. Such an extension is necessary because of the interrelatedness of the semantic with these other forms of participation. The Word is not known apart from the flesh.[15]

So, in the light of Polanyi's understanding of language, Torrance's exposition of semantic participation in revelation must be expanded to include correlate participatory functions. Torrance has shown us that the trinitarian communion of Father, Son, and Holy Spirit is a communion into which human persons are also drawn. The community of this communion is the church. As this community's forms of life are established in this relationship into which it has been drawn, it is necessary for the language that it adopts to be transformed through participation in this relationship. But it is not only its language that must be open to such reverent reconfiguring; its other forms of life must also come into view. *Metanoia* is not limited to semantics!

In the remainder of this chapter I will attempt to identify particular *loci* in which Polanyi's insights offer promising lines of development, and to work these out in some detail. These will have to stand as representative examples of what would comprise a much more extensive project. In the process of selection, I attempt to indicate something of the variety of ways in which Polanyi's work might be taken up. This will serve to suggest the breadth of possibilities that might be followed up as a development of the present work.

---

14. In the development of many skills (in medicine and the natural sciences, for example), there is the need to acquire physical sensitivity and dexterity. Such skills can only be developed by way of hands-on experience.

15. See 1 John 4:2–3.

Epistemic Participation

The Historical Jesus

In chapter 2 I drew attention to a tendency for Barth's two-natures doctrine to underplay the significance of the life of Jesus of Nazareth in articulating his doctrine of revelation. I noted in that context Hart's comment: "If Barth's *Logos* becomes *sarx*, the particular way in which the 'becoming' or the union between the two is consistently construed in his theology nonetheless risks reducing it to the point where it loses all purchase in the real world, thereby robbing it of any genuine redemptive and revelatory force, and finally robbing theology of both its theme and its form as talk about God."[16]

Nevertheless, Barth speaks of Christ's priestly office in his discussion of "the readiness of man." As I noted in chapter 1, Barth affirms that "In our flesh God knows himself. Therefore in Him it is a fact that our flesh knows God Himself."[17] Part of what is implied in our affirmation that God was in Christ is that in him we see the readiness of man for God. "In Him the enmity of man against the grace of God is overcome."[18] Christ becomes our "kinsman redeemer," and in our incorporation into his life we may speak of our readiness for God—not as an autonomous human capacity, but on the basis of our being "in him." Placing emphasis upon this incorporation does not imply a marginalization of the particularity of Jesus Christ. As God's hypostatic presence in the realm of creation as a human being, his life is of quintessential importance for an understanding of our own humanity.

It is insufficient simply to say that Jesus of Nazareth is the revelation of God. This would fail to take into account that God is veiled in his unveiling. However, we must take account of the fact that it was *this* man—in all that he said and did—in which God revealed himself and made himself known.

Jesus called and nurtured his disciples in the context of a dynamic community. This was his teaching method.[19] It was in and through their participation in this form of life that the disciples came to participate in what the Father was making known to them in the Son by the Spirit. In this participation, we see a process of human transformation that undoubtedly implies semantic transformation but entails more beside. Polanyi had little time for the concept of revelation[20] and yet, despite this, we may detail aspects of his thought that help illuminate the ways in which the disciples of Jesus came to participate in revelation.

---

16. Hart, *Regarding Karl Barth*, 4.
17. Barth, *Church Dogmatics II/1*, 151.
18. Ibid., 153.
19. In this regard it is important to acknowledge Christ's "office" as nurturer as well as that of priest.
20. In *The Tacit Dimension* he spoke of "the enfeebled authority of revealed religion." Polanyi, *Tacit Dimension*, 62.

One of Polanyi's key insights is that human knowledge cannot be rendered wholly explicit. Indeed Polanyi's view is that "tacit knowing is . . . the dominant principle of all knowledge."[21] What we can come to know focally is facilitated by subsidiary knowledge—knowledge that we indwell. For Polanyi our calling is that indwelling into which we are nurtured during early years of life when, as children, we come to participate in the language, mores, and ethics of the family and society into which we are born. There are circumstances in which a person may come to participate in other forms of life by becoming involved, for example, in a political, cultural, or sporting community. Again, the nature of our participation in such groups cannot be fully represented or described in explicit terms. So, if it can only be partially explained or described, how can the participation come about? In *The Tacit Dimension*, Polanyi discusses the ways in which an apprentice assimilates the skills of a master in the achievement of a physical performance:

> He must try to combine mentally the movements which the performer combines practically and he must combine them in a pattern similar to the performer's pattern of movements. Two kinds of indwelling meet here. The performer co-ordinates his moves by dwelling in them as parts of his body, while the watcher tries to correlate these moves by seeking to dwell in them from outside. He dwells in these moves by interiorizing them. By such exploratory indwelling the pupil gets the feel of the master's skill and may learn to rival him.[22]

The relationship between apprentice and master is not limited to the acquisition of physical skills. Polanyi points out that "Chess players enter into a master's spirit by rehearsing the games he played, to discover what he had in mind."[23] As the apprentice rehearses the moves of the master, which are articulate and explicit, he or she may come to appreciate why they were made *without being able to fully explain why*. Polanyi indicates that this method of imitating a master is the only way for an apprentice to participate in a skill in the way that the master does.

At this point I want to consider the way in which Jesus' disciples learned from him. It is not possible to offer an exhaustive treatment of this theme, but it is possible to proffer some ideas that will be suggestive of fuller development.

At the commencement of his public ministry, Jesus called a group of people around him who were to form an inner circle of his followers. One of the striking elements of this call is that it appears to imply that those who responded to it left their ordinary employment in order to be part of this group.[24] Jesus' method of teaching and nurturing his disciples was one in which they were immersed in a form of life that would be, in many and significant ways, discontinuous with what

21. Polanyi, *Study of Man*, 13.
22. Polanyi, *Tacit Dimension*, 29–30.
23. Ibid., 30.
24. See, for example, Matt 4:18–22.

they had known. The "method" that Jesus adopted was to incorporate his disciples into a community of practice that was participation in the ministry to which Jesus had been called by the Father.

In the context of first-century Palestine, it was not unusual for rabbis to have a following of disciples with whom they would share much of their lives. This aspect of Jesus' relationship with his disciples was not unique. What was unique was the particular form in which this relationship was established, as we shall see. Nevertheless, from the perspective of contemporary Western society, this form of nurture does strike one as being unfamiliar. This is not typically the pattern according to which students are taught—or, perhaps more to the point, this is not the way in which things are *seen* to be. This is not surprising. The dominant conception of knowledge—as that which can be made explicit—renders the need for such a richly relational form of teaching obscure. As a result, the relational aspects of our learning (which will always be present in some way or another) are bracketed-out of pedagogical theory (if they are noticed at all) and discarded as peripheral, incidental phenomena.[25] In circumstances where a more obvious form of apprenticeship has been sustained (in the case of clinical medical studies, for example), explicit epistemological conceptualizations have been set aside in tacit recognition that such a conceptuality is inadequate to get the job done.

The gospels witness to Jesus' practice of teaching his disciples "on the road." What Jesus *did* and what he *taught* were closely connected.[26] One notices this close linking of what Jesus did and what he taught in the brief description of his life in the prologue to the Acts of the Apostles.[27] Jesus taught the Kingdom and in his actions offered signs of its presence and reality. Jesus also taught ethics and the interpretation of Torah, not in abstract but in the context of events in which he was involved. Here we might think, by way of illustration, of the incident of the woman caught in the act of adultery.[28]

What was unique was that Jesus' teachings and acts provided for his disciples, and for others with the eyes to see, intimations of a radically new reality. But this was not a reality that was necessarily apprehended. In order to "see" this new reality it is necessary, according to John's gospel, to be "born again." This is the work of the Spirit of God. A great deal of Jesus' teaching as we find it in the gospels is parabolic. It is significant that this is an indirect form of teaching. The parables contain images of characters, events, and situations with which his hearers could readily identify. But, typically, they are subversive stories in which the hearers' associations and assumptions are called into question. It is their indirectness that

---

25. The importance of this issue has to come to the fore in the context of distance learning and Web-based courses.

26. See, for example, Matt 4:23.

27. Acts 1:1–2.

28. John 8:1–11.

renders the hearer more susceptible to the message they contain. There is no space to expand on this, but a point to be noted is that these stories were told to provide, for those with eyes to see, part of a vision of the Kingdom of God. It is implicit that the Spirit is at work in the telling and the hearing of these stories. The parables provide a vehicle through which the hearer can conceive of the world differently, and thus they provide the means of epistemic transformation.

Such a transformation was also necessary with regard to the disciples' expectations of Messiah and Israel. In Mark's gospel, for instance, it is immediately after Peter's confession of Jesus as the Christ that Jesus confronted him with a vision of the suffering that he would have to undergo. Here, in a very direct way, Peter's conceptions and beliefs were challenged, and he, having received the revelatory insight that Jesus was the Christ, found himself unable to comprehend what Jesus had to tell him. The disciples' confused reception of Jesus' teaching is a recurrent theme in the gospels.

Jesus often taught by example. It was after one of the disciples had seen Jesus at prayer that he was prompted to ask Jesus how to pray.[29] In response, Jesus gave to his disciples the form of the Lord's Prayer. But the disciples would have had a much broader picture of Jesus' prayer life than could have ever been expressed in the words of a formula prayer. They would have known when and where he prayed; they would have known about the physical posture that he adopted, and they would have known something of his attitude towards it and perhaps some insight into how prayer affected him. Presumably it was this knowledge that prompted the question.

Much more could be said about the ways in which Jesus nurtured and taught his disciples. The central point that I want to make is that his "teaching" cannot be understood apart from his invitation to participate with him in a way of life. It was in the life of this small community—in the midst of its relationships, tasks, and tensions—that Jesus taught his disciples. In direct and in indirect teaching, by signs, miracles, symbolic gestures, and all manner of "life practices" Jesus presented a challenge to the way in which they understood their lives, the destiny of Israel, and their understanding of Messiah, and nurtured them in a distinctive pattern of life.

It is evident that not all of what Jesus taught during his time with his disciples was assimilated, and often the disciples were left in a state of confusion. But such transformation as there was, and such transformation as occurred following the death and resurrection of Jesus and the coming of the Spirit at Pentecost, is shaped by the practices in which the disciples were nurtured in the presence of Jesus. Jesus showed his disciples a way of life, and it was this that the disciples learned during their time with him. As a consequence, the disciples' perspective on their own religious heritage changed: they came to see things differently. But

---

29. Luke 11:1–6.

it seems that their conceptual grasp of the meaning of this way of life and their appreciation of the didactic instruction of Jesus was halting and uncertain.

The vitality of the community that Jesus established cannot be understood apart from the relationship between Jesus and the Father. The synoptic gospels demonstrate this by referring to Jesus' habit of withdrawing from the community and the wider public for prayer,[30] and the form and content of that prayer is indicated in John's gospel.[31] There was an important sense in which the disciples were on the outside of the relationship between Jesus and his Father. When, in John's gospel, Jesus is represented as saying to his disciples, "I have food that you do not know about."[32] they do not understand what he is talking about. This is one of the techniques that the gospel writer adopts for demonstrating that the disciples were far less than fully aware of that in which they had become involved. Nevertheless, Jesus taught his disciples to pray, "Our Father . . . ."[33] Under the tutelage and guidance of their master, the disciples came to participate in a form of life—even though there was much that they did not understand and misunderstood.

When washing his disciples' feet, Jesus told the disciples that they did not know what he was doing, but that later they would understand.[34] While the comment relates to a specific incident, it is clear enough from the gospels that there were many occasions when the disciples had little understanding of Jesus' teaching and actions. However, a time was coming when they would understand much more.

The Early Church

Two dominical commands that were given to the disciples, one before the crucifixion and one before the ascension, have been of crucial importance for the church. Let us consider them and the forms of life that have sprung from them.

THE LORD'S SUPPER

The first was given in the institution of the Lord's Supper, which may well have occurred in the setting of an established habit of eating together and table-fellowship. This event is recorded in the three synoptic gospels (Matt 26:26-28; Mark 14:22-24; and Luke 22:17-20) and in 1 Cor 1:23-25. Before his arrest, at the Passover meal with his disciples, Jesus offered them bread and wine as "his body" and "his blood" in the establishment of a "new covenant." Luke and Paul emphasize that Jesus said, "Do this in remembrance of me." There is something

---

30. See, for example, Matt 14:13 and 23, and Luke 5:16.

31. Especially John 17:1-26.

32. John 4.32.

33. Matt 6:9. Thereby Jesus included his disciples in this relational participation with "the Father" and taught them to consider themselves so included.

34. See John 13:7.

to remember and something to do. This is not the place to enter into the debate about the nature of the bread and wine in the Eucharistic celebration. My interest is in drawing attention to some aspects of this event that are not contested.

It is surely significant that at this crucial moment Jesus addresses his disciples at table in the context of a fellowship meal. Jesus tells them that they must repeat what they do in this upper room in order to remember him. Two aspects of this that are both uncontroversial and highly significant are the communal and symbolic nature of the event. The locus of the commemoration is a communal meal, which implies the corporate nature of what Jesus intends. The "remembering" is that of the community as it comes together to share a meal. The other aspect that ought to be noted is its symbolism. Jesus does not explain himself beyond calling the bread his body and the wine his blood. He does not elucidate what is about to happen to him and how this meal relates to it. Jesus' command is simply that they must eat the meal together in order to remember him.

Why a meal? Why bread? Why wine? Why doesn't Jesus offer his disciples a clearly formulated theological explanation of the significance and meaning of the events that are about to unfold? The church has spilt much ink engaged in this task down the centuries. Why wasn't Jesus more explicit? I suggest that no such teaching was given to the disciples because that was not the way in which Jesus wanted to teach them. The kind of "remembering" Jesus required of his disciples was a "doing": the coming together of community for a meal—as they had come together so many times before. In instituting the Lord's Supper, Jesus' primary intention was not to convey concept or theory but to achieve something much more concrete—to cause the disciples to continue to do something in which they had been nurtured by him during the time of his three years of ministry.[35]

There has been much heated ecclesial debate over the Lord's Supper[36] but it is intriguing that, transcending many disagreements, the followers of Christ *have* come together and shared bread and wine in remembrance of him. The contemporary Christian who partakes in the Eucharistic bread and wine may have no *direct* knowledge of the forms of life that the first disciples learned at Jesus' feet but, drawing on Polanyi's understanding of how skills and traditions are transmitted down generations, it possible to see how Eucharistic practice has been passed down the generations. In this way it is meaningful to say that contemporary Eucharistic practice is a participation in that which was originally instituted by Christ. The "remembering" of the contemporary church is through this "doing."

---

35. This is not to deny the crucial significance of the events of Jesus' crucifixion, death, burial, and resurrection. These events would come to be seen by the disciples as decisive for their understanding of Jesus. But even these decisive events have their meaning in the context of what the disciples had learned in the presence of Jesus over a period of three years. If only the final events of Jesus' life—his death, burial, and resurrection—are significant, the very purpose of Jesus' itinerant ministry, including his calling of a band of followers, is rendered unclear.

36. Also, "Eucharist" or "Mass."

I noted earlier that in their participation in the circle of Jesus' close followers the disciples were often confused by what Jesus did and said, and not infrequently they tried to persuade him that he was mistaken. Gospel accounts suggest that the disciples knew very little of what was about to happen to Jesus after the Lord's Supper—much less did they have a theological understanding of what those events might mean. What the disciples did have was knowledge of the way of life in which Jesus had nurtured them, the centrality of Jesus in this, and some awareness of the relationship that Jesus had with the one he called Father.

The disciples, among others, discerned in him one who spoke and acted with authority.[37] They may have substantially failed to penetrate the meaning and coherence of this. Much of what Jesus said and did did not resonate with many of the expectations and assumptions that they held; indeed Jesus said and did many things that disturbed and discomforted them. The gospels claim that after Jesus' death, the disciples resumed their old patterns of life and work in many ways—they were not able to continue or inhabit the way of life in which they had been nurtured without Jesus' presence with them. It was in the outpouring of the Holy Spirit at Pentecost that the disciples were enabled to take up again the forms of life in which they had been nurtured—in the power of the Spirit.

There are some significant parallels here with the way in which Polanyi describes how a child is nurtured in a family and a society and, more specifically, with the way in which language is learned. Children, if they are to learn language, must believe that the sounds that they hear are meaningful. On the basis of such a belief, a child will try to discern patterns of sounds and meanings. For the disciples to understand the meaning of the life that they shared with Jesus, it was necessary to believe that it was meaningful—but its meaning could not be discerned apart from the disciples' incorporation into the trinitarian fellowship. As Jesus' life was marked by his fellowship with the Father through the Spirit, so the disciples—in their post-Pentecostal taking up again the forms of life in which Jesus had nurtured them—were drawn into communion with the trinitarian God.

THE GREAT COMMISSION

A second dominical command issued to the disciples after the resurrection of Jesus is recorded in Matthew's gospel. Before his ascension, Jesus appeared with his disciples on a mountain in Galilee and said to them, "All authority in heaven and on earth has been given to me. Go therefore and make disciples of all nations, baptizing them in the name of the Father and of the Son and of the Holy Spirit, and teaching them to obey everything that I have commanded you. And remember, I am with you always, to the end of the age."[38]

---

37. See Matt 7:29.
38. See Matt 28:16–18.

Although so much might be said of this text, it seems particularly relevant to draw attention to Jesus' command to "make disciples." The implication of this is that the task with which Jesus charges his close circle of followers is to extend their numbers by nurturing others in the patterns of life that he had established. This task is not exclusively—or even primarily—one of communicating concepts, ideas, or doctrines, but one in which this small group of Jesus' followers must apprentice others in ways in which they had been nurtured by him. Jesus' charge is to "make disciples." He commands his disciples to teach new disciples to obey "everything that I have commanded you," but it is difficult, if not impossible, to conceive of what this might mean apart from the life context in which Jesus taught them.

A further point that can be made is that the command that Jesus issues to his disciples is not delimited to any one social, religious, or cultural grouping but to "all nations." The implication of this is that the form of life that the disciples had learned from Jesus, and in which they are to apprentice others, is one of universal rather than parochial significance.

For the disciples, the form of life in which *they* were discipled entailed a reorientation of life. It would be misleading to conceive of this transformation (*metanoia*) as anything other than a transformation of their whole lives. Their religious and theological beliefs (as first-century Palestinian Jews) were challenged, but so were their socio-political conceptions and semantic practices. But such transformations cannot be conceived apart from the way of life (in all its concreteness) in which Jesus had apprenticed his disciples.

In this section I have attempted to describe how Jesus nurtured his disciples, and how they were commanded, in turn, to nurture others.[39] It is implicit that participation in this form of life is a participation in the life of the trinitarian God as well as one of ecclesial fellowship. It is a transformative way of life. I affirm Torrance's claim that this is a community of semantic transformation, but, beyond this, and following the insights of Polanyi, I wish to place some emphasis upon the fact that those who participate in this transformative community know more than they can tell.

Bodily Participation

Without doubting the importance of language in human formation and, indeed, the significance of semantic transformation implied in the Christian gospel, it does seem that Torrance, in *Persons in Communion*, has a tendency to overstate it. This becomes clear when, in drawing upon Polanyi's theory of tacit knowledge toward the end of his book,[40] he concludes with the thought that "The most essential or

---

39. In the final section of this chapter I will show why diversity is necessarily implied in the living of this form of life.

40. In the context of a discussion of Polanyi's *The Tacit Dimension*.

fundamental tool for our indwelling the world would appear ... to be language."[41] But, as was noted in the exposition of Polanyi in chapter 3, Polanyi—while acknowledging the significance of language—speaks of the "*bodily* roots of all thought."[42] Polanyi would not endorse this aspect of Torrance's reading of his work.

Polanyi offers many examples of knowledge that is ineffable. It is not that we may not speak of such knowledge, but that in speaking of it we are only able to convey part of what we know. Through the development of perceptual skills—in certain circumstances aided by the skillful use of tools or instruments—we are able to "make contact with reality" and to know it in ways that transcend our capacity to articulate it. Over against Torrance, I would contend that it is our *bodies*—in the many ways in which we may skillfully use them—that provide us with our most fundamental tool for indwelling the world.

Mark Johnson's *The Body in the Mind: The Bodily Basis of Meaning, Imagination and Reason* offers a substantial treatment of the relationship between our bodies and our knowing that appears to harmonize with Polanyi's claim about the bodily roots of thought. Johnson makes the point that as *rational* animals, human beings are rational *animals*. He claims: "The centrality of human embodiment directly influences what and how things can be meaningful for us, the ways in which these meanings can be developed and articulated, the ways we are able to comprehend and reason about experience, and the actions we take."[43] Even what might be regarded as abstract meanings, Johnson notes, depend upon schemes of thought which derive from our bodily experience.

Johnson argues that the propositional and conceptual content of our speech is possible because of the existence of a complex web of what he calls "nonpropositional schematic structures" that derive from bodily experience. We have a meaningful physical interaction with the world. In part this precedes our attempts to speak, and to establish conceptualizations of it and little (perhaps none) of our conceptual and linguistic engagement with the world can occur without it. Here Johnson affirms the point made by Polanyi about the bodily roots of our knowing. He writes: "Once meaning is understood in this broader, enriched manner, it will become evident that the structure of rationality is much richer than any set of abstract logical patterns independent of the patterns of our physical interactions in and with our environment."[44]

By way of illustration, Johnson discusses the idea of "force" as it is used both literally and metaphorically. He suggests that, although it is a point that is easily overlooked, its usage depends upon publicly shared meaning structures that derive from our bodily experience of force. Such experiences may first occur in the

---

41. Torrance, *Persons in Communion*, 352.
42. Polanyi, *Tacit Dimension*, 15; my emphasis.
43. Johnson, *The Body in the Mind*, xix.
44. Ibid., 5.

womb and proceed to accumulate after birth. A baby's body is subject to various forces (gravity, water in the bathtub, being dressed, etc.). As well as being acted upon by various forces, the baby also learns to exert force as it pushes its bottle away or grabs its soft toy and its parent's spectacles. "We develop patterns of interacting forcefully with our environment."[45] The baby will sometimes succeed in an attempt to exert force and will sometimes fail. But in these experiences, all of which precede the process of language acquisition, the baby is learning about the meaning of force in relationship to its environment. Johnson makes the important point that

> In each of these motor activities there are repeatable patterns that come to identify that particular forceful action. These patterns are embodied and give coherent, meaningful structure to our physical experience at a *preconceptual* level, though we are taught names for at least some of these patterns, and can discuss them in the abstract. Of course, we formulate a *concept* of "force," which we can explicate in propositional terms. But its meaning—the meaning it identifies—goes deeper than our conceptual and propositional understanding.[46]

All the words and ideas that cluster around the concept of "force" cannot be understood apart from these bodily experiences[47] of force that accumulate from the earliest experiences of our lives. Johnson suggests that such early encounters "reveal patterned recurring relations between ourselves and our environment. Such patterns develop as meaning structures through which our world begins to exhibit a measure of coherence, regularity, and intelligibility."[48] This suggests that in speaking of "force," we speak of a concept that is meaningful to us. But it is only meaningful to us because of the various bodily experiences of force that are part of our early life experience. In the absence of such bodily experiences, the concept of force would be void of meaning. Thus the concept, malleable and useful as it may be for the purposes of articulate communication, is rooted in an understanding of force that is bodily.

This is just one example of how a concept can be meaningful only because of the bodily experience out of which it arises. What our bodily indwelling means to us transcends what we are able to tell but, if Polanyi and Johnson are correct, our concepts can be meaningful only insofar as they arise out of this body-involved way of knowing. As such, I would affirm not only that all knowledge is personal but that it involves our bodily engagement with the world. Knowledge does not exist in abstract apart from persons, and persons depend upon their bodies in order to come to know things.

---

45. Ibid., 13. We come to indwell those patterns.
46. Ibid.; Johnson's emphasis.
47. With all their developing "knowings" and "know-how."
48. Johnson, *The Body in the Mind*, 13. This will inevitably include a substantial tacit component.

I will now extend the idea of bodily-rooted knowledge to subjects of significance within the ecclesial context. I will consider the significance of the eating of bread and the drinking of wine in the Eucharist and the use of water in baptism but, before dealing with these themes, I will consider the significance of song in the context of the church's liturgical practice.

Why Sing?

Steven Guthrie, in an article entitled "Singing, in the Body and in the Spirit," asks why the use of song is so widespread in ecclesial practice. "In a liturgical universe of extraordinary diversity, music is one of the handful of practices which has been and remains an almost universal feature of Christian worship."[49] Why sing?

Guthrie reminds us that within the Christian tradition, the attitudes towards singing of some significant authorities have caused the place of music in ecclesial worship to be cast in a somewhat ambiguous light. Augustine acknowledges the capacity of music to intensify the force of the word that is conjoined with it. But, according to Augustine, there is a danger: "my physical delight [*delectatio carnis*], which has to be checked from enervating the mind [*mentem*], often deceives me when the perception of the senses [*sensus*] is unaccompanied by reason [*rationem*], and is not patiently content to be in a subordinate place."[50] The pastoral conclusion that Augustine reaches, in respect of singing in church, is that it "is to be approved, so that through the delights of the ear the weaker mind may rise up towards the devotion of worship."[51] But his ambivalence about the matter is evident in his subsequent remark: "Yet when it happens to me that the music moves me more than the subject of the song, I confess myself to commit a sin deserving punishment, and then I would prefer not to have heard the singer."[52] Augustine's ambivalence towards music derives from what he perceives as its potential to promote the desire for sensual satisfaction, and his belief that human beings ought to be led by rational thought rather than bodily sense.[53] John Calvin also has an ambivalence towards music in worship. While warmly commending its use, he also warns that the worshipper must guard against being more moved by the sensual experience of the music than by the spiritual meaning of the words. He cautions: "such songs as have been composed only for sweetness and *delight of the ear* are unbecoming to the majesty of the church and cannot but displease God in the highest degree."[54] Guthrie also draws our attention to the thoughts of Dietrich

---

49. Guthrie, "Singing, in the Body and in the Spirit," 633.
50. Quoted in ibid., 634.
51. Quoted in ibid.
52. Quoted in ibid.
53. It is clear that Augustine's view of the relationship between bodily sense and rational thought is quite at odds with the one explored by Mark Johnson in *The Body in the Mind*.
54. Quoted in Guthrie, "Singing, in the Body and in the Spirit," 636; Guthrie's emphasis is preserved.

Bonhoeffer on the subject in which, again, the subservience of the music to the words is emphasized. "All devotion, all attention should be concentrated upon the Word in the hymn . . . [W]e do not hum a melody; we sing words of praise to God, words of thanksgiving, confession and prayer. Thus the music is completely the servant of the Word."[55]

Such views cast the value of music in Christian worship in a most uncertain light. For Augustine its potential for stirring the emotions—which may be of benefit, especially for those of more limited rational powers(!)—is attached to an inherent risk that it may also promote sinful sensuality. For Calvin there is the fear that music will be a distraction and become an end in itself rather than a medium for worship, and for Bonhoeffer the positive function of music is less clear than its negative propensity for distracting attention from the words that it accompanies. On such a view, the value of music seems to be in question. It may distract from the meaning of the words, and, although it can stir the spirit, it can do so only with the concomitant danger of promoting carnality. So, why sing? Would it not be safer and more sober to avoid music in Christian worship?

In contradistinction to this ambivalent evaluation of music, Guthrie reminds us of the exhortation in the Ephesian epistle to "sing psalms and hymns and spiritual songs among yourselves, singing and making melody to the Lord in your hearts."[56] Guthrie makes the significant point that the author's exhortation to engage in music follows on directly from an exhortation to renounce debasing sensual activity.[57] He writes "to a Christian community surrounded by ignorance and immorality; to a people who were themselves prone to the blindness and indulgence of their former way of life; at the conclusion of a passage warning against irrationality and sins of the flesh—Paul urges singing and music making."[58] Guthrie notes that this line of reasoning appears to run counter to the positions that we have reviewed. He writes: "To put it very crudely, Augustine says: 'Irrationality is bad. Sensuality is bad. Therefore be careful about music.' Paul on the other hand says, 'Foolishness is bad. Sensuality is bad. Therefore you had better sing.'"[59]

If Guthrie's exegesis is correct, the author of Ephesians is suggesting that music, far from being a snare, is an antidote to dehumanizing, sinful sensuality. Consequently he develops the thesis that "the children of light are singing people, not *despite*, but *because* music engages body and sense."[60] This is a flat contradiction of the many elements in Christian theological tradition that have to a greater or lesser degree regarded bodies as an impediment to the sanctifying work

---

55. Quoted in ibid.
56. Eph 5:19; see also Col 3:16.
57. See Eph 5:3-18.
58. Guthrie, "Singing, in the Body and in the Spirit," 638.
59. Ibid.; Guthrie assumes Pauline authorship of the epistle.
60. Ibid., 639; Guthrie's emphasis.

of the Spirit. Guthrie suggests that the biblical tradition "does not limit or even focus the redemptive activity of the Holy Spirit on the 'mind' ('Come, visit every pious mind'). Rather, the Holy Spirit of God is also revealed as the incarnating Spirit—the One who creates, vivifies, and restores bodies."[61]

For Guthrie, to conceive of sanctification as a process of mind transformation that is in danger of being impeded—or even reversed—by sensual experience is mistaken. It is *both* body and mind that must be transformed through the sanctifying work of the Holy Spirit. Further, in view of the text from Ephesians, it appears "the sensualist, the one who has abused body and sense, more than anyone needs to have body and sense engaged by the Spirit."[62] For this reason, the author of the epistle exhorts his readers to song. The senses are not to be suppressed; they are to be redirected and transformed.

The imagery that is adopted earlier in Ephesians serves to reinforce this interpretation. The sinfulness of a distorted sensuality—engaging in what is sometimes described as "excess"—has the effect of desensitizing (resulting in loss of sense), which is dehumanizing.[63] The sanctifying work of the Spirit is one of "resensitizing"—of regaining sense—in order that true humanity may be restored. The author of Ephesians suggests that songs of praise may be part of that reorientation.

One of the most intriguing and suggestive parts of Guthrie's paper is his exploration of how our bodies are used in singing in the ecclesial context. He states that "[S]*ensitivity and responsiveness to the created order and to other human beings* . . . *characterizes the Holy Spirit's work among the children of light.*"[64] This is precisely what happens in good music making, where the body-involving aspects of our participation are of very considerable significance:

> As we sing together we attend to the activity of our own bodies in making sound, and we regard and respond to our own song as we hear it resonate in the space around us. We hear and attune ourselves to the sound of others' voices. We respond not only to people, but to the physical qualities of the sound we are creating with others and the physical and acoustical properties of the space in which we sing. Moreover, we submit ourselves together to a tempo, a pattern of melody and rhythm, and we respond dynamically to the shape and movement of our musical interaction.[65]

What Guthrie is saying is that in our music making we must be *sensitive*—to our own bodily participation, to those with whom we make music, to the sounds we make, and to the physical environment in which this happens. This is a way in

---

61. Ibid., 640.
62. Ibid., 641.
63. See Eph 4:19.
64. Guthrie, "Singing, in the Body and in the Spirit," 642; Guthrie's emphasis.
65. Ibid.

which persons can be in communion; it is an activity in which we encounter and respond to one another and, if the music is good, one in which this occurs with a measure of sensitivity. Guthrie claims, "It is not accidental that the commands to sing in Eph 5:19 lead on to the exhortation in verse 21: 'Submit to one another out of reverence for Christ.'"[66] Commenting upon the phenomenon of congregational singing, Guthrie notes that "From the many voices that sing together, a new entity emerges—the voice of the church; a sound which has qualities and properties which the individual voices of which it is composed do not have."[67] Consequently it can be seen that music is—or can become—a means of creating unity.

The structure of the argument in the Ephesians epistle leads towards an affirmation that "the Spirit uses song in leading us from a life of self-absorbed sensuality out into a life of others-orientated sensitivity."[68] Clearly there are many other activities that are communal and require for their performance an embodied, interpersonal sensitivity, but music—not least congregational singing in the church—provides a compelling example of the phenomenon.

It is not that in singing the church and its members look to their own activity or performance as the source of transformation, but that it is an important locus in which God's transforming presence and activity through the Spirit are known. As such, it is one of the ways in which we ought to speak of the church's participation in revelation.

Why Bread, Wine, and Water?

I have already considered some questions of epistemic participation and transformation associated with the sacramental life of the church. I will now reflect, briefly, upon the significance of the "physicality" of these practices.

I contend that one of the significances of the re-enactment of the Last Supper in the Eucharist is intrinsically linked to its physicality. Why does the church "do this in remembrance"? Why is it not sufficient to have a public reading of the gospel and a sermon in which the theological significance of the Last Supper is articulated? Undoubtedly one reason is that it is an act of obedience in response to what is understood as a dominical command. But I think it is possible to say more. Drawing upon Mark Johnson's analysis, it is important to note the significance of the fact that since the form of remembering that Jesus required of his disciples was a meal, its meaning to us will be connected to ideas that cluster around our understanding of meals. We might readily think of some of these ideas: sustenance; satisfaction of hunger, the quenching of thirst, table fellowship, opportunity for discussion and the sharing of stories, and celebration. There are doubtless many others. All these

---

66. Ibid.
67. Ibid., 644.
68. Ibid., 642.

ideas we associate with "meal," and inevitably the breadth and depth of such associations transcend what we are able to articulate of them. But more specifically for the first disciples of Jesus, the eating of bread and the drinking of wine is a symbolic reminder of that way of life in which Jesus had nurtured them and in which they, in turn, now nurture others in response to the Great Commission.

The second dominical command concerns water and baptism. Those who respond to the invitation to Christian discipleship are to be baptized in the name of the Father, Son, and Holy Spirit. Again so much might be said about this, and we have space only to offer a few suggestions about how this practice is to be interpreted and understood. Why use water? Is it not adequate for one who comes to faith to make a public statement or sign a document affirming allegiance to the Christ? Again we might say that it is adopted in the church in obedience to the dominical command. But it seems that, as with the Lord's Supper, what is required by the command reflects an appreciation that as a physical action, the rite of baptism makes connections with deeply rooted bodily experience. The most obvious symbolic connection is with washing, by which we remove dirt from our bodies. This is extended, symbolically, to the washing away of sin.[69] This, as with eating, is a bodily experience into which we enter from earliest childhood—even before its purpose is explicitly known to us. Whatever else we may wish to affirm of baptism, an association with this bodily experience with its tacit associations will be present. A further particular association that overlays the symbolism of washing and cleansing is the idea that in going down into the water the person being baptized is identified with the death and burial of Christ; and, in emerging from the water, with the resurrection of Christ from the dead.[70]

My purpose here, as will be apparent, is not to develop a sacramental theology but merely to acknowledge that the physical elements of bread and wine in the Eucharist, and water in baptism, are meaningful to us in that they draw, in symbolic association, upon bodily experiences and the body-involving knowledge—predominantly tacit—associated with them. In sustaining this emphasis, we circumvent the mistaken and misleading belief that our abstract, theoretical, or doctrinal articulation is meaningful and perhaps in some sense more pure *apart* from its association with such bodily "know-how."

Polanyi's claim that all knowledge is *personal* implies (and this point is one that he often makes explicit) that all knowledge is knowledge of embodied persons. Thus to conceive of knowledge apart from such embodiment can only serve to distort our understanding of it.

One of the consequences for the church of the general failure to appreciate the significance of our embodiment, and of the tendency to conceive of knowledge as (exclusively) that which can be articulated, is that it has led to an impoverished

---

69. See, for example, Acts 22:16.
70. See Rom 6:3–4 and Col 2:12.

view of the physicality of sacramental practice. There may even be some element of embarrassment associated with it. If we embrace the view that all true knowledge can be articulated, it is difficult to see what significance bread and eating, wine and drinking, or water and baptizing can have.[71] The church may continue to use bread and wine at the Eucharist and water at baptism (in various volumes) in obedience to the dominical command and in continuity with an unbroken tradition, but, in the absence of an acknowledgement of the importance of "body-involving" knowledge, it will be hard pressed to find other cogent reasons for its practice.

In this section I have sought to incorporate the insights of Polanyi and Johnson with regard to the bodily roots of human knowledge in order to suggest some preliminary answers to the deceptively problematic questions about the practices that the church has adopted in its sacramental life and in its use of song in worship. Only by supplementing Torrance's account of semantic participation with what I have called (somewhat unsatisfactorily) "bodily participation" (and transformation) has it been possible to do this. As in the previous section, I have shown that our participation in revelation is far from exhausted in its semantic aspect.

Hermeneutical Participation

It is important, as I have argued, to recognize the significance of the trans-linguistic or pre-linguistic aspects of our knowledge. But, as we reflect upon the sacramental practice of the church, we need to recognize that both Eucharist and baptism are set in a liturgical context that is substantially linguistic. The sacramental liturgies locate baptismal and Eucharistic events in the broader narrative of the Judeo-Christian history and tradition. Torrance talks of the "'skill' of interpreting the world from the perspective of the paradigm associated with the ontological and existential realities held forth in baptism."[72]

Rather than dealing with eucharistic and baptismal liturgies, in the concluding section of this chapter I will briefly consider the broader issues associated with the "interpretation of the world," of which Torrance speaks. Here I am concerned with what might be called "hermeneutical" participation. At this juncture, the question of the ecclesial community's interpretation of its Scripture is posed.

There is no scope to deal with the issues of biblical interpretation and hermeneutics in any depth. The limit of what I can hope to achieve in the present context is to outline some ways in which the canonical Scriptures can be conceived as forming and shaping the ecclesial community and, thereby, its self-understanding. I will attempt to indicate the function of the tacit dimension in this process. In concluding the chapter in this way, it will be possible to open up the question of

---

71. As it is difficult to see what music can add to the words of a hymn or a song in terms of human knowledge.

72. Torrance, *Persons in Communion*, 339.

the place of the imagination in this interpretive work in preparation for the final chapter, in which some aspects of the function of imagination in our participation in revelation will be explored.

The New Testament scholar N. T. Wright has suggested a paradigm for biblical interpretation that I think is particularly helpful.[73] Wright, in an attempt to establish the sense in which the biblical texts can be understood as authoritative, rejects approaches that amount to biblicistic proof-texting,[74] and suggests an approach in which we reflect upon the significance of the predominance of "story" in the biblical literature—not least in the New Testament. Wright offers the following suggestion for the interpretation of the biblical literature:

> Suppose there exists a Shakespeare play, most of whose fifth act has been lost. The first four acts provide, let us suppose, such a remarkable wealth of characterization, such a crescendo of excitement within the plot, that it is generally agreed that the play ought to be staged. Nevertheless, it is felt inappropriate actually to write a fifth act once and for all: it would freeze the play into one form, and commit Shakespeare as it were to being prospectively responsible for work not in fact his own. Better, it might be felt, to give the key parts to highly trained, sensitive and experienced Shakespearian actors, who would immerse themselves in the first four acts, and in the language and culture of Shakespeare and his time, *and who would then be told to work out a fifth act for themselves.*[75]

In this scenario, the first four acts play a decisive role in shaping the fifth. The credibility of the rendering of the fifth act could be questioned on the basis that it is incommensurable or inconsistent in some way with the earlier part of the play. But the fifth act could not, of course, be criticized for failing to *repeat* the earlier parts of the play; indeed, an authentic, or at least a credible, fifth act could not possibly be a repetition of what had gone before. What would be required of the actors would be "a free and responsible entering in to the story as it stood, in order first to understand how the threads could appropriately be drawn together and then to put that understanding into effect by speaking and acting with both innovation and consistency."[76]

This model of biblical interpretation, far from being a matter of looking up right answers (or something of the sort), is a creative entering into and extrapolating from the biblical text. To use Polanyi's terminology, we would have to say that authentic biblical interpretation comes not from following a rule-based stratagem but from an imaginative extrapolation facilitated by a profound indwelling of the

---

73. See Wright, *New Testament*, 139–43.

74. In particular, the view that the Bible contains a store of eternal, absolute propositional truths which need simply to be identified and applied in each new situation.

75. Wright, *New Testament*, 140; Wright's emphasis.

76. Ibid.

text. It is a question of "faithful performance." "A good fifth act will show a proper development, not merely repetition of what went before."[77]

Wright makes the point that there might be an analogy here with any work of art or story that is left incomplete.[78] However, he suggests that this analogy is particularly apposite. He explains:

> Among the detailed moves available within this model . . . is the possibility of seeing the biblical story as itself consisting of five acts. Thus: 1-Creation; 2-Fall; 3-Israel; 4-Jesus. The writing of the New Testament—including the writing of the gospels—would then form the first scene of the fifth act, and would simultaneously give hints (Romans 8, 1 Corinthians 15, parts of the Apocalypse) of how the play is supposed to end. The fact of Act 4 being what it is shows what sort of a conclusion the drama should have, without making clear all the intervening steps. The church would live under the 'authority' of the extant story, being required to offer an improvisatory performance of the final act as it leads up to and anticipates the intended conclusion. The church is designed, according to this model, as a stage in the completion of the creator's work of art.[79]

This model suggests that in biblical interpretation we are not looking to quarry timeless truths, or for pre-packaged authoritative answers to questions but, rather, trying to discern our vocation as the people of God, and the appropriate practices, skills, commitments etc., to be associated with it. On such a view, it is not possible to sustain (for example) the view that the Bible is an inerrant source of guidance that tells us what to do in all circumstances. The model opposes the kinds of ideas of biblical interpretation—much influenced by the objectivizing epistemological strategies of the Enlightenment discussed earlier—that from the text "objective truths" can and, indeed, ought to be distilled out. The problems of the interpretation of an ancient text (including those associated both with the historical and contemporary horizons of its meaning) suggest caution in speaking of "the plain meaning of the text." Trevor Hart writes, "The Bible does not often wear its meaning obviously, like a flower waiting to be plucked from its stem."[80]

Kevin J. Vanhoozer, in an essay entitled "The Voice and the Actor,"[81] suggests an approach to biblical interpretation that parallels Wright's approach in some important respects. Vanhoozer's concern is to guard against, on the one hand, a "de-verbalizing" of revelation that places exclusive emphasis on the *acts* of God,[82] and on the other, an "over-verbalizing" that places an exclusive emphasis upon

---

77. Ibid., 141.
78. As it may also be the case for other inherited traditions.
79. Wright, *New Testament*, 141–42.
80. Hart, *Faith Thinking*, 136.
81. Published in Stackhouse, *Evangelical Futures*, 61–106.
82. A move of which some believe Karl Barth is guilty.

the written witness. He believes that it is important to hold word and act together. "Divine revelation . . . is God in communicative action."[83] It is out of this concern that Vanhoozer suggests the metaphor of drama for the gospel. He writes, "The task of theology . . . is to enable hearers and doers of the gospel to respond and correspond to the prior Act and Word of God. The Triune God is the primary speaker and actor, but the people of God have been given the privilege and the responsibility not only of thinking God's thoughts after him but of speaking God's words and acting God's acts after him as well."[84] But what is the process that enables this thinking, speaking, and acting "after God"? Vanhoozer's response to this question (in which his proximity to Wright's position is apparent) is to say that it occurs "through an apprenticeship to the biblical texts."[85] It is through this apprenticeship that we gain theological wisdom.

Redemption is, according to Vanhoozer, a "drama."[86] The drama comprises both the initiative of God and the human response. The purpose of theology is to aid disciples "to participate fittingly in the drama of redemption by making canonically competent judgments about what to say and do as disciples of Jesus Christ in new situations."[87] Rather than thinking of Holy Scripture as a sourcebook from which we simply read off truths and directives, it is conceived as a collection of texts that contribute to a way of seeing things. As such, Christian wisdom—which Vanhoozer calls a spiritual and intellectual "habitus"—is gained "through an apprenticeship to the diverse forms of biblical literature."[88]

Vanhoozer regards authentic human participation in the drama of redemption (an equivalent term for "participation in revelation") in terms of "faithful performance." Summing up his position, he writes:

> Being biblical is not a matter of repeating biblical passages word for word, or even of summarizing the use of particular terms found throughout the bible, but making judgments that are informed, reformed, and transformed, as the case may be, by the wisdom embedded in biblical literature. Canonical-linguistic theology cultivates Christian wisdom: the ability to fit appropriately into the drama of redemption by saying and doing the right thing, by exemplifying right practical reason—in sum, by performing the wisdom of Christ.[89]

---

83. Stackhouse, *Evangelical Futures*, 72.

84. Ibid., 69.

85. Ibid., 82. Note the resonances with Polanyi's ideas *and* terminology here.

86. And it seems implicit that revelation, and human participation in it, can also be understood in this way.

87. Stackhouse, *Evangelical Futures*, 104.

88. Ibid.

89. Ibid.

This apprenticeship occurs in the context of ecclesial communities. Vanhoozer suggests (following Lesslie Newbigin) that the local congregation is the "hermeneutic of the gospel," in that it lives out the meaning of the text. But as Vanhoozer and Wright both maintain, the "faithful performance" has no fixed and determined abstract form against which the correctness of any *particular* ecclesial performance can be judged and evaluated. It is, rather, an improvisation that is based upon what has gone before. Such an improvisation is facilitated by an indwelling of the biblical texts as they have found form and expression within faith communities. Faithful performances are anything but a matter of repeating "the letter of the law"; they are the imaginative and creative responses to what is given in the Word and act of God. As such, they are, among other things, "risky" undertakings for which the communities and individuals involved must accept responsibility.

One of the consequences of this view is that we must expect to find distinctive and differentiated "performances" in different places and at different times. It will be apparent that that not all performances will be the same; but the existence of diversity, although it is likely to be the source of tensions and suspicion, does not necessarily imply disunity. Vanhoozer suggests a "plural unity." He comments: "I for one would be sorry if everyone thought just like me. I would deeply regret it if there were no Mennonite, or Lutheran, or Greek Orthodox voices in the world. Why? Because I think that truth would be better served by their continuing presence."[90] As such, Vanhoozer recognizes the plurality of ecclesial contexts that provide the possibility for such performances. It does not follow from this that "anything goes," but it does require that we recognize the significance of those contexts (ecclesial and otherwise) in which persons are nurtured.

In the models that Wright and Vanhoozer offer, the pneumatological may not be to the fore, but it is not difficult to see how this is necessarily a crucial aspect of the overall picture. The "performance of the gospel" as a participation in revelation is simply not possible apart from its incorporation into the "performance" of Jesus Christ. The ecclesial community participates, through the Spirit, in that which is offered by the Son to the Father. Its performance in temporal existence is provisional. It exists in anticipation of eschatological fulfillment.

Concluding Comment

In this chapter I have not offered anything more than a small number of suggestions of how the epistemology of Michael Polanyi might be brought to bear upon our understanding of participation in revelation. Many of the themes expounded in chapter 3 have been revisited in this chapter in order to demonstrate something of their potential for clarifying what is involved in participating in the revelation

---

90. Ibid., 80.

of God. In particular, the bodily roots of human understanding (with all the practices and skills that are implied in them), the significance of participation within a community for human epistemic transformation, and the importance of the tacit dimension have come to the fore.

In the latter part of this chapter, I have begun to bring out more explicitly the importance of imagination in the church's interpretation of Holy Scripture as it participates in the revelation of God. In the final chapter I will seek to give fuller expression to this facet of human participation.

The theme of imagination has had a checkered history in theology. The final chapter will include an exposition of the work of Gordon Kaufman (for whom imagination is a central theological theme). My conviction is that this is a wrong turn and an example of how far astray from the truth the theme of imagination can lead. Following a critique of Kaufman, I will make a counter-suggestion that I think is both harmonious with the understanding of participation in revelation that has been developed, and a reinforcement and extension of several other themes already explored in this book.

CHAPTER 6

Revelation and Imagination

Introduction

IN THE FINAL section of chapter 5, in the discussion of hermeneutical participation in revelation, the question of imagination was explicitly raised. The substantially overlapping models of "dramatic performance" proposed by Wright and Vanhoozer suggest that the ecclesial interpretation of Holy Scripture and, indeed, ecclesial life be understood in terms of "improvisation" seeking "faithful performance." On such a view, it is implicit that the church's participation in revelation involves a significant imaginative component.[1] In bringing my arguments to a conclusion, I will seek to offer some preliminary suggestions about what might be said about imagination as a component of participation in revelation.

As an extended preliminary to this, I will consider in some detail the work of Gordon Kaufman, who has written substantially on the role of imagination in theology. My reasons for selecting Kaufman's work for framing my approach to the question of imagination are several: Kaufman is a significant figure in contemporary American theology today and, as David Bryant suggests, "his emphasis on the imaginative nature of theological work confronts us, in a way that we cannot ignore, with the question of what it means to say that theology is a human enterprise that involves imagination. That is, he has made it clear that theology must accept the imagination as a central component of its work and must come to terms with the implication of this increasingly inescapable fact."[2]

But despite Kaufman's affirmation of the place of imagination in theology, even the most perfunctory reading of his proposals reveals a profound incommensurability with the thesis that I have been developing. He conceives the

---

1. This does not suggest that issues relating to imagination are not implied elsewhere—only that they remained largely implicit.

2. Bryant, *Faith and the Play of Imagination*, 54.

relationship between imagination and revelation in terms of mutual exclusivity, and Kaufman's enthusiastic employment of the former is, consequently, made at the cost of his rejection of the latter.[3] If we are to speak of an imaginative participation in revelation—which is my intention—it will be necessary to demonstrate that the dichotomy between imagination and revelation that Kaufman adopts can be subjected to an effective challenge.

This chapter will begin with an exposition of Kaufman's understanding of theological imagination in which I will allow Kaufman to speak for himself with minimal interruption. This will be followed by an assessment and critique of his position.[4] In the context of this critical review of Kaufman's work, I will develop some of the contours of an alternative conceptualization in which it is not only possible but necessary to speak of the imaginative component of our participation in revelation. In this task I shall, once again, draw upon the epistemological insights of Michael Polanyi.

I turn now to an exposition of Kaufman's views.

Gordon Kaufman and the Theological Imagination

Theology as Imaginative Construction

In the following exposition I will outline the principal strands of Kaufman's thought pertinent to the concerns of the present work. I will focus primarily on his book *The Theological Imagination: Constructing the Concept of God*.

In the preface to *The Theological Imagination*, Kaufman states: "I have become persuaded that theology is (and always has been) essentially a constructive work of the human imagination, an expression of the imagination's activity helping to provide orientation for human life through developing a symbolical 'picture' of the world roundabout and of the human place within that world."[5] This is the heart of Kaufman's proposal and the fundamental presupposition of his theological method. Theological work is concerned with the "concept of God," and this concept is a human construction through and through. This is so, according to Kaufman, because

---

3. Note that, in an earlier phase of his theological development, Kaufman adopted a positive attitude towards the concept of revelation. For an account of his earlier position, see, for example, ibid., 13–32.

4. Such a task is rendered difficult because of the idiosyncrasy of Kaufman's theology and, in my opinion, by the variety of ways in which he is mistaken. An important example of this is Kaufman's reading of Kant. Although I make no claim to expertise in Kant's philosophy, it is apparent that Kaufman's reading is often far from reliable. However, rather that attempting a critique of Kaufman's reading of Kant, I will allow Kaufman's position as he presents it to be the point at which I interact with him.

5. Kaufman, *Theological Imagination*, 11.

> God is not a reality immediately available in our experience for observation, inspection, and description, and speech about or to God therefore is never directly referential. Thus, we are unable to check our concepts and images of God for accuracy and adequacy through direct confrontation with the reality *God*, as we can with most ordinary objects of perception and experience; instead, our awareness and understanding here is gained entirely in and through the images and concepts themselves, constructed into and focused by the mind into a center for the self's devotion and service.[6]

Kaufman acknowledges that this process must not be understood individualistically. One does not construct the concept of God "from scratch." Inevitably one builds on the work of others and of previous generations. A plethora of ideas is inherited from those believers, prophets, poets, and thinkers who have gone before us. Above all (and problematically as far as Kaufman is concerned) there is the influence of the Bible. "[T]he Bible's significance for Western thinking about God has gone far beyond mere informal influence of this sort. The Bible was long regarded as the locus of God's revelation to humanity (the 'word of God'); it therefore carried an authority powerful enough to override ordinary human experience and rational argument."[7]

It was through this function of the Bible that God's being and activity came to be conceived (quite wrongly in Kaufman's view) in objective terms. It was because the Bible imposed itself as a primary source of normative images that other possibilities were thwarted. Rather than seeing the writings of the Bible as part of an ongoing process of imaginative theological construction, the scriptural record was cast into the role of an authority and came to function as a limit, and so hiding (or disguising) the constructive nature of theology.

Concomitant to this objectification of the biblical tradition is the positing of God as an unconstructed objective being. Kaufman believes that in the highly unified worldview of any monotheistic religion, the reification of the concept of God into an independent existing being is likely. It is, nevertheless, a serious theological error:

> It is a mistake ... to regard qualities attributed to God (e.g., aseity, holiness, omnipotence, omniscience, providence, love, self-revelation) as though they were features or activities of such a particular being. Rather, in the mind's construction of the image/concept of God the ordinary relation of subject and predicate is reversed. Instead of the subject (God) being a *given* to which the various predicate adjectives are then assigned, here the descriptive themes themselves are the building blocks which the imagination uses in putting together its conception.[8]

---

6. Ibid., 21; Kaufman's emphasis.
7. Ibid., 23.
8. Ibid., 29; Kaufman's emphasis.

Kaufman accepts that much of such God-language was, indeed, adopted in the belief that it was somehow referential but disposes of this as a "mistaken understanding." The presence of such a strategy in Christian history should alert us, all the more, to the need for a critical attitude towards our inherited vocabulary.

Although he does not argue the point, Kaufman does not believe that the concept of revelation is viable. But he *is* aware of the fundamental question that this raises, and asks: "If we can no longer assume that theology is working directly from an authoritative divine revelation, how are we to proceed?"[9] He also asks, "Is it really possible to set out a meaningful concept of God once the radically constructive character of theology is acknowledged?"[10] Clearly he believes we can, but, he contends, we are only justified in doing so when we have recognized and acknowledged the fundamentally constructive nature of the task. It is now necessary to consider what is implied by Kaufman's use of the term "construction" in his proposal for establishing the concept of God.

It is worth noting that part of the difficulty in grasping what Kaufman has to say is to be located in his eccentric employment of familiar theological language and terminology. One must always keep in mind that, for Kaufman, all theology is imaginative construction. Theology, in its talk of God, constructs and, for Kaufman, this means that it doesn't refer—at least not in the way that it has generally been assumed to refer in the history of Christian theology.

Constructing the Concept of God

Kaufman believes that the concept of God can provide possibilities for humanity that are otherwise absent. Crucially, the concept of God can serve the purposes of humanization. He explains: "To speak of God's 'reality' or 'existence'—i.e., to speak of the validity or truth of the theistic perspective—is to maintain that the modes of life made possible, when existence is oriented according to this perspective, are a full and genuine realization of the actual potentialities of human nature, are in accord, that is to say, with 'how things are.'"[11]

In constructing the concept of God, Kaufman stresses the need both for transcendence and immanence. God is both the mysterious one who is beyond all human knowing and the one who is the humanizing center of orientation for human life.

With regard to transcendence, Kaufman avers: "What seems to be at stake here is a claim that human individuals and communities need a center of orientation and devotion outside themselves and their perceived desires and needs if they are to find genuine fulfillment. As finite beings seeking security and satisfaction,

---

9. Ibid., 30.

10. Ibid., 31.

11. Ibid., 49. Kaufman's concept of "how things are" is linked to an idea of evolutionary emergence which will be discussed below.

Revelation and Imagination 201

we all too easily make ourselves the center of life, rearranging all else so that it simply conforms with our wishes."[12] It is this relativizing image that counters our human narcissism and confronts the "turned-in" character of human existence. The point is not that the image of the transcendent God points to some being to be understood on its own terms, but rather that "it functions as the principal focal point of an overall world-picture, and it is in terms of that interpretive frame that it must be understood."[13] The God of the Bible functions as the principal actor in that vast historical movement from the creation to the eschaton.

Kaufman suggests that "it is as true to say that the meaning of human life is found within the ongoing movement of (God's) history as to say that it is found in relation to God—for the two expressions come down to the same thing. Living within the world-view that has God as its focus is no different from living in significant relation to that God who is the focal center for this world-view."[14] However, in the contemporary situation—and mindful of the dangers of reifying the concept of God into an independent being—the former alternative is preferable, "For it provides a way to speak of an independence and otherness and even aseity over against the human—the requisite condition for breaking our narcissism and anthropocentrism and drawing us out of ourselves—without positing a particular existing being (named 'God') as that in which this otherness is lodged."[15]

If the concept of transcendence is important in constructing the concept of God, the concept of "immanence" is no less so. Here we have to do with God's active concern for the fulfillment of life. Kaufman points to evolutionary processes that led to the emergence of the human species, and the emergence of values and ideals in human existence as realities in which we discern the fatherly guidance and care of God. "One can . . . speak of a movement of cosmic history that has eventuated in the production of the human and the humane, and one might hope for a further development of this historical tendency towards a more genuinely humane society—what in the traditional mythology was expected as the 'kingdom of God.'"[16] God symbolizes the evolutionary-historical process in which human life and, in time, humane life emerges. Hence, in looking beyond ourselves, we have intimations of the possibilities of the future.

The ideas of transcendence and immanence are both important. Kaufman believes that the concept of God, constructed in this way, can be both meaningful to and serviceable for humanity. "The image . . . of a divine Person who has created us, who sustains us, who loves us and cares for us, and who is seeking our full realization (our salvation), presents vividly and meaningfully to human

---

12. Ibid., 35–36.
13. Ibid., 37.
14. Ibid., 38.
15. Ibid.
16. Ibid., 40.

consciousness that to which we should be devoted, if the further realization of our human potential is to be achieved. 'God' is a symbol that gathers up into itself and focuses for us all those cosmic forces working toward the fully humane existence for which we long."[17]

Christology

Kaufman identifies three categories that are of fundamental importance for theists: God, humanity, and world. But in Christianity there is a fourth category, Jesus Christ. He allows that, in some sense, it is this category that qualifies the other three in the case of Christian belief. But is this concept helpful in contributing to a concept of God that is truly humanizing?

> [We must ask] whether the Christian fourfold categorical scheme is any longer viable or whether the time has come drastically to transform it. How does the Christian world-view stand up in comparison with Buddhist and Jewish, Marxist and liberal humanist and other perspectives? Has the time come to drop the category God or the category Christ—or both of them—from the fundamental places they occupy in the Christian scheme? Should they be replaced by other symbols with quite different metaphorical foundations and metaphysical implications; or should the categorical scheme be expanded beyond four to include important dimensions of life and reality which these categories cannot accommodate? Or has the time come to dispense with the Christian categorical scheme altogether in favor of some more adequate framework for orienting human life?[18]

Once the fundamentally constructive nature of the theological enterprise is embraced, the possibilities of radically reconstructing the tradition are apparent. Indeed, "Whether or how 'Jesus' can properly continue to be central in a contemporary theological position is something to be established, not something to be taken for granted."[19] Whether the concept Jesus is to be retained or not is *our* decision. Kaufman writes, "if Jesus Christ is to be given a significant position—or any position at all—in our theology, this will be because of needs and reasons which we ourselves, in a contemporary attempt at theological understanding and construction, find compelling."[20] In Kaufman's view, the contemporary consciousness has *carte blanche* to dispose of received tradition as it sees fit—be that to adopt, adapt, or reject it. The function of inherited tradition is to serve the purposes of humanity, and those purposes are conceived quite independently of any inheritance from tradition.

17. Ibid., 50.
18. Ibid., 121.
19. Ibid., 125.
20. Ibid., 128.

Although the constructive nature of this process is clearly expressed by Kaufman, the criteria that he offers are exceedingly vague. He suggests, for example, that "[W]hen we adopt a model or an image of the human and make it normative in theological construction, we must be able plausibly to claim (a) that it 'truly' or 'accurately' expresses or represents human nature, its potentialities and its problems, and (b) that it can be intelligibly understood in the context of, and in significant interrelationship with, what we take to be the 'real world.'"[21]

Kaufman affirms that Jesus is a historical figure (however difficult it may be to establish the facts of his life). The difficulty is in establishing how to construct a theology in relation to this figure. Kaufman is extremely critical of the "mythic" picture of Jesus as a divine being who came down from heaven and was resurrected after his death. Kaufman criticizes Barth in this regard:

> In the present century Karl Barth has gone the farthest in trying to develop a theology expressing this traditional understanding of Jesus Christ. However subtle and sophisticated Barth's working out of the details may be, for him faith is understood essentially as buying into and accepting this traditional Christian myth, and the work of the theologian is directed largely to analyzing and imaginatively elaborating the meaning of that myth for our understanding of God and humanity.[22]

He suggests that such an approach is untenable since it grounds the theological enterprise in an arbitrary starting point that must be accepted fideistically. "Once it is recognized that theology is (and always has been) an activity of human imaginative construction, it is no longer acceptable to begin our theological work with an authoritarian starting point, however venerable and revered that foundation may be."[23]

It is an error to attribute definitive significance to an inherited tradition. Whether it be the canon of Scripture, the creeds, the teachings of the Church Fathers, or the theology of the Reformers, what we are dealing with are human constructs. However valuable or functional that tradition may (or may not) have been in another epoch, it must not be afforded an over-privileged position in our own. "To give the expressions and constructions of earlier generations such authoritative and uncriticizable standing—once we have recognized that this is what we are doing—is out-and-out idolatry, an intolerable position for theology seriously attempting to speak of *God*."[24] Kaufman makes the blunt comment: "[M]ost Christian talk about Jesus as divine or 'Jesus as God and Savior' is idolatrous."[25]

21. Ibid., 134.
22. Ibid., 138. The "mythic" in Barth's writing—insofar as Kaufman explicates the term—is to be associated in particular with the idea of incarnation objectively conceived.
23. Ibid.
24. Ibid.; Kaufman's emphasis.
25. Ibid., 205.

What Kaufman sees in the historical figure of Jesus is the exemplification of self-giving love; a life given in service to others. But other examples or paradigms are available to us: Julius Caesar, Socrates, Buddha, Henry Ford, etc. We *may* choose to commit ourselves to one of these or, indeed, to a paradigm that is less individualistic, in which various different images of community are in view.

Kaufman suggests that every religion offers some form of "salvation." Implicit in the notion of salvation is the idea that our humanity is either distorted or insufficiently developed. The purpose of religion is to draw us toward resolution. This is what religion is *for*. Kaufman says that the only God we can afford to worship is the God who will further our process of humanization, the God who will make possible the creation of universal and humane community. Kaufman believes that the image of a suffering God—the Christ of the cross—*is* serviceable in this endeavor.

A difficulty with Kaufman's position is that his concept of "humanization" is profoundly underdeveloped.[26] It is difficult to imagine any religious or secular worldview that would claim to *oppose* the process of humanization. The problem is in establishing, with any degree of unanimity, what "humanization" means; what might facilitate it and what might hinder it.

Kantian Influences

In the chapter "Metaphysics and Theology," Kaufman lays claim to a Kantian influence in his project.[27] He explains that

> Kant saw that the central ideas with which metaphysics works—ideas like "God" and "world" and "self"—function differently in our thinking from concepts dealing with objects of direct experience, concepts like "tree" or "man." While the latter are used to organize and classify elements of experience directly, thus helping to make experience itself possible and serving as vehicles through which experience is cognized, the former "metaphysical" notions function at a remove from direct perception or experience: they are used for ordering and organizing our conceptions or knowledge (rather than what is directly experienced) and function, thus, principally as "regulative ideas."[28]

The concept of God is, for Kaufman, a human construction. "God" is the mind's highest and most profound creation. It is through this concept that every dimension of life is brought into unity. He goes on to say, "To regard God as some

---

26. This is, perhaps, unsurprising, as any such development would imply—whether explicitly or implicitly—a *particular* understanding of human nature.

27. As I mentioned above, Kaufman's reading of Kant can be questioned, but this is not a task that I will attempt to take up.

28. Kaufman, *Theological Imagination*, 242.

kind of describable or knowable object over against us would be at once a degradation of God and a serious category error."[29] Kaufman believes that Kant made a key contribution to theology: "For our purpose, the importance of Kant was his discovery that such central metaphysical concepts as God, self, and the world are imaginative constructs, created by the mind for certain intramental functions."[30]

Here the question of metaphysics might be raised. Kaufman believes that the ideas of metaphysics evolve over the generations as humanity seeks to make sense of its experience in terms bequeathed to it by its ancestors. Concepts serviceable in one particular historical epoch may be quite unserviceable in another. A style of metaphysical conceptualization that was appropriate in the Middle Ages may be most inappropriate for understanding the culture and reality of our own time. But what is metaphysics trying to do? Kaufman suggests that metaphysics endeavors to expose the structures of meaning and concepts that underlie the patterns of thought and practice (including customs, institutions, etc.) of a culture. In bringing such cultural presuppositions to conscious awareness, it is possible to gain some freedom from them and thereby take on a more responsible role. In this way metaphysics helps liberate humanity from determination by the powers and forces of that nature from which it has emerged. Kaufman comments: "[T]he breadth and abstractness of this question [of how conceptualizations promote human freedom] is immense, and assessing different metaphysical positions with reference to it will not be easy, but surely the diverse claims of Whitehead and of Heidegger, of James and Marx and Hegel, can be analyzed in terms of their effectiveness in raising human consciousness about its overall situation and thus in furthering human liberation."[31]

Metaphysicians are concerned with reality and truth claims, but, according to Kaufman, they face substantially the same epistemological problems that confront theologians. He writes: "In the case of ordinary sciences, analysis and experimentation are carried on within a framework of concepts and theory that determines the objects to be investigated, specifies the methods and objectives of the investigation, and defines what will count as true or valid results. In the case of metaphysics, however, none of these matters are specified; they are themselves the very subjects to be investigated."[32] In the realm of metaphysics, Kaufman explains, we are forced to acknowledge the centrality of imagination. "The elaboration of a metaphysical position . . . is not so much the working out of the scientific theory of the nature of the whole as it is the expression of a *faith* that this or that model or metaphor drawn from experience can properly serve as a paradigm in terms

29. Ibid., 244.
30. Ibid.
31. Ibid., 257.
32. Ibid., 246.

of which the world can be grasped."[33] Kaufman describes the kind of check that can be placed upon the metaphysician as "quasi-empirical,"[34] and he is optimistic about the possibilities of this form of verification. Empirically convincing metaphors must be the basis of the principal metaphysical concepts, and those concepts must order and interpret the actual facts of experience in a convincing way.

If the task of both theology and metaphysics is constructive and imaginative, how is it possible to distinguish between the two disciplines? Kaufman's answer to this question is that theology, unlike metaphysics, constructs its concept of the world "under God." The concept of God is that which distinguishes theology from metaphysics. To do away with God is to do away with theology. Nevertheless, metaphysics and theology are confronted with methodological problems that are epistemologically similar. For Kaufman, the value of a theological worldview (a particular imaginative construct of the concept of God) is to be determined on the basis of whether it is true to reality.[35] Metaphysics does not occupy a privileged position with respect to theology. Any metaphysical construct must be evaluated on exactly the same basis.

Kaufman suggests that if metaphysics and theology appear to be very different, it is because theology has attempted to ground its work in Holy Scripture and tradition. As we have seen, Kaufman views this as an error because the writings of Holy Scripture and the testimony of tradition are themselves instantiations of imaginative construction. What the authors of the Scriptures and creeds were doing is on a par with the work of contemporary theologians. To attribute an authority or a priority of the writings of the former over the latter is to misconceive the constructive nature of theological work. "None of . . . [the] biblical authors or the anonymous myth makers who live behind their work, have seen God 'face-to-face' and are thus in a position simply to report what they have experienced."[36]

Kaufman suggests that in our time the metaphysicians have fared rather better than the theologians in terms of establishing respect in the academy. The diagnosis he offers for this is that metaphysics has felt free to employ a wide variety of metaphors and concepts *because it was explicitly aware of the imaginative process in which it was involved.* Theology was largely ignorant of the imaginative nature of its work and, assuming that it was in various ways constrained by tradition, failed to grasp fully the nature, and thereby the possibilities, of the work in which it was engaged. Kaufman summarizes his point when he writes:

> It is my contention . . . that the allegedly "scientific" character of metaphysics, which gave it a claim to cognitive superiority over theology, is a myth (as many contemporary philosophers would also acknowledge), and that

---

33. Ibid., 247; Kaufman's emphasis.
34. See ibid., 249.
35. By which Kaufman means that it has a capacity to facilitate "humanization."
36. Kaufman, *Theological Imagination*, 250.

the theologians' claim of a direct revelatory foundation for their work is equally a myth. When this is recognized, it becomes clear that metaphysics and theology are in fact very similar activities. Both are concerned with imaginative construction of a concept or image of the overall context (the "world") within which human life transpires, and neither can claim to base that construction on direct inspection of "the nature of things," for the simple reason that such direct inspection is impossible.[37]

The Problem of Pragmatic Criteria

Kaufman is aware that in his pressing pragmatic criteria, the continuing viability of the "religious outlook" will be continually called into question:

> [I]f . . . Marxist or materialist conceptions encourage and enable human life of a better and more fulfilling quality, in the long run they will be the ones that prevail, and the theistic view will gradually die out. To the extent that the Christian claim, that true human fulfillment is to be found in the self-sacrificing love epitomized in Jesus' crucifixion, has led to repression of the human (Freud) and to slavishness (Nietzsche), it stands today under heavy criticism for its pretensions. If the Christian understanding of life and the world is not to become increasingly irrelevant in modern culture, or even totally to die out, a much more realistic reconception of its central claims will need to be made.[38]

According to Kaufman, both metaphysical and theological concepts must be tested by the effects that they have upon the character and quality of human life. One of the consequences of this is that only religious views held by a significant proportion of a population are pragmatically testable. Other views, regardless of their potential for humanization, are—for all practical purposes—redundant. This is why Kaufman believes that the concept of "God" is of such significance for the West. It is on a level unparalleled by any other metaphysical concept. Kaufman makes the claim that (despite shortcomings and failures) the Christian church and theology *have* made significant contributions to human growth and liberation in the past, whatever may happen in the future.

Theology would dissolve if the symbol of "God" was jettisoned, and Kaufman feels that it would be inappropriate to make such a move in our present situation. This does not mean that this symbol should not be subjected to radical revision, and he believes that the continuing value of the concept of God is contingent upon the effectiveness of such revisions. The humiliation of theology before the philosophers in recent centuries is, in large part, due to the fact that

---

37. Ibid., 254.
38. Ibid., 257–58.

theologians have not felt sufficiently free to reconstruct, in a radical way, central theological conceptuality.

Concluding Thoughts

Kaufman believes that the concept of God (as a human construct) continues to be a fruitful one. But theology must be judged "in terms of the adequacy with which it is fulfilling the objectives we humans have set for it."[39] "[A]ll religious institutions, practices and ideas—including the idea of God—were made to serve human needs and to further our humanization (what has traditionally been called our "salvation"); humanity was not made for the sake of religious customs and ideas."[40]

Kaufman remains optimistic about the possibilities of the concept of God, and he concludes his work with certain confessional affirmations. "God," being the ultimate point of reference for all understanding, is also the object of devotion for all human life. If anything that is not God is made into the absolute point of reference, it will necessarily become an idol. Whereas idolatry is destructive and dehumanizing, the concept of God is idolatry's negation. "[B]y 'God' we mean that reality which rescues us from all these enslavements into which we continually fall, that reality which brings human life to its full realization."[41]

To the extent that parts of our lives remain unrelated to God (those things for which God is not the ultimate reference point), we are not worshippers of God. God is the one who relativizes all false absolutes. He is the one who unmasks the idols. As the concept of God becomes clearer to us, we see more clearly where we have been inhuman, depersonalizing and destructive of our humanity.

Critique of Kaufman's "Theological Imagination"

Introduction

As I noted at the beginning of the chapter, Kaufman is a theologian who has played a significant role in placing imagination on the theological agenda. I wish to affirm such a move, although, for reasons that have already been mooted, I have some serious concerns about the way in which he does this. I would echo David Bryant's sentiments when he writes: "The issue is not whether faith is imaginative but what the imagination is and how it operates, that is, whether faith is a

---

39. Ibid., 264. Kaufman does not say how "we humans" determine what the objectives will be, but one might hazard a guess that they will probably have much to do with the generic and ubiquitous goal of humanization.

40. Ibid. Again Kaufman does not identify the human needs that are to be served in order to further the process of humanization.

41. Ibid., 268.

construction of the subject's imaginative inventions or the result of an imaginative attunement to the disclosive power of the Christian tradition."[42] This is a possibility that Kaufman does not appear to consider.

At the beginning of the chapter, I noted that one of the most fundamental incompatibilities between Kaufman's position and the one I am seeking to develop is that it conceives of imagination in such a way that revelation is necessarily eclipsed by it. Part of the task of the remainder of this chapter is to show why it is not necessary to be constrained by such a dichotomy. To this end, the first question I want to ask is whether, when we speak of God, there is a referent.

God: Is there a Referent?

Kaufman warns against the objectification of the concept of God for two reasons. Firstly, he claims it mistakenly takes the concept of God to correspond to an available referent along the lines in which we know ordinary objects (a dog, a man, a book, a tree, etc.). Kaufman rejects this and claims that the "available referent" is not an "existent being" but a human construct—and *only* a human construct. Secondly, he believes that in reifying the concept of God, the essential procedure of imaginative construction in theology is obfuscated. Once God has been objectified, this "object" can be (and has been) enshrined in a tradition and functions as an authority that delimits the scope of the theological enterprise, eclipsing and thwarting its creative and imaginative function.

For Kaufman, the "available referent," in speaking about God, is a human construct that enables us to see all other aspects of our reality in humanizing perspective.[43] In this way finite objects do not become idols. In as far as all aspects of our lives are brought into relationship with this concept of God, we are saved from the dehumanizing effects of idolatry. Kaufman simply presupposes that if God does exist independently of our imaginative concept of him, there is no means of either knowing or speaking about such a being. The pertinent point to be made is that, for Kaufman, the "God" of whom we speak in theology could not have such a being as its referent.

But why is it not possible to affirm, as Kaufman does, a transcendent God— one by whom everything else in our lives is to be understood—while maintaining that this God can be the referent of this term? Kaufman appears to believe that in his asserting that the concept of God is a human construct, it is implied that revelation can have no place in theology. But what if God is a self-existent being who is able to reveal himself to humanity?[44] Commenting on Kaufman's position,

---

42. Bryant, *Faith and the Play of Imagination*, 162.

43. Kaufman's use of the term "available referent" in this context appears awkward and unsatisfactory.

44. This is precisely the position which Paul the apostle, for example, held: "For I want you to know, brothers and sisters, that the gospel that was proclaimed by me is not of human origin; for I did

Alvin Plantinga asks: "If God is omnipotent, infinitely powerful, won't he be able to manifest himself in our experience, bring it about that we experience him? He will be unable to do so, presumably, under those conditions, only if it is logically impossible (impossible in the broadly logical sense) that an omniscient and omnipotent being should be able to make himself heard. But so far as I can see, there isn't even the slightest reason to think that; certainly Kaufman gives us none."[45] Indeed. And more generally, Kaufman offers us very little by way of explanation of why the possibility of revelation is ruled out.

If Kaufman is saying that finite humanity has no capacity to know a transcendent God, he articulates a position in harmony with that of Karl Barth. But, as Plantinga helpfully points out, the critical question is whether the transcendent God has the capacity to reveal himself to humanity. Kaufman does not give this matter serious consideration.

Kaufman explains that, as distinct from objects such as a dog, a man, a book, a tree, etc., there is no "direct" experience of God. We do not "see" God as we see these other objects. Kaufman concludes that, on the basis of this distinction, if we are to speak of God we must speak of a concept the content of which is *exclusively* our own imaginative work. His assumption appears to be that revelation, if it is to mean anything akin to its traditional understanding, must be conceived in terms of God making himself known in the way that a dog, a man, a book, or a tree are known. This is why Kaufman rejects the idea of the revelation of God.[46] However, it will be recalled from the first chapter of this book that while Barth affirms that God does indeed make himself known in the sphere of fleshy reality, the means by which this occurs must be radically distinguished from the means by which other objects are known.[47] This is a view that is widely held within the Christian tradition.

If it is (logically) impossible for a self-existent God to make himself known to humanity, then it is not unreasonable to suggest, as Kaufman does, that to construct a theology on the basis of the idea that God has revealed himself is inauthentic, self-deceptive, and, indeed, idolatrous. However, Kaufman does no more than assume this to be so. What Kaufman does achieve is the mapping-out of the implications of this assumption. This is perfectly cogent. What is not cogent is the way in which he presents his program as a refutation of revelation and of the authenticity of belief in a pre-existent God. But Kaufman has simply not made

---

not receive it from a human source, nor was I taught it, but I received it through a revelation of Jesus Christ," Gal 1:11–12.

45. Plantinga, *Warranted Christian Belief*, 34.

46. It might be noted that quantum physics deals with concepts that cannot be perceived like a dog, a man, a book, a tree, etc. But this does not mean that such concepts are "purely imaginative" in Kaufman's sense of the term.

47. Here I have in mind the role of the Holy Spirit as the subjective reality of revelation, and the paradoxical nature of revelation in which God is veiled in his unveiling.

this case, and his "argument" will not be convincing to those who do not already share his basic assumptions.

Starting Points

Kaufman is critical of Barth, who has gone to such lengths to establish a traditional "mythical" view of Jesus Christ. "[F]or him faith is understood essentially as buying into and accepting this traditional Christian myth, and the work of the theologian is directed largely to analyzing and imaginatively elaborating the meaning of that myth for our understanding of God and humanity."[48] Kaufman's charge against Barth is that "Such a procedure forces us to ground our theological work on an *arbitrary starting point* which must be accepted fideistically."[49] As such Kaufman accuses Barth of idolatry.[50]

I have already claimed that Kaufman has not *demonstrated* the incoherence of the concept of revelation; he has *assumed* it. If there is a revelation of the Word of God, as Barth holds, to allow such a revelation to be the starting point for our understanding of God seems far from arbitrary. It is worth noting that Barth attributes to Holy Scripture—as the prime witness to revelation—the status of canon because it imposes itself as such.[51] Revelation is an event in which we are confronted by God. If we are to talk of "grounds," there are no grounds on which Barth's understanding of canon can be accredited and established outside its own sphere: it is self-grounding. In *this* sense Barth's position might be described as "arbitrary." But to say this is to say no more than we would have to say of any disclosure event. Our understanding of things that are revealed or made known to us will generally—and appropriately—start with the event in which the disclosure occurs.

Kaufman believes that Barth's theology is idolatrous and his method arbitrary. But what is his alternative proposal? If we ask Kaufman about where one starts in constructing the concept of God, he replies that the fundamental criterion is "humanization." Kaufman believes that this criterion is not arbitrary because it is "true to the way things are."[52] If we ask Kaufman, "How are things?" he explains that there are cosmic forces that are carrying us towards a more humane existence

---

48. Kaufman, *Theological Imagination*, 138. It is interesting to note that Kaufman does recognize the imaginative component of the work of a theologian such as Barth even if he does regard his basic theological orientation as misconceived.

49. Ibid.; my emphasis.

50. Bruce McCormack, reflecting upon Barth's zealous and lifelong commitment to promoting fidelity to the First Commandment, describes Kaufman's accusation as "one of the richer ironies of the history of theology." See McCormack, "Divine Revelation and Human Imagination," 451.

51. See Barth, *Church Dogmatics* I/1, 109.

52. See Kaufman, *Theological Imagination*, 134.

(for which we long).[53] For Kaufman, it is because of this that we look to the historical figure of Jesus and see in him—in his life and works—something "expressive of an *agape* at the deepest levels of Reality."[54] But this view of reality is not a percept: it is not like a dog, a man, a book, or a tree. What is more, many people see the world very differently.[55]

Kaufman's assertion is that the process of humanization is somehow written into the evolutionary process. As such, it is appropriate to use the concept of humanization as the starting point in constructing the concept of God. He doesn't, however, make a case that this "movement of cosmic forces" is self-evident (and is doubtless wise in his choice not to do so), but the question inevitably arises as to how Kaufman knows this to be the case. Certainly he makes no attempt to ground his conviction, and hence the criterion is set forth in a way that looks, itself, suspiciously arbitrary. As McCormack points out: "The tension (contradiction?) in Kaufman's thought is that he is *both* denying the referential character of God-talk and at the same time, affirming that the symbol of 'God' refers to a metaphysically real ground of reality."[56] Consequently, it is hard to see why Kaufman's starting point is any more grounded than Barth's. Indeed, one wonders whether it is considerably less well grounded.

Kaufman sets the problem up in terms of starting points. If we follow him in this regard, it must said, quite frankly, that if theology is to be done at all, it has to start somewhere. The concept of revelation seems to provide a starting position that is at least as plausible as that of the concept of humanization, if not more so. But is Kaufman's framing of the problem satisfactory? For him, it is crucial for theology to have the correct starting point, and for Kaufman, this point is a *concept*. I want to say that we do not start with concepts at all. We do not *start* with concepts, theories, thoughts, or ideas about God; we *start* (if it is helpful to adopt the word in this context) with our participation in a form of life. It is only out of this participation that our conceptual understanding can arise. As such, I contend that the starting point of theology is not *the concept* of revelation but the life of the church as it participates in revelation.[57]

I will have more to say about the priority of the conceptual in Kaufman's theology later in the chapter.

---

53. See ibid., 50.

54. Ibid., 144.

55. It must surely be acknowledged that there are other views of the world. For many, the preponderance of evil and suffering precludes any idea of progress towards "humanization" (whatever that might be), regardless of whether or not there are "cosmic forces" at work. ("Change and decay in all around I see . . ."—Henry Francis Lyte.)

56. McCormack, "Divine Revelation and Human Imagination," 441; McCormack's emphasis.

57. Whether it is necessary or even appropriate call this a "starting point" is another and less significant matter.

Kaufman and Kant

Kaufman's reasons for opting for "imaginative construction" flow from a particular form of Kantian commitment. As I have noted, following Kant, Kaufman draws a clear distinction between the central ideas of metaphysics ("God," "the world," etc.) and concepts relating to objects of ordinary experience ("a dog," "a book," etc.). The latter are used in a "direct" way to organize experience, but the former cannot be used like this. They operate at a remove to order conceptions of knowledge. Kaufman believes that we can only describe something when there is a correspondence between concepts and percepts. The concept of "God," which is central to theological language, is a regulative idea and does not correspond to a percept, and hence, for Kaufman, it cannot be descriptive; it must be imaginatively constructed. The concept of God must always be a construct of the imagination.

But how viable is this dichotomous understanding, in which concepts that relate to percepts are conceived as descriptions, while regulative ideas (and here we have the concept of "God" in mind in particular) are regarded as purely imaginative constructs? In attempting to answer this question I intend to draw, again, on the insights of Michael Polanyi.

Polanyi's triadic epistemological framework demonstrates, as was explained in chapter 3, that the perception of "ordinary objects" ("a dog," "a book," etc.) occurs in the *action* of a perceiver.[58] Focal knowledge is achieved by drawing upon subsidiary knowledge that, in the act of perceiving, cannot be articulated. The "from-to" nature of human knowing implies that in order to perceive or know, we necessarily rely upon knowledge that, in the act of knowing, functions tacitly—as an extension of ourselves. In the same way we use the spectacles we wear, we do not focus *on* such knowledge; we focus *with* it. So, as we have seen, Polanyi claims that we "indwell" such knowledge. We cannot—at least insofar as we continue to indwell such knowledge—*demonstrate* its veracity; we can only *trust* its veracity.[59]

This insight calls into question the kind of distinction that Kaufman draws.[60] Polanyi notes, however, that Kant did have some partial insight into this epistemological dynamic even though it was not integrated systematically into his theory. Polanyi comments:

> Kant . . . occasionally admitted that into all acts of judgment there enters, and must enter, a personal decision which cannot be accounted for by any

---

58. One difficulty embedded in his "Kantian scheme," of which Kaufman appears be unaware, is dramatically illustrated by the self-perception of the Bororo—a tribe of the Brazilian rainforest: they regard themselves as a species of red parrot. Although they are, in Kaufman's terms, "objects of direct experience," the way in which the Bororo see themselves is very different to the way in which others see them.

59. In *Personal Knowledge*, Polanyi frequently describes such knowledge in terms of "articulate systems."

60. Which he believes he borrows from Kant.

rules. Kant says that no system of rules can prescribe the procedure by which the rules themselves are applied. There is an ultimate agency which, unfettered by any explicit rules, decides on the subsumption of a particular instance under any general rule or a general concept. And of this agency Kant says only that it 'is what constitutes our so-called mother-wit'... [A]t another point he declares that this faculty, indispensable to the exercise of any judgment, is quite inscrutable. He says that the way our intelligence forms and applies the schema of a class to particulars 'is a skill so deeply hidden in the human soul that we shall hardly guess the secret trick that Nature here employs.[61]

This was a matter that puzzled Polanyi. He continues:

One may wonder how a critique of pure reason could accept the operations of such a powerful mental agency, exempt from any analysis, and make no more than a few scattered references to it. And one may wonder too that generations of scholars have left such an ultimate submission of reason to unaccountable decisions unchallenged. Perhaps both Kant and his successors instinctively preferred to let such sleeping monsters lie, for fear that, once awakened, they might destroy their fundamental conception of knowledge. For, once you face up to the ubiquitous controlling position of unformalisable mental skills, you do meet difficulties for the justification of knowledge that cannot be disposed of within the framework of rationalism.[62]

This is the problem that Polanyi addresses in his theory of tacit knowledge. In it he challenges the kind of clear distinction that Kaufman draws between our concepts of "ordinary objects of perception" (which seem to make no demands upon the imagination), and regulative ideas such as "God" (which necessarily do). The triadic structure of Polanyi's epistemology shows that in *all* human knowledge and perception there is present an integrative process in which the knower draws upon indwelt, tacit knowledge in an *imaginative act*.

Polanyi deals with the theme of imagination in some depth in his final book, *Meaning*. In order to illuminate the point being made here, I will offer a brief exposition of Polanyi's understanding of the place of imagination in epistemology.

Polanyi and the Imagination

As I noted in chapter 3 under the subheading "The Ubiquity of the Tacit," it is important to emphasize that in the integrative process in which things are perceived and known, there is an action that is performed by the perceiver or knower in relation to what is known. In describing the process by which subsidiary knowledge

61. Polanyi, "The Unaccountable Element in Science," 1.

62. Ibid., 2. It may be that Polanyi overstates his case here, as it is not clear that he takes into consideration Kant's treatment of imagination in his *Critique of Pure Reason*.

is integrated into focal knowledge, Polanyi emphasizes the centrality of human mediation in the process. "[T]his pair is not linked together of its own accord. The relation of a subsidiary to a focus is formed by the *act of a person* who integrates one to the other. The from-to relation lasts only so long as a person, the knower, sustains the integration."[63]

For Polanyi, this process always involves imagination. Of course, not all integrations require the same degree of imagination. For example, the level of imagination required to make a significant scientific discovery is far greater than that required to recognize an object typically part of day-to-day experience. Nevertheless, human imagination is implied in *any* integrative act.

The example of scientific discovery is a significant one. Since, as it would appear, Kaufman believes that the knowledge of which science speaks is not purely imaginative but "refers," what Polanyi has to say about scientific discovery may be of considerable importance. How does the imagination work, according to Polanyi, in the pursuit of scientific discovery? Polanyi explains: "The scientist's imagination does not roam about, casting up random hypotheses to be tested. He starts by thrusting forward ideas he feels to be promising, because he senses the availability of resources that will support them; his imagination then goes on to hammer away in directions felt to be plausible, uncovering material that has a reasonable chance of confirming these guesses."[64] Here the *disciplined* use of imagination comes to the fore in a way that finds no parallel in Kaufman's discussion.

The process is purposeful, not random or arbitrary, although the scientist will not be able to offer anything other than a sketchy account of how it is that he or she is going about the task. This is because he or she is drawing upon vast resources of scientific theory and experimental skill (knowledge that is indwelt) that functions as subsidiary knowledge in the task. First of all, it is clear that this imaginative work is profoundly constrained by the reality that it seeks to uncover. "When the imagination goes into action to start a scientific inquiry, it becomes not only more intense but also more concrete, more specific. Although it thrusts towards a target that is as yet empty, the target is seen to lie in a definite direction. The target represents a particular problem, pointing vaguely, but still always pointing, to a hidden feature of reality."[65]

Discovery, if and when it comes, does not come as the inevitable outcome of a sequence of logical deductions but as an achievement of a rich and imaginative indwelling of the scientific traditions—theoretical and practical—out of which

---

63. Polanyi and Prosch, *Meaning*, 38; Polanyi's emphasis.

64. Ibid., 58.

65. Ibid., 58–59. Polanyi acknowledges not only the importance of imagination, but *intuition* also. "It seems plausible to assume ... that two functions of the mind are jointly at work from the beginning to the end of an inquiry. One is the deliberately active powers of the imagination; the other is a spontaneous process of integration which we may call *intuition*." Ibid., 60; Polanyi's emphasis.

hitherto unnoticed connections are discerned or unrecognized patterns seen. What is achieved represents "a leap of a logical gap."[66]

In view of this account of discovery, Polanyi asserts, "Scientific inquiry is . . . a dynamic exercise of the imagination and is rooted in commitments and beliefs about the nature of things."[67] It is out of an essentially trusting and imaginative indwelling of the scientific tradition that significant scientific discoveries have been and will continue to be made. In this, Polanyi claims, we ought to discern profound continuities between knowledge gained in the sciences and the humanities. He writes:

> The understanding of science we have achieved . . . enables us to see that the study of man in humanistic terms is not unscientific, since *all* meaningful integrations (including those achieved in science) exhibit a triadic structure consisting of the subsidiary, the focal, and the person, and all are thus inescapably *personal*. This observation . . . can be understood to constitute the first step in bridging the gulf that supposedly separates scientific from humanistic knowledge, attitudes, and methods. In view of what we have now seen . . . we can surely bridge this gulf completely. We now see that not only do the scientific and humanistic both involve personal participation; we see that both also involve an active use of the imagination. That the various humanities are heavily entangled with the imagination has always been very clear to almost everyone; but that imagination has an essential role to play in science as well has rarely even been glimpsed.[68]

Polanyi does not deny the distinctions that must be made between the subject matter of science and of the humanities, but he does show the ubiquitous presence of the imagination in both, and the presence of imaginative human participation as a facilitator in our endeavors to make contact with reality. Given the ubiquity of both personal and imaginative participation, Polanyi is able to conclude that "meanings created in the sciences stand in no more favored relation to reality than do meanings created in the arts, in moral judgments, and in religion. *At least they can stand in no more favored relation to reality on the basis of the supposed presence or absence of personal participation and imagination in the one rather than in the other.*"[69]

This penetrating analysis of Polanyi's shows that Kaufman's dichotomous schema will not do, nor will his vague and undifferentiated understanding of imaginative function.[70] Against Kaufman it is now possible to affirm, firstly, that

---

66. Ibid., 62.
67. Ibid., 63.
68. Ibid., 63–64; Polanyi's emphasis.
69. Ibid., 65; my emphasis.
70. McCormack points out that it is entirely unclear what controls exist to regulate the use of imagination in Kaufman's theology. See McCormack, "Divine Revelation and Human Imagination," 434.

imagination—in the varying ranges of its powers—is present in all of our attempts to "refer" and, secondly, that imagination is a function of our disciplined indwelling of received traditions, with all the skills and know-how that this implies.

Kaufman adopts an essentially critical stance towards the various expressions of the Christian tradition on the basis that they offer arbitrary and even idolatrous starting points. Instead he proffers the suggestion that there are forces at work that will bring about a more humane future. This, he claims, is "true to the way things are." Unfortunately he does not expand upon this statement or make any attempt to substantiate it. In view of the horrors of the twentieth century—with wars of unprecedented destruction, the Holocaust, and the promise, with the dawn of the twenty-first century, of a new era of international terrorism—I am persuaded that Bruce McCormack is nearer the mark in his suggestion that the evidence is against this claim, and that Kaufman's view amounts to little more than "a shallow optimism."[71]

I believe that Kaufman is fundamentally mistaken in claiming that we must choose between revelation and imagination.[72] He implies that if God *did* reveal himself, the revelation would be a percept akin to those of other "ordinary objects." This is presumably the reason why he makes the point that the biblical authors did not see God "face to face." But such a notion is far from the understanding of revelation that I have been developing (or, indeed, of that which has been widely held within the Christian tradition). I have argued that God's presence in the sphere of contingent reality is, necessarily, a paradoxical one. God is veiled even in his unveiling; he hides himself even as he makes himself known. God is present to us—and really present—but present as that which is "not God." Hence in his revelation, God takes on form, but the form cannot be equated directly with revelation.[73] However, the form that God does take (and we think of this primarily in the event of incarnation) carries great significance for us.[74]

Revelation is not an alternative to imagination; it is—and it must be—(among other things) God's appeal to our imagination. There is no possibility of participating in revelation apart from a profound imaginative engagement with it. In assuming non-divine form, God adopts something akin to the strategy of the poet. The poet's work draws upon the poet's imagination, but it also calls forth an imaginative response from the reader. It is apparent that to take the poet's words literally is to miss the point. The poet has something to say that transcends what the words (used in a "direct" way) can do. But the poet has only words to do the job, and so they must be used in such a way as to point beyond themselves to the

---

71. Ibid., 441.

72. In practice, Kaufman does not so much suggest a choice as assume that a necessary affirmation of the role of imagination in theology implies a rejection of revelation.

73. John 5:37: "You have never heard his voice or seen his form . . ."

74. John 14:9: "Whoever has seen me has seen the Father."

meaning that the poet intends. The similarities between poetics and revelation now come into view—as does the inherently imaginative nature of our participation in poetics and revelation.

I have already made reference to the importance of Jesus' parabolic teaching, in which he adopts familiar images with which his hearers can readily identify, in order to convey a radically new and subversive message. The parables of Jesus do not teach in a direct way but invite those with ears to hear to begin to learn how to think along new lines that are opened up by them. Jesus' parables of the Kingdom do not describe God's eschatological purposes for his creation directly, for the obvious reason that they describe a reality that is only partially and paradoxically present to us. So Jesus repeatedly speaks of the Kingdom of God being like this or that. Of course the Kingdom of God is not "this" or "that," but it is a bit like "this" or "that": just use your imagination. And, of course, this invitation to imagine does not stand alone but is made in the context of all that Jesus is saying and doing. The form of life that he establishes both is an embodiment of that which he teaches and becomes for his followers an interpretive paradigm.

It is also apparent, in contradistinction to Kaufman, that the kind of imaginative task in which we are engaged in theology[75] is not the free creativity of human consciousness (whether that consciousness is understood individually or collectively), but the disciplined response to what is opened up for us as human beings in God's revelatory activity in which he draws persons into fellowship with himself.

If we are to understand the function of imagination in general, and its significance for theology in particular, Kaufman's empty and generalizing concept of it must be rejected. It will be necessary, for example, to be far more specific about the *particular* function of imagination in differing contexts, and to be aware of the various kinds of discipline to which it must be subjected in our responsible use of it. Several examples of such practice have already been offered earlier in the book.

In chapter 3 I referred to Polanyi's comments about the role of the judge in the law courts. The judge must be independent, in that he or she serves the law and not the interests of a particular party. The judge is, in this sense, free. But the requirements of justice demand that the judge be both knowledgeable of the law (pertinent to the cases in which he or she must pass judgment) and skilled in the interpretation of it. Where a judgment requires the establishment of new law, the judge, far from being free to do whatever he or she likes, must draw deeply from his or her legal knowledge (most of which will be functionally tacit) in order to a reach a proper decision. This is certainly an imaginative activity but one that requires the disciplined application of a highly developed legal mind.[76]

---

75. Which, as a second-order reflective activity, is always contingent upon a form of life that is itself an imaginative, responsive participation in revelation.

76. This does not preclude, of course, the possibility of an error of judgment.

It is possible to discern something of a parallel task in the work of the church confessor. Barth's description of church confession shows that the articulation of what must be said in a particular place at a particular time cannot be derived by the route of logical argumentation from the text of Scripture alone. I will not repeat the description of chapter 4 here, save to emphasize that the work of the confessor is *necessarily* an imaginative one. In this case, it is an imagination that must be "sourced" by a rich knowledge of the scriptural texts, an understanding of the earlier confessions of the church's history, a well-developed dogmatic understanding of the faith, and an acute awareness of the nature of the particular crisis that confronts the church. This is a task that requires imagination—a highly disciplined, trained, responsive imagination.

Having criticized Kaufman for his failure to recognize the responsive and disciplined nature of the theological imagination, I must now question his overly conceptual understanding of what is implied in the task of theological work. In adopting an essentially negative attitude towards tradition, Kaufman fails to see the primary significance of the forms of life in which we participate. As I seek to bring this chapter to a conclusion, I must take issue with this aspect of Kaufman's work.

Conclusion: Revelation, Participation, and Imagination

David Bryant makes the observation that Kaufman treats tradition "as one of the instruments that controlling subjects use to reach the goals they decide are important."[77] Consequently, "the disclosive power of tradition can play no more than a very subordinate role."[78] Kaufman's prioritization of concepts and conceptual formation runs counter to the conviction for which I have argued—that concepts can only be articulated and authenticated from within a particular life practice as it engages with reality. Bryant makes substantially the same point: "It is . . . a mistake to think of disclosure in primarily conceptual terms, just as it is wrong to limit it to brief ecstatic moments of insight. In this light, it is possible to speak of being grasped by the disclosive power of a tradition even before reflecting on it in any conscious way."[79]

The ecclesial forms of life, in which we may speak of participation in revelation, provide a dwelling place in which we may find our home. From within this dwelling, it will be possible to articulate in conceptual terms something of what this participation means: its phenomenological form, its historical formation and development, its internal rationality, etc. But in view of what has been established, it is necessary to acknowledge that this can be no more than an attenuated

77. Bryant, *Faith and the Play of Imagination*, 46.
78. Ibid.
79. Ibid., 123.

summary of what is known. We know more than we can tell. Furthermore, this task (among others) is an imaginative one, but, over against Kaufman, its essential *responsive* nature must be recognized and acknowledged. Bryant writes, "Christian faith arises out of the disclosive power of the expressions of faith that are found in the Bible and in the rest of the Christian tradition."[80] And, as Barth was so aware, that disclosive power came from disclosive participation in the revelatory activity of God.

The theories of biblical interpretation, put forward by Wright and Vanhoozer (adopting, for example, the theatrical metaphor of improvisation) clearly entail an imaginative engagement with the text. But the kinds of imagination required in biblical interpretation (calling as it must upon the use of many skills acquired and indwelt) are those that are responsive to the text. It is not the case that "any performance will do." What is required is a "faithful performance."[81]

In a faithful "performance" of biblical interpretation the imaginative component of the process is one in which there is a rigorous and nuanced responsiveness to the text. But the interpreter is a *person*—located in a particular place and time (Polanyi would say "calling"). The "situatedness" of the interpreter (as noted in the exposition of Polanyi in chapter 3) is of considerable significance in at least two respects. Firstly, it provides the place, or "dwelling" out of which engagement with the text is facilitated. In the case of an ecclesial reading of the biblical text, it must be noted that the form of life—with its distinctive "language-games," practices, conceptual understandings, etc.—will shape the way in which the text is read, and influence the aspects of the text that will receive attention. To adopt another Polanyian term, it provides a cluster of "articulate systems" that Christians indwell. These are the "happy dwelling places of the human mind"[82] that facilitate a reading of the text.

Although such "indwellings" are necessary for an engagement with the text, what they provide for the interpreter is not an infallible guide. Indeed, they may be in error in any number of ways. To adopt a couple of metaphors, they are tools for getting on with the job, or spectacles that enable one to see. There is no *guarantee* that the tools will be adequate for the job or that the spectacles will be the right prescription (and, even if they are, we might not always use them well). In the reading of the Bible the church looks, listens, and waits for the God who promises to be present to it by the Holy Spirit, in order to hear afresh the word of reconciliation in which it hopes for transformation and renewal.[83] This event, we must

---

80. Ibid., 129.

81. Although it is impossible to articulate fully what is meant by "faithful performance," this does not mean that it is impossible to distinguish between good and bad performances. Rather it acknowledges that the parameters on the basis of which a judgment can be made are significantly tacit, and it is upon this tacit knowledge, we must necessarily draw in making any judgment.

82. Polanyi, *Personal Knowledge*, 280.

83. To extend the metaphors we might say that the tools can be improved, as can our skill in using

emphasize, is not one in which human faculties are eclipsed, but one in which they are engaged by God, and through which new possibilities are opened up. Bryant puts it well when he writes:

> [O]ne experiences a revelatory encounter with God when one takes the God to whom the biblical texts point to be the transcendent reality that grounds, limits, and defines one's world. The involvement of the imagination means that such a revelation does not occur without the constructive engagement of our creative capacities. On the other hand, this constructive engagement occurs within the process of our imaginative *attunement* to the ongoing play of tradition and present situation, so that construction works hand in hand with, and is dependent on, the receptive powers of the imagination.[84]

On such a view of biblical interpretation as a participation in revelation, the imaginative component is integral, but it is one that, far from free creative expression, is disciplined and responsive to the text (in which the interpreter must "dwell" to a considerable degree) if it is to be faithful, authentic interpretation. Revelation makes present new possibilities for human existence, but God does not impose himself and efface human will in making himself known. McCormack comments: "It is an autonomy in which the theologian freely chooses to respond in obedience to that which he/she hears. Such obedience is necessary if arbitrariness is to be avoided."[85] In other words, it is a human autonomy, but the autonomy of one drawn into participation within the orbit of the intra-trinitarian communion.

McCormack complains that "Kaufman does far too little to show concretely how theonomy might condition autonomy."[86] I have noted, at various points, that in his explicit treatment of the theme of revelation, Barth exhibits a tendency to understate autonomy. What is required is a more adequate attempt to show how autonomy is conditioned, and how the themes of autonomy and theonomy are related. This is what I have endeavored to accomplish in the present work.

In this final chapter I have shown that it is not only meaningful but necessary to speak of an imaginative participation in revelation. I have voiced my opposition to theological strategies that would either ignore the role of imagination or displace revelation and assert the autonomy of the theological imagination. The examples I have offered, and the suggestions that I have made, are relatively few. Nevertheless, as well as being significant in themselves, these are suggestive of a much broader development. Indeed, I believe that what I have presented offers some significant pointers toward the construction of an authentic theology of the imagination.

---

them, and lenses can be re-ground to improve our vision.

84. Bryant, *Faith and the Play of Imagination*, 164; Bryant's emphasis.
85. McCormack, "Divine Revelation and Human Imagination," 446.
86. Ibid., 453.

In reflecting upon imagination in this chapter, I have both exposed one particular blind alley in the form of Kaufman's project of imaginative theological construction, and have suggested some more fruitful lines of development.

CHAPTER 7

Closing Remarks

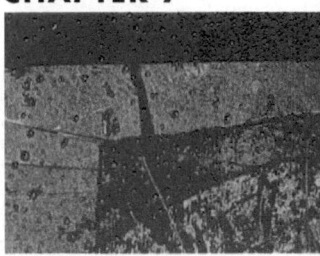

I SAID AT THE outset that this book would not resolve in a grand synthesizing conclusion. The reason for this is not a negative one; it is not—at least not primarily—that the task is too onerous or complex to fulfill within the limited space available. The main reason for ending the book in this way is implied in the methodological stance that I have attempted to adopt in relation to the theme of the work. Theology is, and ought to remain, ongoing and open ended (cf. Barth's *Church Dogmatics!*).

I have argued that a doctrine of revelation must be developed not according to an *a priori* scheme, but as reflection upon what we have come to know of God through what he has revealed to us—and how we have come to know it in the church. Here, as elsewhere, we can articulate and formalize what is known, but in doing so we can only partially represent our knowledge. This is because, as Polanyi has taught us, we know more than we are able to tell.

The crucial tacit component in our knowledge is gained through our engagement with the world as embodied and social persons. Our knowledge is forged through the acquisition of many diverse skills as we are nurtured, trained, socialized, discipled, and apprenticed in the communities that represent the contexts in which our lives are lived. Our participation in these contexts is ineffable.[1] This does not mean that we cannot say things—important and necessary things—about such processes.[2] What it does mean is that what we do say—our "knowledge that"—is, and must always be, sourced by our "knowledge how."

In view of this insight, I have argued that in developing a doctrine of revelation, in which we seek to speak of our knowledge of God, it is necessary to pay attention to the many and diverse ways in which God draws us into fellowship and participation in his own intra-trinitarian life. In agreement with Barth, I say that

---

1. In the sense in which the word has been utilized in the present work.
2. The extent to which we can render our knowledge varies according to the nature of the matter.

such participation is a possibility only in and through the sovereign and gracious initiative of God. But, in that God has been gracious to us, we participate in the life of God through the life of the church and the life of the world. This is the reality of our participation in revelation. It is the task of the doctrine of revelation, as a second-order activity, to reflect upon and articulate this reality. As such, it is necessarily an ongoing task undertaken in the eschatological hope of the consummation of God's purposes for us.

This work has sought to explore some of the possibilities inherent in bringing the thinking of Michael Polanyi and Karl Barth into conversation. In doing this, I have noted some significant kinships between the two thinkers. Both thinkers have contested the distorting rationalisms of Enlightenment thought, and both have sought to adopt *a posteriori* methodologies. It is clear, as I argued in the excursus, that Polanyi's religious and theological writings are seriously misdirected, but it is also clear that his epistemological insights can be[3] a rich source of insight for Christian theology. It is my conviction that the conversation that I have convened between Barth and Polanyi has been a constructive one that promises to bear yet more fruit.

Barth struggled with his concern that theology is always in danger of being distracted from its theme insofar as it engages in dialogue with the sciences. I contend that no such distraction is present in this work. Indeed, in Polanyi's work, the movement is largely in the opposite direction. As a scientist, Polanyi adopts many images drawn from the heart of the Christian tradition in order to subvert the ingrained misconceptions that he discerns in the philosophy of science. As a consequence, he has been accused, by some scientists and philosophers of science[4] of subverting the theme of science by smuggling into its midst alien religious, theological, and mystical themes!

I believe that such concerns—on either side—are misconceived. The conversation between Polanyi and the theologians in general, and with Barth in particular, has already shown its corrective and creative potential. Long may it continue.

---

3. And, indeed, have already been.
4. I am thinking, here, of some who continue to sustain a significantly "objectivistic" view of science.

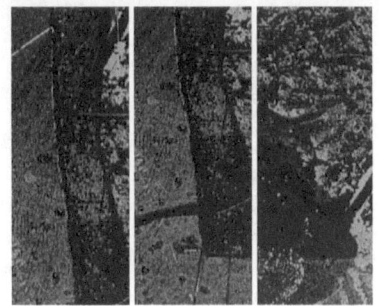

Bibliography

Barth, Karl. *Church Dogmatics: Volume I: The Doctrine of the Word of God, Part 1*. Translated by G. W. Bromiley. Edited by G. W. Bromiley and T. F. Torrance. 2nd ed. Edinburgh: T. & T. Clark, 1975.

———. *Church Dogmatics. Volume I: The Doctrine of the Word of God, Part 2*. Translated by G. T. Thomson and Harold Knight. Edited by G. W. Bromiley and T. F. Torrance. Edinburgh: T. & T. Clark, 1956.

———. *Church Dogmatics. Volume II: the Doctrine of God Part 1*. Translated by T. H. L. Parker, W. B. Johnston, Harold Knight, and J. L. M. Haire. Edited by G. W. Bromiley and T. F. Torrance, 1957.

Bonhoeffer, Dietrich. *Lectures on Christology*. Translated by Edwin Robertson. London: Collins, 1966.

Bradie, Michael. "Polanyi on the Meno Paradox." *Philosophy of Science* 41 (1974) 203.

Bryant, David J. *Faith and the Play of Imagination: On the Role of Imagination in Religion*. Studies in American Biblical Hermeneutics 5. Macon: Mercer University Press, 1989.

Crombie, A. C., editor. *Scientific Change: Historical Studies in the Intellectual, Social, and Technical Conditions for Scientific Discovery and Technical Invention, from Antiquity to the Present*. Symposuim on the History of Science: University of Oxford 9–15 July 1961. London: Heinemann, 1963.

Dulles, Avery. "Faith, Church, and God: Insights from Michael Polanyi." *Theological Studies* 45 (1984) 537–50.

Gill, Jerry H. *The Tacit Mode: Michael Polanyi's Postmodern Philosophy*. SUNY Series in Constructive Postmodern Thought. Albany: State University of New York Press, 2000.

Grant, Patrick. "Michael Polanyi: The Augustinian Component." *New Scholasticism* 48 (1974) 438–63.

Grene, Marjorie. "Tacit Knowing: Grounds for a Revolution in Philosophy." *Journal of the British Society for Phenomenology* 8/3 (1977) 164–71.

———, editor. *Knowing and Being: Essays by Michael Polanyi*. Chicago: University of Chicago Press, 1969.

Gunton, Colin E. *Theology through the Theologians: Selected Essays 1972–1995*. Edinburgh: T. & T. Clark, 1996.

Guthrie, Steven R. "Singing, in the Body and in the Spirit." *Journal of the Evangelical Theological Society* 46 (2003) 633–46.

Hall, Ronald L. "Michael Polanyi on Art and Religion." *Zygon* 17 (1982) 9–18.

Hart, Trevor. *Faith Thinking: The Dynamics of Christian Theology, Gospel and Culture*. London: SPCK, 1995.

———. *Regarding Karl Barth: Essays toward a Reading of His Theology*. Carlisle, UK: Paternoster, 1999.

Jha, Stefania Ruzsits. *Reconsidering Michael Polanyi's Philosophy*. Pittsburgh: University of Pittsburgh Press, 2002.

Johnson, Mark. *The Body in the Mind: The Bodily Basis of Meaning, Imagination and Reason*. Chicago: University of Chicago Press, 1987.

Kaufman, Gordon D. *The Theological Imagination: Constructing the Concept of God*. 1st ed. Philadelphia: Westminster, 1981.

Kuhn, Thomas S. *The Structure of Scientific Revolutions*. International Encyclopedia of Unified Science, Vol. 2, No. 2. Chicago: University of Chicago Press, 1970.

Langford, Thomas A., and William H. Poteat, editors. *Intellect and Hope: Essays in the Thought of Michael Polanyi*. Durham, NC: Duke University Press, 1968.

McCormack, Bruce L. "Divine Revelation and Human Imagination: Must We Choose between the Two?" *Scottish Journal of Theology* 37 (1984) 431–55.

———. *Karl Barth's Critically Realistic Dialectical Theology: Its Genesis and Development 1909–1936*. Oxford: Oxford University Press, 1995.

Moleski, Martin X. *Personal Catholicism: The Theological Epistemologies of John Henry Newman and Michael Polanyi*. Washington, DC: Catholic University of America Press, 2000.

Moltmann, Jürgen. *The Spirit of Life: A Universal Affirmation*. Translated by Margaret Kohl. London: SCM, 1992.

Mullins, Phil. "The Real as Meaningful." *Tradition and Discovery* 26.3 (1999–2000) 42–50.

Newbigin, Lesslie. *The Gospel in a Pluralist Society*. Grand Rapids: Eerdmans, 1989.

Plantinga, Alvin. *Warranted Christian Belief*. New York: Oxford University Press, 2000.

Polanyi, Michael. "Faith and Reason." *Journal of Religion* 41 (1961) 237–47.

———. *The Logic of Liberty: Reflections and Rejoinders*. Indianapolis: Liberty Fund, 1951.

———. "The Logic of Tacit Inference." *Philosophy: The Journal of the Royal Institute of Philosophy* 41/155 (1966) 1–18.

———. "Passions and Controversy in Science." *Bulletin of the Atomic Scientists* 13 (1957) 114–19.

———. *Personal Knowledge: Towards a Post-Critical Philosophy*. London: Routledge and Kegan Paul, 1958.

———. "Science and Reality." *British Journal for the Philosophy of Science* 33/2 (1967–68) 177–96.

———. "Science and Religion: Separate Dimensions or Common Ground?" *Philosophy Today* 7 (1963) 4–14.

———. *Science, Faith and Society*. Chicago: University of Chicago Press, 1964.

———. "Science: Observation and Belief." *Humanitas* 1 (1947) 10–15.

———. *The Study of Man: The Lindsay Memorial Lectures 1958*. London: Routledge and Kegan Paul, 1959.

———. *The Tacit Dimension*. Gloucester, MA: Peter Smith, 1983.

———. "Transcendence and Self-Transcendence." *Encounter* 53 (1970) 88–94.

———. "The Unaccountable Element in Science." *Philosophy: the Journal of the Royal Institute of Philosophy* 37/139 (1962) 1–14.

Polanyi, Michael, and Harry Prosch. *Meaning*. Chicago: University of Chicago Press, 1975.

Prosch, Harry. "Polanyi's View of Religion in *Personal Knowledge*: A Response to Richard Gelwick." *Zygon* 17 (1982) 41–48.

Ryle, Gilbert. *The Concept of Mind*. London: Penguin, 1949.

Schwartz, Fred, editor. *Scientific Thought and Social Reality: Essays by Michael Polanyi*. Edited by Herbert J. Schlesinger. Psychological Issues. New York: International Universities Press, 1974.

Scott, Drusilla. *Michael Polanyi*. London: SPCK, 1996.

Simon, Herbert A. "Bradie on Polanyi on the Meno Paradox." *Philosophy of Science* 43 (1976) 147–50.

Stackhouse, John J., editor. *Evangelical Futures: A Conversation on Theological Method.* Grand Rapids: Baker, 2000.

Thiemann, Ronald F. *Revelation and Theology: The Gospel as Narrated Promise.* Notre Dame: University of Notre Dame Press, 1985.

Torrance, Alan. *Persons in Communion: Trinitarian Description and Human Participation with Special Reference to Volume One of Karl Barth's Church Dogmatics.* Edinburgh: T. & T. Clark, 1996.

Torrance, T. F. "Michael Polanyi and the Christian Faith—A Personal Report." *Tradition and Discovery* 27/2 (2000–2001) 26–32.

———. *Theology in Reconstruction.* London: SCM, 1965.

Webster, John, editor. *The Cambridge Companion to Karl Barth.* Cambridge: Cambridge University Press, 2000.

Wittgenstein, Ludwig. *Philosophical Investigations (Second Edition).* Translated by G. E. M. Anscombe. Oxford: Blackwell, 1958.

Wright, N. T. *The New Testament and the People of God.* Christian Origins and the Question of God 1. Minneapolis: Fortress, 1992.

Zizioulas, John D. *Being as Communion: Studies in Personhood and the Church.* Crestwood, NY: St. Vladimir's Seminary Press, 1993.

www.ingramcontent.com/pod-product-compliance
Lightning Source LLC
Chambersburg PA
CBHW020407230426
43664CB00009B/1219